797,885 Books
are available to read at

Forgotten Books

www.ForgottenBooks.com

Forgotten Books' App
Available for mobile, tablet & eReader

ISBN 978-1-331-13023-9
PIBN 10125688

This book is a reproduction of an important historical work. Forgotten Books uses state-of-the-art technology to digitally reconstruct the work, preserving the original format whilst repairing imperfections present in the aged copy. In rare cases, an imperfection in the original, such as a blemish or missing page, may be replicated in our edition. We do, however, repair the vast majority of imperfections successfully; any imperfections that remain are intentionally left to preserve the state of such historical works.

Forgotten Books is a registered trademark of FB &c Ltd.
Copyright © 2015 FB &c Ltd.
FB &c Ltd, Dalton House, 60 Windsor Avenue, London, SW19 2RR.
Company number 08720141. Registered in England and Wales.

For support please visit www.forgottenbooks.com

YAMAHA Yamaha Worldwide Representative Offices

For details of products, please contact your nearest Yamaha representative or the authorized distributor listed below.
Pour plus de détails sur les produits, contactez votre représentant Yamaha le plus proche de chez vous ou le distributeur agréé indiqué ci-dessous.

NORTH AMERICA

CANADA
Yamaha Canada Music Ltd.
135 Milner Avenue, Toronto ON M1S 3R1, Canada

U.S.A.
Yamaha Corporation of America
6600 Orangethorpe Ave., Buena Park, Calif. 90620, U.S.A.

CENTRAL & SOUTH AMERICA

MEXICO
Yamaha de México S.A. de C.V.
Avenida Insurgentes número 1647,
Col. San José Insurgentes, C.P. 03900,
Deleg. Benito Juárez, México, D.F.

BRAZIL
Yamaha Musical do Brasil Ltda.
Rua Fidêncio Ramos, 302 - Cj 52 e 54 - Torre B -
Vila Olímpia - CEP 04551-010 - São Paulo/SP
BRAZIL

ARGENTINA
**Yamaha Music Latin America, S.A.
Sucursal de Argentina**
Olga Cossettini 1553, Piso 4 Norte
Madero Este-C1107CEK
Buenos Aires, Argentina

**PANAMA AND OTHER LATIN
AMERICAN COUNTRIES/
CARIBBEAN COUNTRIES**
Yamaha Music Latin America, S.A.
Torre Banco General, Piso 7, Urbanización Marbella,
Calle 47 y Aquilino de la Guardia,
Ciudad de Panamá, Panamá

EUROPE

EUROPEAN COUNTRIES
Yamaha Music Europe GmbH
Siemensstrasse 22-34, 25462 Rellingen, Germany

RUSSIA
Yamaha Music (Russia)
Room 37, bld. 7, Kievskaya street, Moscow,
121059, Russia

AFRICA

Yamaha Music Gulf FZE
JAFZA-16, Office 512, P.O.Box 17328, Jebel Ali FZE,
Dubai, U.A.E.

Yamaha Corporation, Audio Products Sales and Marketing Division
Nakazawa-cho 10-1, Naka-ku, Hamamatsu, Japan 430-8650
ヤマハ株式会社
〒430-8650　静岡県浜松市中区中沢町10-1

As of January 2015
AVRO1501A

ZF73310-2

MIDDLE EAST

TURKEY / CYPRUS
Yamaha Music Europe GmbH
Siemensstrasse 22-34, 25462 Rellingen, Germany

OTHER COUNTRIES
Yamaha Music Gulf FZE
JAFZA-16, Office 512, P.O.Box 17328, Jebel Ali FZE,
Dubai, U.A.E

ASIA

THE PEOPLE'S REPUBLIC OF CHINA
Yamaha Music & Electronics (China) Co.,Ltd.
2F, Yunhedasha, 1818 Xinzha-lu, Jingan-qu,
Shanghai, China

INDIA
Yamaha Music India Pvt. Ltd.
Spazedge building, Ground Floor, Tower A, Sector
47, Gurgaon-Sohna Road, Gurgaon, Haryana, India

INDONESIA
PT. Yamaha Musik Indonesia (Distributor)
PT. Nusantik
Gedung Yamaha Music Center, Jalan Jend. Gatot
Subroto Kav. 4, Jakarta 12930, Indonesia

REPUBLIC OF KOREA
Yamaha Music Korea Ltd.
8F, 9F, Dongsung Bldg. 158-9 Samsung-Dong,
Kangnam-Gu, Seoul, Korea

MALAYSIA
Yamaha Music (Malaysia) Sdn., Bhd.
Lot 8, Jalan Perbandaran, 47301 Kelana Jaya,
Petaling Jaya, Selangor, Malaysia

SINGAPORE
Yamaha Music (Asia) PRIVATE LIMITED
Blk 202 Hougang Street 21, #02-00,
Singapore 530202, Singapore

TAIWAN
Yamaha Music and Electronics Taiwan Co., Ltd.
2F., No.1, Yuandong Rd, Banqiao Dist.
New Taipei City 22063 Taiwan

THAILAND
Siam Music Yamaha Co., Ltd.
3, 4, 15, 16th Fl., Siam Motors Bldg.,
891/1 Rama 1 Road, Wangmai, Pathumwan,
Bangkok 10330, Thailand

VIETNAM
Yamaha Music Vietnam Company, Limited
15th Floor, Nam A Bank Tower
201-203 Cach Mang Thang Tam St., Ward 4, Dist.3,
Ho Chi Minh City, Vietnam

OTHER COUNTRIES
Yamaha Corporation, Business Planning Div.
Area Business Development Department
Nakazawa-cho 10-1, Naka-ku, Hamamatsu,
Japan 430-8650

OCEANIA

AUSTRALIA / NEW ZEALAND
Yamaha Music Australia Pty. Ltd.
Level 1, 99 Queensbridge Street, Southbank,
Victoria 3006, Australia

1 MONTH OF FREE READING

at
www.ForgottenBooks.com

By purchasing this book you are eligible for one month membership to ForgottenBooks.com, giving you unlimited access to our entire collection of over 700,000 titles via our web site and mobile apps.

To claim your free month visit: www.forgottenbooks.com/free125688

* Offer is valid for 45 days from date of purchase. Terms and conditions apply.

Similar Books Are Available from
www.forgottenbooks.com

The Spirit of the Hour in Archaeology
by William E. Gates

Archaeological Excavation
by J. P. Droop

Archæology and False Antiquities
by Robert Munro

A Century of Archæological Discoveries
by Adolf Theodor Friedrich Michaelis

Classical Archaeology in Schools
by Percy Gardner

Anthropology and Archaeology
by Daniel Wilson

Introduction to the Study of North American Archaeology
by Cyrus Thomas

Notes on Iroquois Archeology
by Alanson Skinner

A Text-Book of European Archaeology, Vol. 1
by Robert Alexander Stewart Macalister

An Illustrated Dictionary of Words Used in Art and Archaeology
by John William Mollett

The Archæology of the Cuneiform Inscriptions
by A. H. Sayce

Prehistoric Ireland
A Manual of Irish Pre-Christian Archaeology, by Rev. P. Power

Archaeological Notes on Mandalay
by Taw Sein Ko

Archaeology at French Colonial Cahokia
by Bonnie L. Gums

Man and His Past
by O. G. S. Crawford

Schliemann's Excavations
An Archaeological and Historical Study, by Karl Schuchhardt

Some Observations on the Ethnography and Archaeology of the American Aborigines
by Samuel George Morton

A Group of Nation-Builders
O'Donovan - O'Curry - Petrie, by Patrick M. MacSweeney

Archaeological Studies Among the Ancient Cities of Mexico
by William Henry Holmes

The Archaeology and Site History of 75 State Street
by Michael Roberts

THE

Old Kingdom of Elmet:

THE LAND 'TWIXT AIRE AND WHARFE.

A Descriptive Sketch of its Ancient History, Antiquities, Legends, Picturesque Features, and its Flora, being a Companion Volume to "Lower Wharfeland."

BY

EDMUND BOGG,

AUTHOR OF

"A Thousand Miles in Wharfedale."
"Edenvale," "The Border Country," "Lakeland."
"Two Thousand Miles in Wharfedale."
ETC., ETC.

OVER ONE HUNDRED AND SIXTY ILLUSTRATIONS
PREPARED EXPRESSLY FOR THIS WORK.

YORK: John Sampson, Coney Street.
LONDON: John Heywood, 29 & 30, Shoe Lane, E.C.
MANCHESTER: John Heywood, Deansgate.
LEEDS: James Miles, Guildford Street.

Entered at Stationers' Hall.   OCTOBER, 1904.   *All rights reserved.*

Preface.

The Old Kingdom of Elmet:

The Land betwixt Aire and the Wharfe.

The subscribers' edition being almost exhausted, it becomes a pleasure to respond to the call of a larger public for an account of one of the most interesting of the ancient petty states into which the county of York was originally divided. The information cannot be culled from any existing work. From Bede's time onwards every writer has trodden in the beaten track of his predecessors, without attempting to unveil the mystery and silence enshrouding the Kingdom. The material to be relied upon with absolute certainty is scanty indeed, yet the theme is one of absorbing interest. In its place-names is fixed, for all time, the memory of a people—the Celts—whose principality was Elmet: centuries before any historic record, the wooded wolds of Elmet were the stronghold of a dominant or ruling class. Probably it will be the means of exploding a fallacy which I have heard repeatedly expressed, viz.: that all the historic records concerning this Kingdom could be told on a sheet of note-paper! Possibly some future writer may endeavour to complete the work of restoring Elmet to its ancient dignity in history—that of an independent state retaining its integrity long after others had fallen under the iron heel of the Invader.

To be brief, the writer offers his thanks to all who have assisted him in any way, either with pen or pencil.

One error the writer cannot too sincerely regret: on page 132 Byram Hall, home of the Ramsdens, is, by inadvertence, erroneously stated to be the seat of the poet, Lord Houghton, whereas, in fact, the seat of the Monckton Milnes' family was Fryston, across the river Aire.

A minor matter the *two* hundred feet mentioned on page 145, should read *one* hundred.

EDMUND BOGG.

LEEDS,
 October, 1904.

Index to Illustrations.

PAGE		
2	Fossil Remains of Gigantic Animals found in Aire Valley (Zoological Section Leeds Philosophical Hall)	
3	Ditto	
4	Stone Implements of Warfare, Elmet	
7	Flint Arrow Heads, Adel	
8	Devil's Arrows, Boroughbridge	*Percy Robinson.*
10	Bronze Weapons, Elmet	
12	Tesselated Pavement, Aldborough	*S. Wagstaff*
14	Roman Milestone, Castleford	
15	Plan of Earthworks, Barwick-in-Elmet	*G. T. Lowe.*
17	Hall Tower Hill, Barwick-in-Elmet	*G. T. Lowe.*
19	Map of Roman Roads	*G. T. Lowe.*
20	Roman Altars	
21	Section of Roman Road, Aberford	*Owen Bowen.*
22	Line of Roman Road, Aldwoodley	*Owen Bowen.*
23	Roman and Saxon Relics, Adel	*A. Sutton.*
25	Sepulchral Tablets, York	*A. Sutton.*
26	Roman Altars, York	*A. Sutton.*
27	Ancient Coffins, Adel and York	*A. Sutton.*
30	Saxon Crosses, Otley	*A. Haselgrave.*
31	The Ilkley Crosses	*Percy Robinson.*
32	Norse Cross, Leeds Parish Church	*Percy Robinson.*
33	Anglo Danish Cross, Grinston	*E. Bogg.*
40	Pre Norman Arch, Godmundham	*E. Bogg.*
44	Relics, Adel	*A. Sutton.*
46	Ground Plan, Potterton	*G. T. Lowe.*
49	Kneeling Cross, Ripley	*Percy Robinson.*
52	Kirkstall Abbey	*S. Wagstaff.*
54	Kirkstall Abbey	*S. Wagstaff.*
55	Milestone, Black Hill	*A. Sutton.*
56	Ravine, Eccup	*A. Sutton.*
57	Aldwoodley Hall	*A. Sutton.*
59	The Mill House, Adel	*A. Sutton.*
60	Norman Doorway, Adel	*Percy Robinson.*
61	Corbel Ornaments and Door Knocker, Adel	*A. Sutton.*
63	Adel Church	*S. Wagstaff.*
64	Milestone, Aldwoodley	*A. Sutton.*

vi.

PAGE		
65	Sandy Rock, Adel Beck	*Scrimshaw.*
66	Old Tap, Meanwood Hill Top	*A. Sutton.*
68	Shire Oak, Headingley (200 years ago)	*From an Old Drawing.*
69	Shire Oak, 1902	*Owen Bowen.*
70	Burley Grove	*Percy Robinson.*
72	Tudor Framework, Rockley Hall	*Scrimshaw.*
74	Map of Elmet and Ainsty Country	*G. T. Lowe.*
76	Leeds Parish Church	*Albert Bottomley.*
77	Arms of Mowbray and Howard, from oaken beam in old house, Swinegate	*S. W.*
78	Templar Crosses in Leeds	*Sam Harrison.*
80	Bit of Old Briggate	*E. Bogg.*
81	Relic of Lands Lane	*Percy Teasdale.*
82	Pack Horse, Briggate	*A. Sutton.*
83	Old Green Dragon, Guildford Street	*Percy Robinson.*
85	Old Hall Hotel	*A. Sutton.*
87	St. John's Church	*A. Sutton.*
88	Red Hall	*A. Sutton.*
90	Town Hall, from Guildford Street	*Owen Bowen.*
91	Chapeltown	*W. G. Foster.*
92	A Stretch of Elmet from Roundhay Park	*Owen Bowen.*
95	Ingram Hall	*Percy Robinson.*
96	Foundry Mill	*Gilbert Foster.*
97	Wyke Beck	*E. Bogg.*
98	Wyke Bridge House	*Scrimshaw.*
99	Arms in do.	
100	Glimpse of Leeds from Halton	*Gilbert Foster.*
102	Evening Scene, Whitkirk	*Gilbert Foster.*
103	Osmondthorpe	*Scrimshaw.*
104	Ivy House, York Road	*Thos. Dawson.*
105	Old Hall, Knostrop	*William Jones.*
106	The Pleasance, do.	*Louis Grimshaw.*
108	Thorp Stapleton	*Alfred Bottomley.*
110	Templenewsam	*Gilbert Foster.*
112	Arms of Ingram and Slingsby	*S. Harrison.*
114	Whitkirk, from Colton	*Gilbert Foster.*
116	Whitkirk Church	*Gilbert Foster.*
117	Old Barrowby	*W. Jones.*
118	Swillington	*Gilbert Foster.*
119	Garforth Cliff	*Percy Teasdale.*
121	Kippax, from Great Preston	*Gilbert Foster.*
122	Plan of Mound, Kippax	*P. Robinson.*
123	Remains of Cross, Kippax	
124	The Almshouses, Kippax	*E. Bogg.*
127	Old Parish Church, Castleford	*A. Sutton.*
128	Ledston Hall	*E. Bogg.*
130	Norman Doorway and Font, Ledsham	*E. Bogg.*
131	Springtime, Ledsham	*Gilbert Foster.*
132	Micklefield	*Frank Dean.*

PAGE		
133	Garforth	Gilbert Foster.
137	Manstou Hall	A. Sutton.
140	Street Scene, Barwick	W. Jones.
143	Hall Tower Hill and Wendal, from Raikes Beck, Barwick	Gilbert Foster.
144	Trench, south side of Hall Tower Hill	E. Bogg.
145	Street Scene, Barwick	W. Jones.
147	Church, Barwick	G. F. Jones.
148	Crosses in Barwick Church	E. Bogg.
150	Barwick, View of, from the East	A. Haselgrave.
151	Kiddal Hall	A. Haselgrave.
154	Cuckoo in Titlark's Nest, Scholes	E. Bogg.
156	View of Barwick, from Cock Beck	Gilbert Foster.
157	Avenue, Aberford	A. Haselgrave.
158	View, Aberford	W. Jones.
159	Sanny Hick's Anvil	
161	Parlington Park	Gilbert Foster.
162	Aberford, View of	Frank Dean.
163	The Old Windmill, Aberford	W. Jones.
164	Entrenchments, Aberford	G. T. Lowe.
165	A Rustic Corner	S. Wagstaff.
167	Old Belfry, Lotherton	W. Jones.
168	Interior Lotherton Chapel	S. Wagstaff.
169	Norman Doorway, Lotherton	E. Bogg.
170	Lead Church	E. Bogg.
171	Interior do.	A. Sutton.
172	A Peep of Hazelwood	Frank Dean.
173	Hazelwood Castle	G. W. Preston.
174	Chapel, Hazelwood	Percy Robinson
181	Towton Battlefield	Frank Dean.
182	Ditto, from Saxton, looking over the Battlefield	Frank Dean.
183	Towton Bridge, corner of Renshaw Wood	Frank Dean.
186	Renshaw Woodside	Frank Dean.
188	Lord Dacre's Tomb, Saxton Churchyard	E. Bogg.
190	The Dacres Tomb, Lauercost Priory	E. Bogg.
191	Lord Dacre's Cross, Towton	Frank Dean.
193	A Peep of Saxton from Diutingdale	Gilbert Foster.
195	Sherburn, from the North	Frank Dean.
199	Sherburn Church	S. W.
200	Ditto	W. Jones.
201	Norman Nave, Sherburn Church	G. F. Jones.
203	Janus Cross ditto	G. F. Jones.
204	Huddleston, from the Moat	Frank Dean.
205	Huddleston Quarry	Frank Dean.
207	Gateway, Steeton	G. F. Jones.
208	Steeton Hall, showing part Janus Cross	G. F. Jones.
210	Barkston Ash	Frank Dean.
212	Fenton Church, from the North	E. Bogg.
213	Ditto from the South	A. Sutton.

viii.

PAGE		
215	Vine Cottage, Church Fenton	E. Bogg.
217	Gateway, Cawood	Albert Haselgrave.
221	A Bit of Cawood from the Bridge	S. W.
222	A Window in Farmyard	G. T. L.
224	Cawood Castle Gateway, from the South	W. Jones.
227	Ditto from the River	Frank Dean.
228	Bishopdyke	E. Bogg.
230	Street View	S. W.
231	Old Font in Hospital Garden	E. Bogg.
232	Cawood Church	A. Sutton.
235	Wistow Church	Frank Dean.
236	Tablet do.	S. Harrison.
237	West Doorway, Selby Abbey	G. F. Jones.
239	The Choir, Selby Abbey	Valentine & Sons, Dundee.
242	A Bend of the Ouse at Cawood	E. Bogg.
244	The Ouse, near Riccall	Frank Dean.
246	Tombs, Ryther Church	W. Jones.
247	Ditto, before the Restoration	J. Manham.
248	Chancel Arch and Hagioscope	E. Bogg.
251	The Ferry, Ryther	E. Bogg.
253	A Bend of the Wharfe at Ulleskelf	Gilbert Foster.
254	Grinston and Kirkby Wharfe	Gilbert Foster.
255	The Church Tower, Kirkby Wharfe	J. Manham.
256	Ancient Cross, Kirkby Wharfe	E. Bogg.

Contents.

                                                                                            PAGE

INTRODUCTION   1
        PREHISTORIC SKETCH—A GLANCE BACKWARD.
Fossil Remains of Gigantic Animals and Reptiles—Stone and Flint Implements of Warfare—The Dawn of Civilization.

CHAPTER I.   6
        THE BRIGANTES—THEIR KINGDOM AND CAPITAL.

CHAPTER II.   9
        THE INVASION OF THE ROMANS.
Boadicea, Queen of the Iceni—Caractacus, Prince of the Silures—His Fight with the Romans—Cartismandua, Queen of the Brigantes—Her Betrayal of Caractacus and Flight—Roman Advance over the Don and Aire—Penetrate through the Western Gate of Elmet—Earthworks at Barwick, Becca, and Woodhouse Rein, &c., stubbornly defended—The position stormed by Agricola—His March on York and Aldborough—Roman Roads in Yorkshire.

CHAPTER III.   24
        THE KINGDOM OF ELMET.
Its Boundaries and Natural Barriers—The Invasion and Settlement of Engle-folk—Capture of York—Survival of Celtic Place-names—The Liberty of Cawood, Wistow, and Otley—Barwick, the Capital of Elmet—A Story of the Yorkshire Wolds—The Line of Ella—The Rise and Glory of Edwin—The House of Ida and Ethelfrith—Hereric murdered at the Court of Cerdic—Vengeance of Edwin—Invades Elmet—Introduction of Christianity by Paulinus—Coifi destroys the God of the Pagans—The Battle of Heathfield—Edwin defeated by Cadwallader—Penda slain—The Celts invade Bryneich and Deifyr—Defeat and Death of Cadwallader at Heavenfield—Penda invades Elmet—The Great Fight at Whinmoor—Oswy's Victory and Death of Penda—Place-names in Elmet—Ligures, Ludees, Leedes—The Name Elmet—Its Regulus, Recognition, and Strength—The Antiquity of Barwick—Elmet—Churches of All Hallows—Early Christianity, &c.

CHAPTER IV.   54
        HISTORY, ANTIQUITIES, AND GENERAL SURVEY OF ELMET.
Kirkstall—Cookridge—Brearey—Echope and Adel—Roman, Celtic, Saxon, and Norman Antiquities—Adel Crags and the Meanwood Valley—Headingley, a charming suburb—The Wapentake of Skyrack—The Shire Oak—Aire River.

CHAPTER V.   71
        LEEDS.
Early History—Prehistoric Remains—British Settlement on Quarry Hill—No traces of Roman Occupation—Antiquity of the Church of St Peter.—Norman and Mediæval Leeds—Leeds Castle nith—Ralph Thoresby's House—Old Inns

CHAPTER V. *(continued)*.
—Civil War—Turnpike Riots—St. John's Church and John Harrison—King Charles a prisoner at the Red Hall—Notable Men—Startling Growth of Leeds during the Last Century—A Great Commercial City—Potternewton and Chapeltown—The Kitchingmans—The Church—Discovery of a Stone Coffin—Moortown—Street Lane—Elmet Hall—Discovery of Roman Altar and Bronze Axes—Roundhay Park and its environs (of old a hunting-place of kings)—Gipton—Ancient Fortifications—Battle of Whinmoor—Wyke Beck—Foundry Mill and Seacroft—Killingbeck and Wyke Bridge House—Halton—Its claim to antiquity—A Notable Feast—Whitkirk — Evening Scene—Osmondthorpe—Traditions connecting the place to a Royal Villa of Saxon Kings—The Osmund Family—Knostrop Old Hall—Jacobean Interiors —The Home of the late Atkinson Grimshaw—The Ruins of Thorp-Stapleton—Its associations with the Stapletons and Scargills.

TEMPLENEWSAM AND WHITKIRK. 109
Botany—The Templars and Knights of St. John—Lord Darnley and the Ingrams —Colton—Fine View of Whitkirk—Situation of the latter—Manorial Rights and Old Customs—The Scargills' Tomb, etc.—Austhorpe Lodge and the Smeatons—The Moores of Austhorpe Hall—Bullerthorpe Moor—Roman Road —Legend of a Great Disaster—The Lowthers of Swillington—Interesting Church—Great Preston—Its past significance—Charming View of Kippax— The Old Soke Mill—Hairy palms of the Millers—Importance of Kippax in the past—Ancient Mound, 'Cheeny Basin'—Roche Grange—The Church of St. Mary—Remains of Cross, typical of Early Christianity—Memorials to the Slingsbys and Medhursts—Old Almshouses, etc.—Kippax Park and the Blands —The Great Military Road of the Romans (the Ermine Street)—The Don Country—Doncaster, the Campo-Danum of Bede—Key to the North—The Southern Border of the Brigantes—Castleford, the Legiolium of the Latins— Parish Church, occupying site of former camp—Roman Milestone and Altar— Broad Sweep of the Lower Aire Valley—The Western Gate of Elmet—Commanding Ridge of its Frontier—The Aire River, a great barrier—In flood times rendered impassable—Norman Army unable to cross—Mary Pannell Hill—Ledstone Village and Hall—Ledsham—A Charming Spot—The Church and surroundings—'Lady Betty Hastings' Charities—Her Tomb and Monument—Newton, Fairburn, and Brotherton—Thomas de Brotherton—Queens Margaret and Isabella—Byram Hall—Micklefield—Samuel Hick—Stourton Grange and Garforth—Their Significance and Antiquity.

CHAPTER VI. 134
THE VALLEY OF THE COCK.
Round about its Source—Red Hall—Grimes Dyke and Whinmoor—Story of a Famous Battle—Morwick Hall and the Grays Family—Penwell Farm and Penda's Well—Scholes and the Vevers Family—Stanks and Old Manston—An Old-time District—Lasincroft—Shippen and Barnbow—Former Residences of the Gascoignes—Description of the Family—Their Adherence to the Old Faith —The Popish Plot—Sir Thomas Gascoigne—Parlington and the De Parlyngtons —The Despensers—Arms of the Gascoignes.

CHAPTER VII. 142
AROUND BARWICK AND ABERFORD.
Barwick—Its Naturally Strong Position—The Capital of the Ancient Kingdom of Elmet—Traditions of its Kings—Hall Tower and Wendell Hills, places of vast antiquity—Oral Traditions concerning its construction—The Rakes Thoresby's Quaint Reference—The Maypole renewed every third year—Scenes of Great Festivity—'Knocked at Barwick,' a superstition — The Village Cross—Charm and Character of Barwick—The Church of All Hallows—Antiquity and Significance of its early Crosses—Supposed Site of Thridwulf's

xi.

PAGE

CHAPTER VII. *(continued).*
    Monastery—The late Canon Hope—Billy Dawson (a famous preacher)—Mary Morritt, the double-sighted—The Chapels of the Gascoignes and Ellises—Value of the Rectory in 1525—Rare quality of Barwick Lime—Potterton Bridge—Dark Lane—Copple Syke Spring—An Ancient Pack-horse Route—Kiddle Hall and the Ellises—A Skirmish on the Moor—The Haunted Chamber—Whin or Whinney Moor—Old-world Stories, Signs, and Omens—Second-sighted—Potterton—Its Antiquities—Morgan's Cross and King Morgan—Manor Garth—Supposed Site of an Ancient Church—The Hall—Ass Bridge—The Cliff—The Cliff Lady—The Padfoot—Road to Aberford—River Cock—Celtic Earthworks—Becca Banks—Becca Mills—The Hall, etc.

ABERFORD.
    Its Claims to Antiquity—Its Church, dedicated to St. Ricarius—Burial-place of 'Sanny Hick'—Tradition of a Miracle—Healthy situation of Aberford—Longevity of its Inhabitants—The Pinners—A Foul Deed before the High Altar—The Almshouses, a memorial to the Gascoignes—Tradition of a Monastery at Aberford—Evidence of a Fortress, mentioned by Camden—The River Craw—Old Windmill—The Ermine Street—Nip Scaup—High Cross—The Noverleys—The Roman Way—Buckingham's Well—Coaching Days—Old Inns—Bramham Moor—Nevison—Becca and Aberford—Entrenchments—Base of Aberford Market Cross—Its Story of a Great Plague—Flint Implements of Warfare—Coin of Faustina, the infamous Empress, etc.—Lotherton—Its former Owners—An Ancient Chapel and its Story—Lead or Lede—Its connection to Celtic Times—The Manor—The Teyes and Scargill Families—Leland's Description—Chapel of Lead, in the Parish of Ryther—Singular Customs—Two Services held yearly—Origin of Custom unknown—Hazelwood and the Vavasours—Antiquity of the Family Office of 'Valvasor'—The Hall—Extensive Views and Impressions—The Roman Catholic Chapel of St. Leonard—Memorials and Effigies—High Chivalry and Renown of the Old Family—Grant of Stone and Timber to the Fabric of York Minster—A Story from "The Hundred Mery Talys."

CHAPTER VIII. -   179
ROUND ABOUT TOWTON AND SAXTON.
    Newstead and Lead Mill—Castle Hill and Renshaw Wood—Solitary Windings of the Cock Rivulet—Strange Contrasts—Morning before the Battle of Towton—The Ferrybridge Fight—Fitz-Walter slain—Warwick's Resolve—The Bloody Clifford slain at Dintingdale—Prelude of Battle—Position of the Two Armies—Morning of the Great Fight—A Blinding Snowstorm—The Conflict—Defeat of the Lancastrians—The Vale of the Cock a Death Trap—Renshaw Wood—Mayden Castle—Memorials of the Battle: Burial Mounds, Arrow Heads, Battleaxes and Spears—Head of a Maltese Cross, still to be seen on the Battlefield—Lord Dacre's Tomb—Traditions of the Villagers—The Red and White Roses—A Beautiful Memorial—Towton and Early History—Connection with the Fight—Commencement of a Great Memorial Chapel—Village of Saxton—The Salleys and Hungates—The vicissitudes of the latter—The Sexton's Story of the Hammonds and Widdringtons—Teresa Simpson, a tale of penance—The Church of All Saints—A Vast Grave—The Manor Hall of the Hungates—Nor Acres and Dintingdale—Old Traditions, etc.

CHAPTER IX.   197
SHERBURN-IN-ELMET.
    Early Christianity—Athelstan's Gift to the Archbishop—Battle of Brunanburgh Raid of the Scots—The Eastern Fringe of Elmet—Church of All Saints—Its former and present significance—A Memorable Incident—Description of the Church—Chapel of the Holy Angels—Story of an interesting Cross—Huddleston Hall—Its Early History—The Chapel—The Huddleston Family

xii.

CHAPTER IX. *(continued).*

—A Celebrated Quarry—The Trenches—Newthorpe, etc.—Steeton Hall—Its Massive Gateway—Vestiges of Chapel—Story of the Reckett—Wilghbys, Reygates, and Foljambes—Janus Cross—Lunley and Monk Fryston—South Milford and its rural surroundings—Barkston Ash—Head of the Wapentake—A Focus of Great Antiquity—Scarthingwell Hall—Beauty of its situation—Brief Sketch of Fenland—Church Fenton—Early History—The Church—Its Antiquities—Stump of Market Cross—Site of Old Manor Hall—The Moat—Vine Cottage—Unique Rustic Picture—Mysterious Visitants—Little Fenton, Hall Garth, etc.—A Fen Road—Fenton Grange and Fenton Lodge—Biggan Grange and the Haunted Chamber—The Cultivation of the Old Fenland by the Norsemen—An Ancient Road—Mattram Hall, Rust Park, and Bishopdyke.

CHAPTER X. 219

CAWOOD.

Etymology of its Name—Invasion of the Sea Kings—The Castle—A Home of the Archbishops—A Resting-place of Kings and Queens—Bishopwood Chase—Scottish Raid—A Celebrated Feast—Cardinal Wolsey arrested at Cawood—Archbishop Montaigu—Remains of the Castle—Reminiscences—Ferry-boat Accident—Bessie Pilmer—The Port of Cawood—Wistowgate—The Court Leet—Keysbury Hall—Bishopdyke and the Old Soke Mill—Jacky Fowler, *alias* Lord Milton—Pepper and his old-time Stories—Paved Ford over the Ouse—The Church of All Saints—Interesting Examples of Architecture—Archbishop Montaigne's Memorial—Font in Hospital Garden, now used for pump trough—Figures of the Four Evangelists—Old Families still resident in Cawood—Instance of Remarkable Attachment of Animals—Largee Young, the Gipsy Chief, arrested—Vegetable Cultivation—The Goblin Tree—Wistow—Its Situation—Athelstan's Liberty, Peg Fife, Boggart Brigg. Black Feu, and Garmaen Carr—The Maypole and the Fairies—Scalm Park and the Storrs—The Church—Curious Memorial—St. Hilda's Chapel—Olive House and St. Olaf—Selby Abbey—Brief Description—The Missionary, Benedict—His Account of the Landscape around Selby—The Highway of the Vikings—Wistow Lordship—Monk's Lane—Riccall Church—Invasion of Norsemen—Hardrada and Tosti land at Riccall—March through the Forest—Battle of Fulford—Capture of York—King Harold enters York—Battle of Stamford Bridge—Defeat of the Norsemen—Death of Hardrada and Tosti—The Lament of the Vikings—A Dismal Story of Ill-omen—Danesland—Kellfield—The Eagre, or Aigre—The Sea-God of old—The Commercial Inn—The Old Mole Catcher—Story of the Mole.

CHAPTER XI. 245

RYTHER, ULLESKELF, AND GRIMSTON.

The Antiquity of the Ryther Family—Situation of the Village—The Ancient Church—Unique Features—Fine Display of Tombs—Chancel Arch and Hagioscope—A Family of Warriors—Rare Glass—Fine Altar Slabs—Old Font, Memorial to the Prioresses of Appleton—The Castle of Ryther—Remaining Vestiges—The Moat—Hall Garth—Coney Garth—Sketch of the Ryther Family, Fendyke—Wild Hops and Profusion of Flowers—The River Bank—Ulleskelf, a Port of Shipment—An Ancient Settlement—The Hall—Shillito Family—John Leland's Description—A Charming Picture—The Path to Grinston—Delightful Evening Scene—Grin, the Viking—Grinston House—Kirkby Wharfe—The Church—Ancient Crosses—Antiquity of Grimston and Kirkby—Picturesque Surroundings.

THE WILD FLOWERS OF ELMET - 257

BY F. ARNOLD LEES, M.R.C.S.

INDEX.

	PAGE
Aire, River	47, 126
Ancient Animals	1
Ancient Seas	2, 16
Ancient Birds	3
Ainsty	8, 18
Aldborough Pavement	12
Aberford	15, 16, 20
Angles, The	17, 25, 28, 29
Agricola	17
Adel	21, 23, 53, 57, 58, 59, 62, 63, 109
Aldwoodley	21, 22, 53, 57, 64, 109
Athelstan	29, 199, 234
Antiquities	61, 77, 166, 250, 252, 256
Arnley	73
Austhorpe	115
Alnshouses	124
Aberford	124, 128, 135, 157, 158, 160, 162
Animal Fidelity	230, 231
Acclom (fam.)	232
Ægir, The	243
Abbeys	238
Black Fen	234
Benedict, St.	236
Bolton Percy	250
Briggate	73, 75, 77, 79, 80
Botany	108, 130, 138, 139, 188, 189, 208, 252, 256, 257
Barrowby	116, 117
Bullerthorpe	116
Blands, The	124
Brotherton	131
Byran Hall	132
Barnbow	134, 138
Belfry, Old	167
Birds	180, 212
Bondbridge Farn	209
Barkston Ash	210
Biggan	212, 215, 216
Bishopdyke	216, 222, 227, 228
Brayton Barf	217
Bishopwood	218, 222

	PAGE
Bishopthorpe	225
Bowett, Archbishop	225
Boggart Brig	234, 236
Brigantes	6, 7, 8, 12, 17, 43, 49, 56, 61, 127
Bronze Weapons	10
Barwick-in-Elnet	15, 16, 17, 20, 32, 50, 72, 121, 123, 140, 142, 150, 156
Bearruc	16, 144
Becca Banks	16, 18, 157, 163
Branhan	17, 20, 21, 22, 152, 165
Blubberhouse Moor	21
Brandon	21, 58
Blacknoor	21, 55, 57
Bilburgh	25
Bede, The Venerable	26, 32, 38, 47, 51, 72, 100
Brunanburgh	29, 31, 51, 75, 197, 199, 220
Brumby	32
Bernicia	44
Breary	53, 55
Branhope	53
Buckingham, Duke of	54, 164
Burley Grove	70
Cookridge	53, 54, 58
Calcaria	61
Chevin	65
Call-way	75
Crosses, Templars', etc.	78, 115, 123, 145, 148, 166, 187, 191, 203, 256
Castle of Leeds	81
Chapeltown	91, 92, 93
Cobble Hall	94
Colton	113, 114
Colyson, Robt. (Will of)	115
Calder, River	125
Cuckoo (bird)	154
Coins, Old	166
Clifford, Lord	195
Celtic Earthworks	7
Cartismandua	10, 11
Caractacus	10, 11
Castleford	13, 14, 20, 125, 126, 127

xiv.

	PAGE
Cock, River	13, 15, 16, 20, 47, 134, 136. 156, 169, 184, 256
Craw, River	15, 161
Camboduunm	20, 100
Claro	25
Cawood	29, 30, 217, 219, 222. 224, 227, 231, 232, 234, 242
Celts	30, 126
Cerdic	35, 38
Cearl	37
Cadwallader	38, 42, 45. 100
Coifi	39, 41
Canden	40, 43, 50, 160, 177
Crida	41
Cadvan	42
Crossgates	48, 98
Constantine	52, 219
Devils Arrows	8
Danes, The	17, 29, 241
Deira	26, 27, 33, 42, 44
Danish Cross	33
Donesday Book	79, 98, 120, 216
Darnley, Lord	113
Dodsworth	118
Danum (Doncaster)	124, 125
Despenser (fam.)	141, 198
Dawson, Billy	149
Dacre, Lord	187, 188, 190, 191, 195
Dintingdale	193, 195, 196
Earthworks	15, 17, 46, 164, 166, 186
Eastdale Beck	16
Ernine Street	20, 122, 124, 134
Eltofts	22
Engles	27
Edwin	35, 38, 40, 43, 51, 100, 103
Ethelfrith	36, 38, 42, 126
Elnet	24. 25, 37, 48, 49, 53, 71, 117, 122, 123, 146, 197
Echope (Eccup)	55, 56, 57, 59
Elmete Hall	93
Ellis (fam.)	147, 152
Eagre, The	243
Fossil Footprints	3, 4
Fenton	25, 212, 213, 215, 243
Franks, The	58
Foundry Mill	97, 109
Fairfax (fam.)	113, 168
Fonts	130, 214, 231
Fairburn	131
Ferrybridge	131
Fryston, Monks'	209
Flowers, Wild	257
Fenland, The	211, 234
Feast, Celebrated	223
Fleet Dyke	246
Fielden (fam.)	256
Geology	4, 5
Grassington	7, 18

	PAGE
Godmudham	39
Gipton	46, 73, 94, 95, 114
Grimes-dyke	48, 134 135
Gascoigne (fam.)	58, 138, 147, 160, 168, 194, 251
Garforth	119, 133
Gray (fam.)	136
Gawthorpe	141, 251
Goblin Tree	233
Gipsy King	233
Garnan-carr	234
Grinston	252, 253, 254
Grin (fam.)	254
Huugate	187, 192, 194
Hammond (fam.)	192
Hunchel (fam.)	204
Hilda, St.	236
Harold, King	240
Humber, River	241
Hubberholme	245
Hagioscope	248
Harewood	251
Hatfield Chase	14. 43
Hook Moor	15, 161
Hall Tower Hill	15, 142, 144
Huddleston	16, 204, 226
Hazlewood	20, 50, 172, 174, 176
Hedley Bar	20, 164
Helaugh	25, 216
Hereric	37
Heathfield	45, 100
Halton	46, 99, 100, 101
Hell-dyke	48
Hungerhills	48
Helena, Empress	52, 64
Headingley	67, 68, 69
Harrison, John	86
Hastings, Lady Betty	130
Hick, Sanny	132, 159
Hope, Canon	142
Isurium	17, 20
Inns, Old	66, 81, 82, 83, 84, 85, 101, 102, 165, 210
Ingran's Hall	95, 113
Ivy House	104
Ingram, Arms of	112
Julius Cæsar	9, 11
Janus Cross	203
Jackdaw Crag (Quarry)	
Jacky Fowler	229
Kippax	8, 15, 28, 73, 119, 120, 121, 123, 124
Kirk Deighton	25
Kirkby Overblow	25
Kirkstall (Abbey, etc.)	52, 53, 55, 79, 84. 92
Killingbeck	73, 99, 101
Kirkgate	79, 81, 101
Knights of St. John	80, 110
King Charles	88

	PAGE
Kitchingman	92
Knowesthorp	105
Knostrop Hall	106
Kidhall (or Kiddle)	150, 152
Kelfield	242
Kirkby Wharfe	254, 255
Leeds	8, 21, 28, 32, 45, 48, 71, 72, 75, 76, 81, 82, 85, 86, 90, 101, 126
Legeolium	13, 124
Lotherton	16, 50, 165, 167, 168, 169
Lead	16, 49, 169, 170, 180
Leathley	49
Ledshan	49, 129, 130, 131
Ledston	49, 121, 128, 129
Lœgyriaus	49, 129
Laci, Ilbert de	79, 191
Lennox, Duke of	113
Lowthers, The	118
Leathers, The	118
Lasincroft	137, 138
Leland	169, 252
Lunby	209
Little Fenton	215
Leet (Courts)	229
Londesborough (fam.)	256
Micklefield	132
Morwick Hall	136
Maypoles	146
Morritt, Mary	149
Markhan, Sir C.	157
Mayden Castle	180, 182, 185
Milford, South	209, 210
Montaign, Archbishop	224, 232
Moreby (fam.)	232
Molehills	243
Milestone, Ronan	14, 64
Map of Ronan Roads, etc.	19, 74, 164
Mercians	28, 43
Morgan's Cross	37, 46, 154
Market Weighton	40
Monks, British	42
Maserfeld (battle)	45
Manston	45, 134, 136
Manor Garth	46, 154
Meanwood	53, 58, 65
Moortown	65, 93
Mowbray, Arns of	77
Mill Hill	81, 89
Moot Hall	83
Middleton	111
More, John	116
Multure	120
Mary Pannell Hill	128
Newton Kyne	20
Norse Cross	32
Nennius	38, 72
Nornan Porch at Adel	60
Newspapers (Early)	88, 89, 166

	PAGE
Newton	131
Noverley (fam.)	164
Nevison	166
Neville (fam.)	168, 218, 220, 223
Newstead	179
Newthorpe	207
Newbiggyng	216
Nun Appleton	216, 245
Ordovices	9
Old Manston	20
Olicana	21
Otley	29, 30, 146, 218, 234
Osric	43
Oswald	45
Oswy	45, 47
Oswin	47
Oak, Skyrack	68, 69
Osmondthorpe	100, 103
Ouse, River	126, 225, 231, 233, 238, 242, 244
Olaf, St.	236
Ozendike	252
Pack-horse Roads	66
Potterton	16, 46, 150, 154, 155
Place-names	28
Paulinus	38, 40
Penda	41, 43, 45, 48, 135, 137
Powys	43
Parisees	49
Pagenel, M. (Charter of)	79
Potternewton	91
Paynes, The	110
Preston, Gt.	118, 119
Peckfield	129
Parlington	139, 140, 161
Pelagius	155
Peter's Post	177
Porches	60
Pepper, Old	230
Percy (fam.)	246
Plunpton (fam.)	255
Quœnburga	41
Quarry Hill	75
Quarries, Old	117, 205, 226
Rest Park	218
Riccall	220, 238, 241
Rednan, Sir Rd.	251
Ronan Invasion	6, 9, 13, 16, 126, 211
Ronan Roads	15, 18, 20, 22, 23, 58, 73, 163
Rudgate	20
Ronan Relics	23, 26, 27, 166, 185
Regulus	32
Rædwald	39, 103
Ripley	49
Ronan Canps	57, 59
Rockley Hall	72, 82, 83
Rawdon	73
Red Hall	88, 134
Roundhay Park	93, 94, 96

	PAGE
Rath, The	122
Roach Grange	122
Raikes Beck	143, 145
Ricarius, St.	158
Reckett (or Rackett), The	208
Ryther	172, 198, 242, 243, 245, 247, 249, 251, 255
Renshaw Wood	180, 183, 185, 186, 188
Rein (or Rine)	166
Street Lane	93
Shadwell	109
Scargills, The	108, 115, 169, 198
Smeaton John	115
Soc	120
Stourton Grange	132
Shippon	138
Superstitions	146, 153, 155, 208, 234, 243
Saxton	179, 180, 196
Stutton	185
Salley (fam.)	192, 193
Steeton Hall	207
Scarthingwell	210
Saxons (the coming of)	220
Selby	230, 236, 237, 238, 239
Scalm Park	234
Storr, William	234
Stanford Bridge (battle)	240
Shillito (fam.)	252
Stone Implements	4, 7
Silures	9, 10
St. Helen's Ford	20
Swillington	20, 116, 117, 119
Stanks	20, 45, 48, 137
Scholes	20, 45, 116, 137
Seacroft	20, 97, 134
Scarcroft	21, 22, 249, 251
Stubbing Moor	22
Saxon Relics	23, 30, 31, 46, 129, 148, 248
Sherburn	25, 29, 51, 146, 195, 197, 198, 200, 203
Stainforth	43
St. Hilda	47
Skyrack	67, 120
St. Gildas	72
Slack	73
Soke Mill	80, 228, 230
Swinegate	81
Tombs	246, 247

	PAGE
Tadcaster	18, 61, 186, 253
Toulston	20
Thorner	21, 22, 117
Thridwulf	46, 50, 101, 155
Tingwald Hill	65
Thoresby	73, 77, 81, 90, 119
Ten plars	78, 80, 110, 112
Templenewsam	80, 109, 115
Tinble Bridge	80
Thorp-Stapleton	107, 108
Thorp Hall	108
Towton	135, 179, 186, 190
Tithebarns	147
Teyes, or Tyas (fam)	169
Thevesdale	177
Towton Moor (battle)	181, 182, 183
Tunulus	144, 188
Tosti and Hardrada	240, 241
Ulleskelf	25, 252, 253
Venutius	10, 11, 12, 18
Vitruvius	23
Villa Regia	100
Vevers (fam.)	137
Vavasour (fam.)	141, 147, 171, 173, 192, 198, 217
Valvasor, Office of	171, 172
Vine Cottage	214
Wendel Hill	15, 51, 144
Walton	20, 25
Wistow	29, 30, 218, 228, 233, 235
Wittenagemot	39
Whinmoor	45, 46, 48, 96, 98, 109, 115, 134, 153
Whitkirk	45, 79, 94, 102, 114, 115, 116
Winwæd Field (battle)	46, 48, 50, 96
Weeping Cross	49
Wade, Marshal	85
Wykebeck	93, 94, 97
Wyke-brig House	98
Woodlesford	118
Wheler (fam.)	129
Wells	137, 139
Water-mills	209
Wharfedale, Lower	211, 253
Wolsey, Cardinal	220, 223
Wheel Hall	239
York	17, 24, 36, 62, 128
Zoology	154

THE OLD KINGDOM OF ELMET

INTRODUCTION.

A Glance Backward.

TIME, measured by periods of many thousand years, has passed since the districts which form our subject were inhabited by a strange creation of gigantic animals, both graminivora, carnivora, and huge amphibia of weird, misshapen form, and fearful crawling reptiles, loathsome and poisonous. Looking backward through the long dim vista of ages, this picture appears to our mind like a phantasy, strange and shadowy.

The tusked mastodon, now long extinct, many tons in weight, browsed in herds with the mammoth, a huge ungainly quadruped. The woolly elephant and buffalo roamed the forest vales of the Aire and Wharfe, for pasture, with the reindeer, giant elk, herds of oxen and wild horse, etc.* Lions and tigers, of a now extinct species, inhabited the forest region, or made their lair in the rank tropical vegetation. Packs of snarling hyænas and howling wolves hunted for food the larger animals. Boars and enormous bears, the latter larger than the existing grisly or polar, haunted the dens and limestone caverns of Craven.

At that period of time Britain was united to the continent from the Atlantic away into the North Sea by land, and over this bridge of earth the wild beasts from the South and East, and also man, probably migrated

* See Museums—Leeds and York.

West. Down this stretch, where now unceasingly rolls the North Sea, a great continental river pursued its course to the Atlantic, fed by the eastern watershed of Britain on the one hand, and on the other by the waterways of Europe.

Tennyson, who, doubtless, had examined the vast remains of primeval growth to be seen on the Lincolnshire coast (from whence the villagers to this day obtain valuable fuel), possibly had the idea of a submerged forest in mind when he wrote "In Memoriam":

"There rolls the deep, where grew the tree;
O, earth! what changes hast thou seen?"

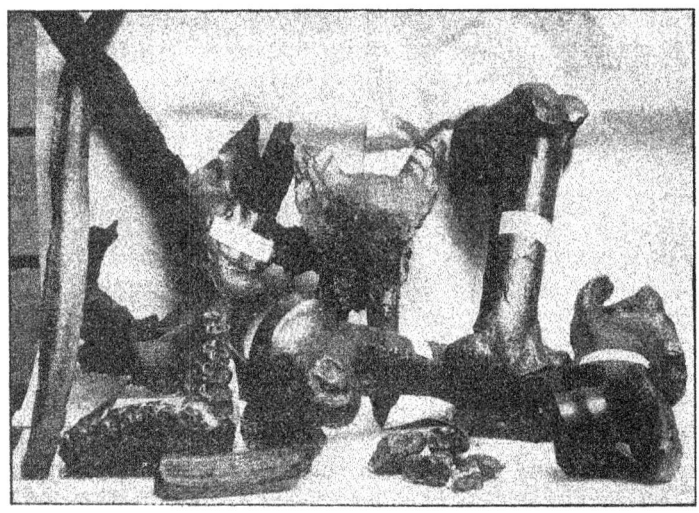

FOSSIL REMAINS OF ELEPHAS ANTIQUES, HIPPOPOTAMUS AND RHINOCEROS, FOUND IN THE AIRE VALLEY.—*(See Zoological Section, Leeds Museum.)*

Remains of submarine forests are to be found all along the east coast of Lincolnshire and Norfolk, and subsidences in the Channel between the mainland and Jersey have taken place within historic times. There is a record that, in 1014, the sea-flood came sweeping over the land and drowned many towns and a great number of people. In Yorkshire, broad inland rivers, lakes, lagoons, swamps, and even seas existed; for instance, down the vales of the Derwent, Mowbray, York, etc. The land-locked waters of the

Upper Wharfe and Aire, at that time united, were of far greater width and depth than to-day, and the current more rapid; these facts are plainly written for those who care to examine the rocks, and higher levels of old-world deposits. The surroundings of river, lake, and swamp were alive with huge amphibious creatures, half serpent, half fish. The cold-blooded plesiosaurus, with fascinating eye, arched its long flexible neck from among the reeds on the swampy shores of the wide-spreading Ouse. Huge batrachia, frog-like in form, hopped about the banks of the Wharfe and Aire, and have left their footprints in the soil behind. Monster fish lizards swam along the surface of the inland waters; and hideous saurians, in scaly covering of mail, haunted the shores of river and swamp. The hippopotamus and woolly rhinoceros wallowed in the mud of the Lower Wharfe,

FOSSIL REMAINS OF MAMMOTH (ELEPHAS PRIMIGENIUS) AND HIPPOPOTAMUS, FOUND IN THE AIRE VALLEY, WORTLEY.—*(See Zoological Section, Leeds Museum.)*

Aire, and Ouse. Such were the wild beasts and reptiles, whilst the shades of night seemed to evoke from the lower world monstrous birds of the owl and bat-like species, the vampire and flying dragon. Buckland says: "With flocks of such like creatures flying in the air, and monstrous plesiosaurus in the sea, and gigantic crocodiles and tortoises crawling on the shore of primeval lake and river, air, sea, and land must have been strangely tenanted in the early period of our infant world."

It is at the latter part of this period, known as the "Post-tertiary," that the biped figure of man appears dimly on the horizon, his arms of defence a knotted club, wrested from the trees of the tropical forest, and, peradventure, with a stone fastened by withes at the end—probably the only rude weapon of man in the early stone age, or "Paleolithic." Century after century roll past in startling numbers—how many the greatest scientist cannot tell us; climatic changes are gradually taking place, many of the larger animals become extinct, and the Almighty Ruler altering the face of Nature, in the succession of ages, more suitable for the dwelling of man in this district. Primeval forests, seeds of our vast coal measures, are slowly, but surely, sinking; the great Eastern Plain, little by little, subsiding below water level, and gradually forming the German Ocean.

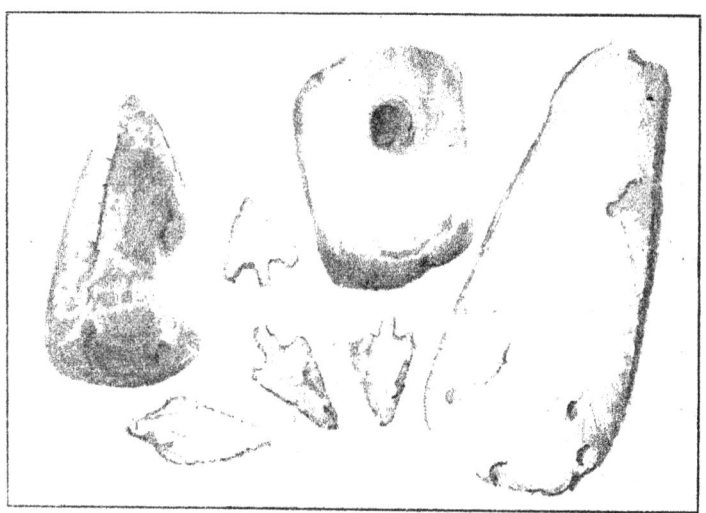

STONE IMPLEMENTS OF WARFARE, FOUND IN ELMET.

Ages still glide slowly by, tropical animals have moved southwards towards the equator—before the atmospheric succession and the final severance of continents—only the fittest survive; but the fossiliferous remains of all the colossal beasts previously mentioned are to be seen in our museums to-day; many specimens have been unearthed in the vicinity of Leeds.[*]

[*] See case, Leeds Museum ; also specimens in the Rooms of Philosophical Society, York.

Slowly, but surely, man is emerging from the darkness of the primeval world, his weapons of flint and stone becoming more useful and artistically formed; the deep sombre woods (his former dwelling-place) are changed for caves, screened with boughs, or a circular hollow, and roof of wattle, or one leaning against an overhanging rock,—such are known as rock shelters. Man's barbaric costume, formed from the skins of wild beasts, held together with pins of bone; from whence we see the slow, but gradual transition upward to the manufacture of rude pottery and beautifully polished stone axes, spears, and arrows (barbed and otherwise), wonderfully fashioned, which are still plentifully distributed over the eastern side of Yorkshire.

Centuries glide away, other people appear upon the scene, and also pass away, leaving slight vestiges of their existence, except burial mounds, bones, and weapons. The wheel of time still revolving until the discovery of bronze marks an epoch in the world's history, and opens out a new era in manufacture, both of weapons and domestic utensils. The gradual progress of man's advance to civilisation is now defined more strongly, and the dawn of the iron age marks the greatest stride upward for man, socially and intellectually. And about this period, and a few centuries previous to the Christian era, we find the original inhabitants of Yorkshire thrust out of their possessions or enslaved by the Brigantes, a strong, hardy race of people, hailing from southern Europe; and from the stubborn resistance which those people offered to the invading legionaries of Imperial Rome, the historic period of Yorkshire properly commences.

CHAPTER I.

THE BRIGANTES.

NEARLY all writers of Yorkshire history agree that the Brigantes, the most important of British tribes at the Roman invasion, and located chiefly within the boundaries of our present Yorkshire, originally immigrated from southern Europe. There are several places on the continent with only slight variations, bearing the above significant name, an appellation formerly given to the hillsmen or highlanders. This does not prove that the districts, either in Britain or on the continent, inhabited by the Brigantes, were strictly mountainous. Brynaich, reaching from the Tyne to the Cheviots, a land of brown heath and mountain, was the northern limit of their possessions. Pliny mentions "the Brigiani, a people dwelling on the western side of the Cottian Alps."*

Between the Brigantes and the tribes located 'twixt the Humber and the Thames was a certain affinity and racial connection; also a great similarity of name and custom. For instance, the Brigante and the Parisi, the latter a semi-independent branch (an offset of the tribe who afterwards gave their name to Paris), occupied the land lying between the Derwent, Humber, and the sea, chiefly the Holderness and South Wold district. The Coritani were a people dwelling in the district lying immediately to the south of the Humber, between the valley of the Trent and the sea. The Iceni, a tribe immortalized for all time in the annals of history, occupied the district between the Fen country, the Wash, and sea coast of Norfolk and Suffolk, to the south of whom, and reaching down to the valley of the Thames, lay the country of the Trinobantes.

These little kingdoms were shut in, on one hand, by immense dark

* The word "brigand" is not improbably derived from the name of the Brigantes; or, perhaps, from Briga, a border town near Nice. The word "brigant" first appears in the sense of a light-armed soldier, and then it takes the meaning of a robber. Next we find "brigante, a pirate"; and the pirate's ship is called a brigantine, of which the word brig is a contraction.

forests, the one to the south, thirty miles or more in width, stretched along the valley of the Thames, nearly from sea to sea. Another forest ran north across the Fen country, and along the valley of the Trent, remains of which we find in the forest of Arden and Sherwood; whilst further north was the great forest of Elmet, reaching from the Don, over the Aire and Wharfe valleys, to Knaresborough, and, beyond, to the more inaccessible moorland of north-east Yorkshire; and still further, rendering the difficulties of approach more dangerous to a hostile army, were the vast stretches of solitude and fen-land, swamp, morass, and rivers overflowing like a sea at flood-time, inundating the land for miles around. Such were the conditions of the country, and the disposition of the several British tribes, occupying the eastern part of Britain, about the period of the Roman invasion.

We have previously spoken of the Brigantes as a tribe: strictly speaking they were a nation, the most powerful, numerous, and warlike of the whole Celtic people at that time inhabiting thi island. Their territory stretched from the Humber's flood to the watershed of the Tyne, embracing what afterwards became the kingdom of North-Humber-land, which included the counties Palatine of Lancaster and Durham, and the hill fastnesses of Cumberland and Westmoreland, the Pennines, from the wilds of Stainmoor to the Peak district. The river Don, in all probability, formed the boundary of the kingdom to the south, to the north of which are still to be traced numerous earthworks, attributed to the Brigantes; but in their great fight with the legions of Rome, the lines of the Aire and Calder were also of paramount importance.

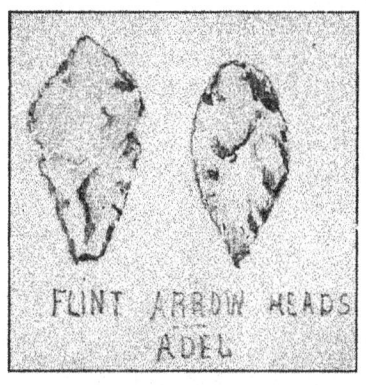
FLINT ARROW HEADS
ADEL

The capital of this great people is considered by all historians to have been on the Ure—"Isuer Brigantum," built on the angle of land lying between the little river Tut and Ure, and adjoining what afterwards became the Isurium of the Roman, now Aldborough; but the Celtic earthworks above Grassington, and those in Grasswood, adjoining, prove the latter district to have been also a great centre of the Brigantes, probably equal, and of even more strategical importance than Isner.

Sixteen miles lower down the Wharfe Llecan (British), Olicana (Roman), now Ilkley, another strong station; still further down the river we find Bardsey (Celtic), and the fortified ridge and coomb, now Compton; lower still we have Calcaria. Nine miles east from the latter station, across the Ein-Stiga (Ainsty) stood Eborach (York), situated in the angle, as it remains to-day, at the confluence of the Foss and the Ouse. Sixteen miles south west from York are the huge earthworks of Barrach (Barwick), from whence runs the long irregular line of entrenchments above the valley of the little river Cock (the Cocru of the Celt), stretching two miles east, beyond Aberford (another strong position), at the confluence of the tiny river Crow and the Cock. Kippax and Caer-Loid-Coit (Leeds) have also been strong positions, guarding the passage of the Aire; and away south-west on the Calder was the important station of Cambodunum; to the south, protecting the passage of the Dun (Don) was Caer-Dune (Doncaster), Caer-Conon (Conisborough).

To the north of those mentioned, and particularly on the wide moorland stretching from the east coast to the Pennine Range, are numerous remains of Celtic settlement and earthworks, this district being the last strong place of refuge for the harried Celt, in his great struggle with the Roman, as it was also in after centuries with the Engle folk. Such were the disposition and chief centres of the Brigantes at the commencement of the Christian era, and at this period, when they appear upon the stage of the world's history, they were not barbarians, but in a fairly advanced stage of civilisation.

THE DEVIL'S ARROWS, BOROUGHBRIDGE.

CHAPTER II.

The Invasion of the Romans.

LED by Julius Cæsar, the conquering legions of Rome turned their attention towards the subjection of Britain, 55 years before the advent of Christ. This invasion or invasions (there was another attempt the year following) did not penetrate beyond the Thames valley, and was of no great importance. Nearly a century later, Aulus Plautius in command of four legions (40,000), and followed soon by the Emperor Claudius, again invaded Britain, and the task of subduing and bringing the various tribes under Roman domination was seriously begun.

It does not come within our province to relate how the Romans fought their way, step by step, over swamp and desolate moorland, and through the great forest belt of the Thames valley, defeating the Atrabates and the Trinobantes; nor does it belong to these pages to explain the great revolt and swoop of the renowned Boadicea, Queen of the Iceni; how her tribe smote with sudden vengeance the Romans for their cruel slaughter of Druids of Anglesey, and of the swift and terrible retribution which followed—eighty thousand Britons were slain, and Boadicea, who could not survive the disaster, fell by her own hands : by this deed, the Iceni dwell in the pages of history for all time, although passing thence into oblivion as a people.

Apart from the Brigantes, the Silures and the Ordovices were the most valiant and difficult of conquest. Their Caers were situated amongst the most inaccessible hill fastnesses of Wales, and for some years, Caractacus, Prince of the Silures, waged an unequal contest with Rome. From motives of policy, the Celtic prince ultimately withdrew his army from his own country (South Wales), and selected a most impregnable position among the hilly fastnesses of the Ordovices (North-east Wales), a formidable retreat, and there offered battle to Ostorius Scapula. This grand old chieftain did all in his power to resist his adversaries, yet nothing could withstand the onslaught of the advancing legion, who with closed ranks and holding their shields high, forming a roof above their heads, swept aside all opposition, and victoriously penetrated the British camp. Amongst the captives was the wife of Caractacus and other members of his family, yet the Silures and their allies were not easily vanquished, the bitter conflict was prolonged for many a year in the hilly fastnesses of the west; thirty pitched

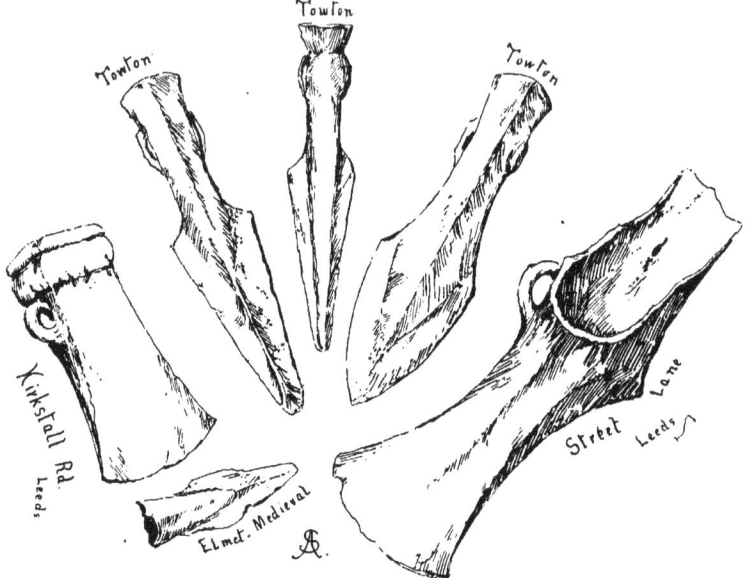

BRONZE WEAPONS, FOUND IN ELMET.

battles, we are told by the Roman historian, were fought before the Celts, inhabiting Wales and the country bordering on the Severn valley, would yield their independence—in fact, at no period during the Roman occupation of this island, was their power supreme in Wales. Here in this lone, wild mountain land, impregnable by nature, the nationality of the Celt has survived unto our time.

Amongst those who gave assistance to the Silures were a strong force of Brigantes and the Coritina, led by Venutius, probably a prince of the latter tribe, and husband to Cartismandua (of infamous memory), Queen of the Brigantes. This army of auxiliaries surprised and gained at least one complete victory over the Romans. Soon after the latter event, a bitter quarrel arose between Cartismandua and Venutius. The story runs that the false Queen, of Cleopatra type, had taken to herself another lover during Venutius' campaign in Wales. Be this as it may, the outcome of the trouble was a split and civil war amongst the Brigantes. With the assistance of other tribes, and the disaffected Brigantes, Venutius made war on Cartismandua. The battle going against her, she craved assistance of the Romans for help to prop up her tottering power; and probably for the first time cohorts of imperial soldiers passed the natural lines of defence—the valleys of the Don, Aire, and Wharfe—and thus gained admission into Isner, the capital. Had the Britons been united at this juncture of affairs, determined to resist the invader with their united strength, the legionaries would probably have never penetrated through the strong natural boundaries of the kingdom (the waterways running east and west from the Pennines, making this the northern boundary of their empire; instead of, as afterwards, the Tyne and Irthing valleys), or, at least, would have found the conquest of this strong people one of far greater difficulty, requiring all the strength which Rome would have been able to despatch for that purpose.

It was at this time, when that grand old type of soldier, Caractacus— so long the glory of his nation and the terror of the enemy—fought his last fight and fled north, across the Severn and through the Cannock Forest and over the Pennines to the capital of Cartismandua, doubtless, longing to have another opportunity of striking, for freedom, the invaders of his country. Sad to relate, his hopes were cruelly dispelled; for the terms of stipulation, made between the Queen and the Romans for the assistance of the latter, was the infamous betrayal of her kinsman—for the prince was a relation of hers—into the hands of the enemy, to enhance the triumph and glory of the victorious army on their return and parade through the streets of Rome.

This took place about the year A.D. 51; but the gallant deeds of this brave soldier prince, and his undaunted reply before the tribunal of Cæsar, shine out with a brilliant lustre across the gulf of eighteen centuries. For has he not been the model for the historian, the poet, the artist, and the composer, whilst the name of the false-hearted Queen has been branded with infamy?* Her further history can be told in a few words.

* How like her prototype, Cleopatra of the Nile, was this queen. The three attributes of feminine distinctiveness were lacking in each: that which marks the woman, the wife, the mother, were cast aside. Spurred on by a sordid, selfish ambition, each could walk complacently over the troubles and ravages of their bleeding country into the arms of the strong one—the conqueror—whoever he might be.

Unable to hold her own against Venutius, even with the assistance she invoked, she fled south with the cohorts of Didius about the year 54, and so passed into obscurity for ever.

Venutius, who seems to have been a great leader and a worthy representative of Caractacus, now became King of the Brigantes, and successfully maintained his own against the efforts of the enemy, keeping the kingdom intact for a period of sixteen years, until A.D. 70, when the conquest of the North British was begun in such earnest, as could only end in subjection or death. Yet for the space of ten years the bitter fight was waged, until the strength of the nation gradually waned before the superior power of Rome.

So much for written history. We must now examine and endeavour to point out the evidences of this great struggle.

About the year A.D. 70, Vespasian, having become emperor, sent over into Britain well-equipped armies commanded by Petilius Cerealis, who pressed home the attack on the Brigantes with a firm resolve to bring them into complete subjection. And it is from this date that we catch the echo of the almost ceaseless tramp of the legionaries, with all their military accoutrements and panoply of war rolling north.

Between the hill fastnesses of peak and forest to the west, and the impassable fen-land around the mouths of the rivers on the east, ran a strip or neck of land, the only passable road to the north at that period, across which, and to the north of the Don, the Brigantes made a strong line of entrenchments, so formidable as to stay for some time the advance of the

TESSELATED PAVEMENT FROM ALDBOROUGH, DEPICTING THE CAPITOLINE WOLF, ROMULUS AND REMUS.

invaders; along the valley of the Don and its tributaries, forming a remarkable natural barrier, and the first line of defence, we can imagine the Brigantes waiting in readiness to check the advancing foe.

Many battles were fought; but how the Celtic "Caer-Dune" (Doncaster), inclosed with ditch and rampart, was stormed we cannot say, for no complete story of the bitter fight for possession has been handed down to our time. The struggle at the fords, the gates to the north, would be most protracted and severe.

Slowly, but surely, the Romans pressed back the defenders to their second line of defence, the vales of the Aire and Calder and the high lands, extending like a frontier wall north-east of the Aire for several miles. From Doncaster, the Eagle banner of the legions was planted at Legeolium (Castleford), from hence the Roman road (still to be distinctly traced) runs high and straight above the low-lying lands of the Aire valley, and pierces the bold frontier wall—a defensive boundary and the western gateway into the wolds of Elmet. Here again the British may have taken their position for the defence of the Elmet country; and there are not wanting evidences of the great struggle for existence and supremacy.

From the high vantage ground, the harried Celt would naturally watch the advance of his foes. Here pressing home a charge; now retreating, or lying in ambush; every yard of ground from the river line being bitterly contested.

Through the dim haze of centuries we can almost hear the dire tumult of the struggle. For the Britons fully realized that once the enemy gained possession of this line of defence, it would presage disaster and ruin to their kingdom.

Still northward rolled the din of war and strife, until the third line of defence—the valley of the little river Cock—was reached. Along the northern bank of this river there runs, for several miles, a huge rampart and ditch, strengthened here and there by a double line at this day. From the top of the vallum to the bottom of the ditch is, in many places, from twelve to twenty feet in depth. At the base, in the deep hollow scooped out by the natural process of time, slowly runs the little river; at that period, dammed back by natural obstructions, in addition to the blocking of the waterway with flood-gates, by the defenders, the beck would be swollen in width and depth to a large river, a hundred yards or more across, a formidable retreat with the high rampart added, strong enough to check, for some considerable time, even an army of Rome. And making the difficulty of approach to the line of defence all the more dangerous and deadly, was the great forest of Elmet, stretching in one unbroken line from the Don across the valleys of Aire, Calder, and Wharfe, to what, in after centuries, became known as the wide forest of Knaresborough; whilst over the lower reaches of these rivers, from the Trent and along the Ouse valley to the Lower Nidd, there existed a wild trackless waste of marsh, forest, and fen-land, the southern part of which is still known as Hatfield Chase, formerly tenanted by innumerable flocks of wild fowl, and where the aborigines, who understood the intricate mazes, could glide swiftly hither and thither amongst reeds and mud in their light coracles, as much at home and at ease as the wild fowl; forest and swamp forming extensive coverts where

ROMAN MILESTONE FOUND AT CASTLEFORD.

the harried Briton could flee for refuge or lay in ambush, ready to pounce on the Roman soldier when at disadvantage. This was the state of Yorkshire at the invasion.

Leaving garrisons to keep the road clear and guard the fords at Danum, Doncaster, and Castleford, the Romans plunged right into the heart of Elmet, following the line of road as it runs to-day, probably at that period a British trackway, direct to Isurium. Just to the left at Kippax are vestiges of a Celtic fort or rath, and other evidences of fortification along the edge of this hill frontier, but not of sufficient strength to arrest for long the progress of an army, only to be brought to bay on reaching the environs of Aberford. The prefix, aber, is Celtic, and means a confluence of two streams which are to be found here, in the angle of which, and on a high sharp ridge, the town stands. Here, guarding the line of road and passage of river, the Britons held a strong position, well chosen, naturally a defensive site; close by, on the north, runs the Cock; and a deep indent or ravine on the east, down which filters a small stream rising on the confines of Hook Moor, known as the Crow or Craw (to crawl). It is only by examination of this angle of land

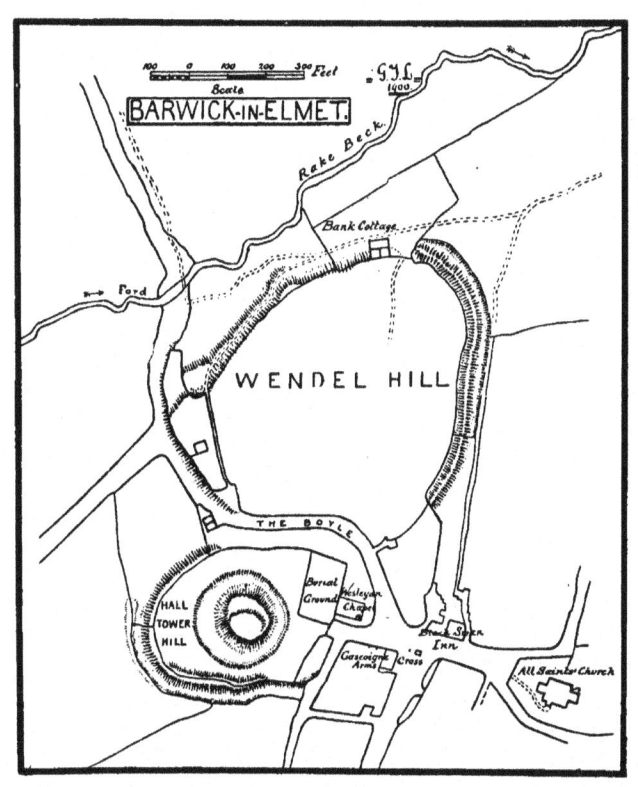

PLAN OF EARTHWORKS BARWICK-IN-ELMET.

at the confluence of the streams, that one recognises the defensive advantages of this strong position at Aberford in the past. Two miles west, situated in the fork of two main streams, the river Cock and Eastdale Beck, is the Berrauc of the Briton, and Barwick of to-day; from a natural and strong military point, the position here has been most wisely chosen. The stronghold is composed of a centre mound and double trench and rampart, the outer ditch also enclosing a large space, comprising several acres; at the northern extremity, the ground falls sharply down from the fighting platform to the swampy ground of Eastdale or Rake Beck, nearly 300 feet below, practically forming an impassable barrier on this side.

As Barwick will be again mentioned in the following pages during our description of Elmet, we leave it for the present, and glance at the rampart and ditch which has been continued on the south side along the edge of the bank, high above Eastdale Beck. Here, in the past, existed a large swamp or lagoon. Continuing along this bank for some two or three hundred yards beyond the Potterton Road, the defensive line descends into the valley bottom, crosses the stream, climbs the opposite slope, turns at a sharp angle to the right, and passes along part of the Potterton estate in an irregular line, to the north of the beck. From thence the rampart enters a woodland ridge, known to-day as Becca Banks, and so on just above the river Cock to Aberford; it crosses the Roman highway at the latter place, and continues a mile or more along the north bank of the river. Whilst three hundred yards east from Aberford, another trench and vallum commences at the beck on the south side; runs up the incline to the brow of the slope, turns a sharp angle to the left, enters Raper Hills, crosses the Saxton road, and terminates abruptly opposite Lotherton. This line of earthworks at the finish points direct to Huddleston, about two miles away, where are still to be seen, in the woods, remains of trenches supposed to have been formed by the Brigantes in this great struggle.

Apart from the above-mentioned, between Lead Mill and Aberford are fragments of other earthworks. The Britons may have protected the shallower parts, and the fords, with stakes shod with iron, as Bede informs us was done at the fords on the Thames, to withstand the Roman advance. It is quite evident that a line of forts and earthworks have extended from the swamps of Aire valley, between Leeds and Castleford, on the west, to Sherburn on the east, and the position of the trench and the fighting platform, in every instance, faces the south; all point to the fact that from that quarter the enemy came. "Were those invaders the Romans?" some may naturally inquire. The question is easily answered. It could not be the Angles, for those people came from the east and spread over the wolds, or extended westwards from the Humber, along the waterways of the Don and the Aire. The Danes, who came in war galleys, chose for their highway into the county riverway and creek. The Romans, on the other hand, were great road builders, and were the only invaders who fought their way direct from south to north, and in less than half-a-century from the second invasion, had practically conquered the island, from the Channel to the wall

G. T. Lowe.]   EARTHWORKS, BARWICK-IN-ELMET, FROM THE WEST.

barrier, raised to protect the northern frontier of their empire; and the great highroad which we find to-day, running over the wolds of Elmet right through Aberford, over Bramham Moor to Isurium and York, is the work of their hands.

From the foregoing remarks I think it will be apparent that the Brigantes have held the valley of the Cock with a tenacious grip, and it has been the scene of the main struggle, in fact, the "Albuera of the campaign." How the line was broken no record tells. The final conquest was reserved for Agricola, A.D. 78-80. His army marched in two columns, one striking north, the other operating north-east from the borders of Wales. Faithful native guides conducted them by ancient trackways, through the almost inaccessible forest and mountain passes, etc. Thus equipped, he went through Yorkshire with a stern and steady tramp, and probably swept aside the opposition at Becca Banks, and also broke the Bramham Moor camp; then, instead of fighting along the Rudgate to Isner, turned aside, and gained York by a flank march from Tadcaster, across the Ainsty, and probably passing from thence, both by road and the riverway, to storm and capture Isner, the capital of the Brigantes.*

It would have been some pleasure to have known the end of Venutius, the gallant Celtic prince, but on this point history is silent. He may have fled with those who would not stoop to the yoke of the invader, and found refuge amid the hills and deep ravines of the upper dales, which for at least another generation remained unconquered. The vast remains of Celtic occupation point to such a city of refuge at Grassington, where for some time the Brigantes kept up some state and show of independence. At length, overstepping the limits of prudence, the latter made war on a tribe under Roman protection, and, becoming emboldened by success, cut up a cohort of imperial troops. This deed brought down on their heads the strong avenging arm of Rome, and the Brigantes, as a united and independent people, from this date ceased to exist.

THE ROMAN ROADS.

That the Romans were great road makers, requires no further proof than that the remains of such can still be traced after a lapse of 1,600 years. All roads in the north centred in and radiated to and from York. Those which principally concern our subject are immediately to the south and west of the ancient city. Possibly some of these roads were partly built on the line of ancient British trackways, which, however, unlike the Roman ways (which nearly always ran direct from point to point), deviated according to the circumstance and nature of the ground.

* "At the return of summer," says Tacitus, "Agricola assembled his army. On their march, he commended the regular and orderly, and restrained the stragglers; he marked out the encampments, and explored in person the estuaries and forests. At the same time, he perpetually harassed the enemy by sudden incursions; and, after sufficiently alarming them by an interval of forbearance he held to their view the allurements of peace and repose. By this management, many states, which till this time had asserted their independence, were now induced to lay aside their animosity, and to deliver hostages. These districts were surrounded with castles and forts, disposed with so much attention and judgment, that none of the newly explored part of Britain was left unguarded."

THE OLD KINGDOM OF ELMET.

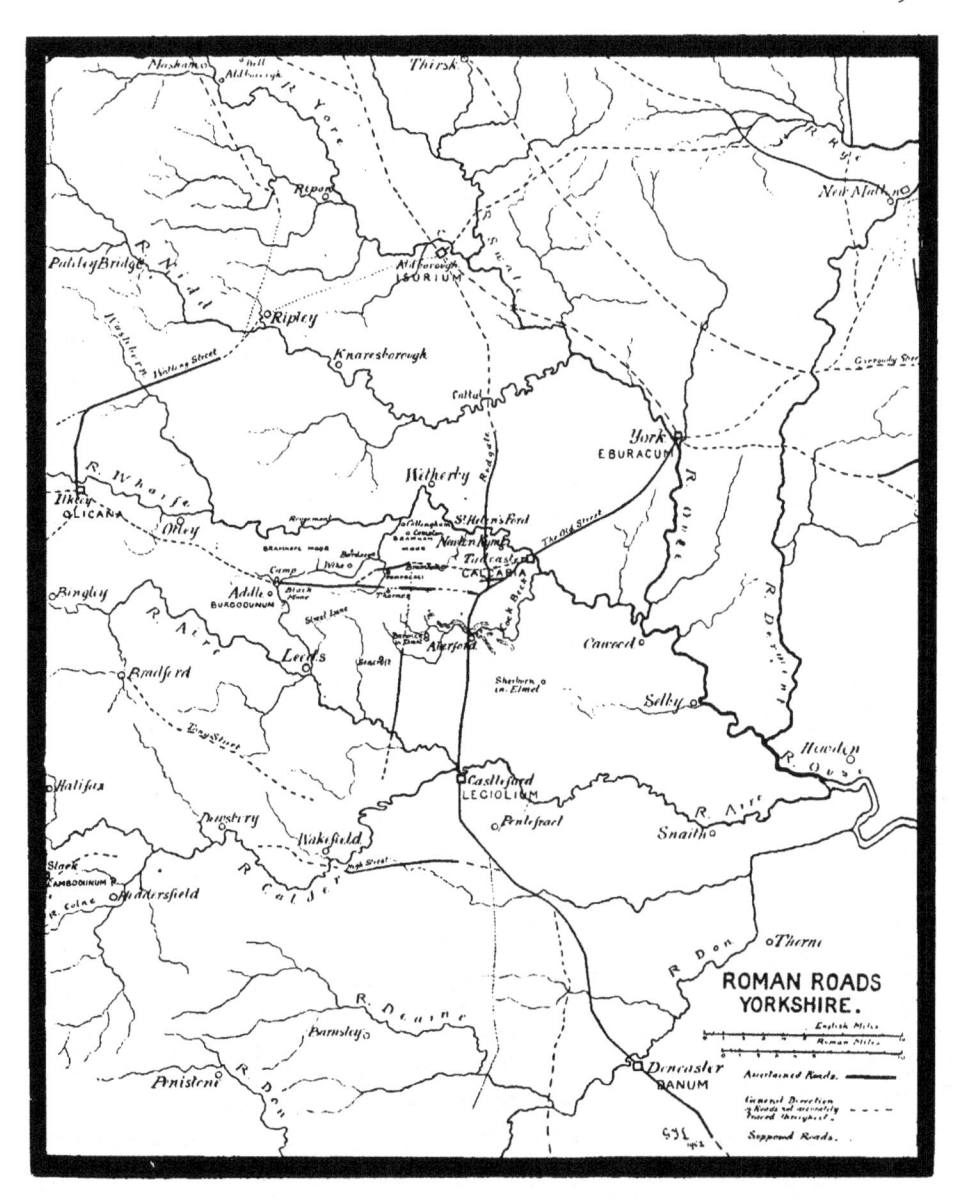

20   THE OLD KINGDOM OF ELMET.

One of the four main trunk roads of Roman construction—the Ermine* Street—ran direct through Elmet, crossing the Don at Doncaster, the Aire at Castleford, and the Cock at Aberford. Hereabouts the old road is easily traceable, and still called "Roman Rigg." From thence, passing through the Hazlewood estates and fringing Bramham Park, a branch diverges sharply to the right, just beyond Hedley Bar, for Tadcaster; passing over the Wharfe, opposite the site of the present church, and across the Ainsty to York.

The other road, the Rudgate, Celtic, Rhyd-a-ford (possibly an early British way), ran by Toulston down to the Wharfe, past Newton Kyme, and crossed at St. Helen's Ford; thence over the western fringe of Ainsty, leaving Walton (Wheales-tun) to the left, and over the Nidd at Cattal, and forward, by way of Whixley and Little Ouseburn, to Aldborough —the Isner of the Briton, and Isurium of the Roman.

Another lesser road ran from Mancunium (Manchester) to Cambodunum (Slack), and over the Aire near Swillington, and into the Elmet. This via-road or street can still be distinctly traced running for some distance on, and then parallel with the present road. Thence continuing through a stretch of wood, belonging to Templenewsam estate, and over the fields to the Selby Road. The track is still visible—one of the fields here is called "Roman Rigg" Field. The road line now passes the West Yorkshire Colliery, runs between Old Manston and Stanks, where it crosses the river Cock. Near this crossing, the rigg, or bank, is very high; from hence we have traced it over two fields, pointing in a direct line to Scholes; it is finally lost by the wood, adjoining the Seacroft and Barwick highway. Although the line of road here becomes invisible, there

---

* Korme, the Men of Earn or Fen-land, the Ermings, through which this road passes from the south. Thus the name, which at first had been given to a portion of the road, which bordered the Fens, was at length given to the whole line of road.

is no reason to doubt that it joined the road leading from Adel over Bramham Moor, remains of which are discovered just to the east of Thorner.

Another military way, which crosses Elmet, ran from the main street, crossing from Deva (Chester) by way of Olicana (Ilkley), over the Blubberhouse Moor to Isurium. Deviating from the above road, the one under our present consideration ran east, from Ilkley, along the high ridge above the Wharfe, over Guiseley Moor, Carlton, and Bramhope, past Cookridge, to the Roman camp at Adel, which is still traceable. From hence, the

[By *Owen Bowe*]
SECTION OF ROMAN ROAD, NUT HILL, NEAR ABERFORD.

line of road continues along the ridge of high lands of Aldwoodley, crossing the Leeds and Harrogate highway, thence over Brandon and Blackmoor, where many relics appertaining to this way have been turned up of late years; also the debris and remains of furnaces used for smelting purposes.

From Blackmoor to the Leeds and Wetherby road, one can walk on the Rig. Near Scarcroft, the road splits into two branches, one running on the lofty ridge past Eltofts Wood and through Thorner, and beyond, the track crosses the south side of Bramham Park, and hereabouts joins the Ermine Street, three miles south of Tadcaster. The other branch previously mentioned, is clearly to be traced in the meadow, south side of Scarcroft, where it is cut by the present Wetherby Road. From thence it ran north of Wothersome, over Stubbing Moor, and forward to Bramham, joining the Rudgate in the vicinity of Toulston.

[*By Owen Bowen.*
ON THE LINE OF THE ROMAN ROAD, ALDWOODLEY, LOOKING WEST TOWARDS THE CHEVIN.

An old man, upwards of fourscore, told us that sixty years ago he assisted in the breaking up of Stubbing Moor, and at that time the site of the road was for some distance laid bare, and a vast quantity of large irregular blocks of stone were carted away.

At other places on this street, portions of the road, in the shape of paving stones, some even six feet in length, and a foot or eighteen inches broad, have been laid bare by the plough and spade, principally on Blackmoor, Brandon, and at Aldwoodley. These stones, relics of the road, are to be found in several situations, and are objects of various comment to the interested wayfarer.

ROMAN AND SAXON RELICS AT ADEL.

VITRUVIUS'S DIRECTIONS FOR MAKING A ROMAN ROAD.—The foundation began by making two parallel furrows, the intended width of the road, and then removing all the loose earth between them till they came to the hard solid ground, and then filling up this excavation with fine earth, hard beaten in. This first layer was called "pavimentum." Upon it was laid the first bed of the road, consisting of small squared stones nicely ranged on the ground, which was sometimes left dry, but often a large quantity of fresh mortar was poured into it. This layer was termed "statumen." The next was called "rudus," or "ruderatio," and consisted of a mass of small stones broken to pieces and mixed with lime in the proportion of one part of broken stones to two of lime. The third layer or bed, which was termed "nucleus," was formed of a mixture of lime, chalk, pounded or broken tiles or earth broken together, or of gravel or sand and lime mixed with clay. Upon this was laid the crust surface or pavement of the road. It was composed sometimes of stones, set like the paving-stones in our streets, and sometimes of flag-stones cut square or polygonally, and also, probably oftener, of a firm bed of gravel and lime. The roads were thus raised higher than the surrounding ground, and on this account the mass was termed "agger." The smaller roads were of simpler construction.

CHAPTER III.

The Kingdom of Elmet.

OUT of the chaos following the collapse of the Roman power in Britain, there came forth on the page of history the little kingdom of Elmet, appearing only like the glimmer of a small star when surrounded by those of greater magnitude, rising forth into life, as it were, to battle for the old order of things, withstanding the shock, inrush and tumult of barbarian hordes from other lands, thirsty with long waiting for the final severance of the Roman from the Briton. So it stands forth out of the chaos and dismembered fragments of Romanised Celtic Britain.

The chronicles of this tiny kingdom are of the briefest, but those who care to study its history must seek for information in the strong and natural defensive advantages of the district, the river boundaries surrounding it on all sides, and in its tumuli, raths, mounds, and intrenchments; also in the Celtic names of its rivers and mountains, etc. From its rise to its overthrow, extending over three to four centuries, Britain was environed by enemies. Pirates from Ireland invaded the western coast, Pict and Scot raided and burnt down to the very walls of York, and the Angles, who came in their war keels, ravaged the Yorkshire coast line, spreading desolation and ruin over the wold country. Then began that long and bitterly contested fight, lasting over centuries, a war of possession and dispossession, a pushing back of the Celtic people, and a gradual settling down on the land by the Anglo-Saxon race. It was this period which produced such great men of Celtic stock, as Aurelius Ambrosius, Vortigern, Uther-Pendragon, Merlin the bard, and the immortal Arthur

The Scotch chronicles say that in 521, King Arthur kept Christmas at York, surrounded by his courtiers and famed knights of the Round Table. No other city in Great Britain can dwell on such historic scenes of the past as the ancient city of York, and the visit of this prince adds another link to its long chain of famous personages and strange scenes enacted there.

THE OLD KINGDOM OF ELMET. 25

Tennyson, in that soul-inspiring theme, "The Passing of Arthur," has breathed around this old hero of glamour and romance a beautiful, yet strange and weird spirit of immortality.

It is not possible to exactly determine the extent of the kingdom of Elmet: perhaps it is best measured by natural surroundings, being situated in a boundary of river, swamp, moor, forest, and mountain. In its most prosperous era, the greatest width from east to west comes under fifty miles, probably reaching from Sherburn on the east to the hill fastnesses lying between the head-waters of the Aire and Nidd.

Starting from Sherburn, along the border of the Fen district, where in later centuries the Angle raised his Fentown (Fenton), and the Norseman Ulla, Ullaskelf—the boundary follows the line of the Wharfe past Tadcaster, with the outlying Celtic stations of Bilburgh, Helaugh, and Walton, and so on to Kirk Deighton and Kirkby Overblow, and possibly reached north in its most palmy days as far as Knaresborough, which gives name to the Claro Wapentake. The word "Claro" is a corruption of the Celtic word "Caer-haug'r" (the hill of the Caer). Thence the natural boundary runs over the high ridge of moor dividing the watershed of the Wharfe and Nidd. Beyond this high ridge the Angles seem scarcely to have penetrated, the British having held undisputed possession until the period of Norse invasion; the place-names along the north bank of the Wharfe are, with few exceptions, all of Norse derivation.

Fragments. Sepulchral Tablets.
YORK

The natural boundary on the western side of the kingdom spreads towards the wild mountain range, the head-waters of the Wharfe. Skipton stood within its western fringe; thence the boundary passed over the moors in the direction of Keighley and Bingley; following the basin of the Aire (a natural barrier) to where it merges into the great Ouse plain between the western fringe of Elmet and the northern rheged (a frontier) or Celtic kingdom of Cumbria; which reached from the mouth of the Ribble to the Westmoreland Fells, a wild district, wild even to-day, and here the Celtic blood is still more pure than in any other part of Yorkshire. Here in the early centuries ruled smaller chieftains, yet in subordinate authority to the power of Elmet, whose influence reached to the confines of Cumbria. Such was the kingdom of Elmet at the commencement of the sixth century, by the end of which it had already been shorn and much narrowed in its proportions.

Roman Altars. Found at York.

The Anglian people were at this period rapidly settling between the Aire and Calder; Ethelfrith, the conquering King of Deira, who, Bede says, was the most severe scourge the Celts ever met with, boldly fought his way up the river valleys, and led his army over the wild moorlands of north Yorkshire, passed down the vale of the Ribble, reached the Dee country by a rapid march, gave battle to the north Welsh, gaining a decisive victory, capturing the important city of Deva (Chester), and thus severed the connection and line of influence and communication between the Britons of North Wales, Cumbria, and Elmet.

The great enemy to the State seems chiefly to have come from the East; even as early as the fourth century, small war bands of Angles landed at various points along the Yorkshire coast, and from that date to the capture and sack of York, one hundred and fifty years later, or to even a century later still, when Edwin overran Elmet. The danger to the kingdom seems ever to have been increasing from the East, from the beautiful moorlands of Brynaic and chalk wolds of Devyr, with its long frontier of shimmering ocean.

It was here by the North Sea the Celts encountered the first brunt of heathen fierceness, and from hence the Engles passed westward, ravaging and harrying the wolds and moorlands, yet the conquest of Yorkshire was not the work of a year or even a century. For many a year the Britons held the Angles pinned to the eastern wolds. and when at length driven from their beloved " Devyr "—Saxon Deira, they fell back behind the line of the Derwent, a natural and for long an effectual barrier, stretching from the moors of North York to the huge swamp and fen-land of the Ouse. How long the war bands of the Engles, or Deirans, as at this period called, were held to the east of this line of the Derwent we cannot say. Through the lapse of centuries we can almost hear the tumult of the struggle. Its very length tells of the stubbornness, resistance, and obstinacy of the Celt, who retired slowly and sullenly backward, step by step.

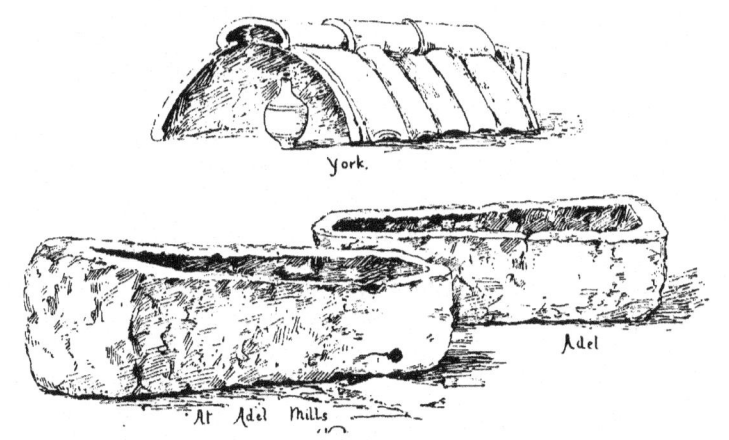

ANCIENT COFFINS, FOUND AT ADEL AND YORK.

Then came the final rush and swoop on the old city of York, for three centuries the home of Rome's famed legion, the residence of Emperors, and for long the capital of Britain. Standing in the angle of land between the confluence of the Foss and the Ouse, its natural and artificial defences can be easily studied to-day. But the city of the Romans, with its wealth, its temples and other noble buildings, villas, baths, its tesselated pavements, and marble statues, and all the refinements of civilisation, art, and luxury, fell beneath this great swoop of the Engle folk; and the treasures of palace and temple, the pomp and luxury of imperial Rome, were trodden beneath the heel of the

Pagan, or, broken and otherwise mutilated, were buried beneath the ruin (wreck, and burning, and the accumulation of debris and desolation following in the wake), to be unearthed in after centuries as evidences of York's former greatness.

Still the Elmet kingdom remained intact for at least another hundred years, wedged in, as it were, between the Deirans and Mercians, its cordon of foes gradually coiling round and hemming its defenders in on every side. To the west, however, the line of the Aire was at least for three centuries the eastern frontier of the Engle folk. Settlements in the Wapentake of Claro were even of a much later date, and then only very precarious; in fact, the vestiges of the Engle in this Wapentake are only very faint, and only slight in Skyrack Wapentake.

From the mouth of the Wharfe to Arthington, their power has been small indeed, for the latter place is their first settlement; and from thence to Addingham, seventeen miles further, we find the same dearth of Angle colonisation. On the east bank of the Aire we have also this circumstance: Swillington marks their first settlement from the mouth of the Aire upwards, being situated near the site of the Roman vicinal, Headingley being the second, also standing near the line of road from Ilkley to Adel.

Between the north-east bank of the Lower Aire, from Ledstone or Kippax to the north watershed of the Wharfe, the place-names reveal in their Celto word combinations Celtic occupation and rule, coeval with the Norse invasion and occupation; hill, valley, and river, in many instances, remain purely Celtic; for instance, the "chevens" (cefn), "bryns," "lyns," "pens," "dunes" or "duns," the "combes" and "coeds." In fact, if we examine the high ridge running from Bramham to Ilkley, along the south side of the Wharfe, we shall find in many instances a survival of Celtic place-names. Even our great industrial city of Leeds holds in its name, along with several other places, the memory of a Celtic people—the Leods or Ludees. In the name of its river, the Aire—the "bright shining water" (now, alas! black), we have another evidence of their occupation. In fact, the names of our rivers and streams all reveal their Celtic story; the word Wharfe we obtain from the same people, whose poetical tongue had, in obedience to a poet's eye, combined the root word ch-wefru or g'arw—the "hurrying, gushing, violent water." To the same eye and tongue, the Angle owed the name of the river Nidd (Nawdd)—the "dark, obscure, secluded." To the Celt, also, the invader owed his Crimple (the crwm-pwll)—"bending, winding pool, properly descriptive of the shimmering waters of that twisted knoll-bent pool."

Turning for the present to the south-west fringe, and extending our research across the vale of the Calder to the Don, we there find numerous evidences of early Angle colonisation. From Snaith, perhaps the most eastern of Engle settlements, to Cononley, a distance of forty miles, the valley of the Aire, to the south and west, has been permanently occupied since the end of the sixth century

Between Snaith and Woodlesford there are the Anglian stations of Pollington and Kellington, Knottingley and Darrington; beyond, we have Drighlington, Stanningley, Manningham, and Bingley. On the Calder, we find Horbury, Dewsbury, Almondbury, Littleborough: Further south still, reaching to the valley of the Don, we find quite a cluster of "worths" and "burghs"—Coningsburgh, Sprotborough, Greasborough, Worsborough, Masborough, Stainborough, Kexborough, and Hemsworth and Badsworth or Brodsworth; besides a host of "hams" and "tons," all pointing to a line of river frontier, and to the wedge of Saxon colonisation thrust in between the Celts of Elmet and their kinsmen to the west.

There is one great historic fact in connection with Elmet, which probably marks the boundaries and limits of the ancient kingdom more clearly than any other, and the outcome of King Athelstan's great victory over the combined army of Danes and Scotch at Brunanburgh, viz., the creation of the "liberty" of Cawood, Wistow, and Otley, including the palace and lordship of Sherburn, with all the villages and hamlets appertaining thereto, with full power and rights vested in the Archbishop. This policy of Athelstan showed great forethought, as well as a gracious and kingly act.

The Danes and their allies had for long been a thorn in the side of the Angle kings. Anlaf, the Norse leader in this battle, was the pretender to the kingdom of Northumbria, and a Pagan or Christian by turns, according to circumstances. The sea kings, and other princes of the north, were all very jealous of Athelstan's great power, and nearly always in open or covert rebellion, continually threatening his over-lordship and supremacy.

All through the centuries of harrying and plunder, by Angle and Dane, the Celt had survived, and still clung tenaciously (although spirit-broken and considerably reduced both in number and power) to the little kingdom of Elmet, probably fighting on the side of Athelstan, in that king's great battle against the confederacy of the north.*

* In a great genot, held at Nottingham by Athelstan, A.D. 930, there attended, among others, three Welsh princes. This is not the only instance of the generosity of this famous king, for his magnanimity and generosity extended, on many occasions, even to his great enemies.

The Celts of Elmet were of Christian faith, and had been so, more or less, since its introduction into the island by the Apostles, during the Roman domination; thus the reason for the creation of the "liberty" of Cawood, Wistow, and Otley was twofold: firstly, the existence of the Christian Celt in Elmet; secondly, its erection as a menace and buffer to the semi-independent and unruly Danes, who at this period had become all-powerful in Northumbria, and who were now either thrust further back by this wedge of Angle and Celt, or compelled to submit to the power of Saxon arms. Further, the boundary of the "liberty" appears almost identical with the boundary of the Elmet.

The great barony of the Archbishop, over which he ruled with almost kingly power, included in the "liberty" of Cawood, Wistow, and Otley, also the palace and lordship of Sherburn-in-Elmet. The dissociation of the members of this "liberty" has always been an insuperable perplexity; why places so remote should be linked in a common bond, has been the source of much comment.

FRAGMENTS OF SAXON CROSSES, OTLEY.

Cawood and Wistow extend from the Wharfe to the northern fringe of the great Bretune, where Selby now stands, a territory afterwards filched from the Brets, with its old ecclesiastical organisation, for the establishment of Norman monasticism. The Otley portion of the "liberty" lies away from the eastern fringe at least thirty miles.*

Whence came the chain of association? What was the connecting link? Their oneness came from the Christianity which had never died at

---

* The ancient parish of Otley, as it existed in the years following the preaching of Paulinus, who set up the cross at this place, and the extent of the parish he then created stretched from the watershed of the Nidd to the banks of the Aire. Its members were Bayldon, Hawkesworth, Burley, Denton, Lyndley, Farnley, Newhall, Menston, Weston, and Guiseley, the latter, whose name, the "Gisel-lega"—"district of the king's office"—marks its importance.

Sherburn and Barwick; the connecting link was the little kingdom of Elmet. The eastern boundary of the "liberty" of Cawood, Wistow, and Otley in Wharfedale, is yet the strongest delineation of the zone of influence so long maintained at Barwick.

The members of the Archbishop's barony of Sherburn prove the same thing on the eastern flank of the ancient kingdom, their southern boundary, in turn, being determined by that of the barony of Drax, which stretched widely along the north bank of the Aire from Drax, through Leeds to Bingley. Both these fragmentary baronies teach the same lesson, of which the core lies in the kingdom of Elmet.

The battle of Brunanburgh was fought in 937, but where the exact field was, appears beyond determination.* For the time being, it entirely shattered the great power of the Norsemen, and consolidated that of the Celts, still clinging to the land, though scattered and drooping under the scourge of Norse invasion. Taking the fullest advantage of such an opportunity, Athelstan erected the "liberty" of Cawood, Wistow, and Otley, making the Archbishop lord over the territories where Celtic nationality had still life, though feeble power. Hence the disjointed nature of such a barony.

THE ILKLEY CROSSES.

This is no place to review the keen contentions as to the actual site of the battle, nor would it be profitable to do so. The word Brunanburgh is Angle, meaning the fortress at the burns or streams. The name, therefore,

* A mile north-west of Bolton Percy there is a Brumber Hill and Brumber Grange ("ber" is distinctly Norse). It is just possible this spot may have been the site of battle.

seems to attach the battle to a place where Anglian speech prevailed, and it is very probable, for several reasons, that the action was fought in the neighbourhood of Wharfedale. One very peculiar circumstance is found in the mention of the place as Brumby (a Norse expression), in the Saxon poem celebrating the victory. The stone memorial cross now in Leeds Parish Church is said to have been raised to the memory of Anlaf, son of Silxtryg, the Norse leader in this great action.

From our digression we must now return to the regular order of events—the conquest of Elmet by Edwin; his death at the great fight at Heathfield; the reconquest of Elmet and the invasion of Northumbria by Cadwallader and Penda; and the causes which led up to the above series of events.

Around these incidents and sidelights of history we obtain glimpses, though feeble and glimmering, of the Royal House of Elmet. That there existed a "Regulus," or petty king, in this little principality, during the Roman administration, there is not the least doubt; and his authority, after being to some extent diminished, was left respected by treaty arrangement, the price of his alliance and that of his tribe. What had remained intact during Roman rule, was found too strong to be overthrown during the first inrush and onslaught of the Angles, and so the kingdom remained intact for a period of two hundred years or more, until the days of King Edwin, who, Bede says—"with great power commanded all the nations, as well of the English as of the Britons who inhabited Britain, except the people of Kent." With all deference to the immortal Bede, there were other exceptions to Edwin's supremacy, notably that of Penda, who, after his accession to the throne of Mercia, 626, allied with Cadwallader, the Briton, began a great strife for supremacy, which only ended in the death of Edwin at Hatfield.

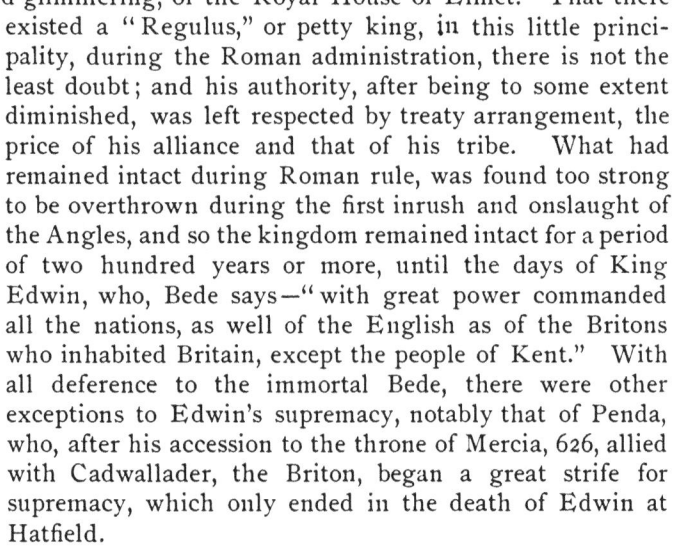

It may be that our views of Elmet are a trifle magnified, yet, doubtless, Celtic royalty held their court at Barwick (their capital or oppidum),* in rude pomp and barbaric splendour, in the far-off days of

NORSE CROSS,
in Leeds Parish Church.

* Oppidun — town (as opposed to Rone, *urbs*); among the Britons—a fortified wood.

unwritten history; and, apart from this Regiunculus, being the last to come under the yoke of the invader, the Britons of Elmet retained the worship and form of an earlier Christianity, brought hither centuries before the time of Augustine and Paulinus.

A MEMORABLE, OFT-TOLD STORY OF THE YORKSHIRE WOLDS.

The newly-formed kingdom of Deira, that is, the district between the Humber and Tees, and the kingdom of Bernicia, the latter lying between the Tees and the Tweed, were both Angle kingdoms under separate rule, until they came into collision towards the end of the sixth century, when the struggle for supremacy began between Ethelric, son of Ida (founder of the northern kingdom), and Ella. This strife filled the slave market of Rome with captives, brought thither for sale from the moors and wolds of Deira. The following incident is in connection with the above-mentioned strife.

While yet a simple priest, the afterwards famous pontiff, Gregory the Great, was one day passing through the slave market of Rome (situated at the end of the ancient Forum). His attention was forcibly arrested by some slaves there for sale, with bright complexions, shapely figures, and fair long hair.

"Whence came these youths?" he asked.

"From Britain," was the answer.

"Are the people Christians, there?" he inquired.

"No, Pagans."

"Alas!" said he, "how grievous it is that faces fair as angels' should be in subjection to the devil."

He next inquired the name of their tribe.

"Angles," said the dealer.

"Ah! that is well. Not Angles but angels they are in looks, and co-heirs of angels they ought to be. Where in Britain do their people dwell?"

ANGLO-DANISH CROSS, GRIMSTON.

"In Deira," was the reply.

"Then our duty is to deliver them from God's ire. And who is the king of Deira?"

"Ella," said the merchant.

"Then," replied Gregory, "Alleluia must be sung in his country."

The sequel to the above incident will be told in the story of Edwin.

In 558, immediately after the above scene occurred in the market place of Rome, in the above description of which the curious word-play of Gregory is so graphically told, the aged king of Deira passed away. At his death, the strength of his kingdom seems to have suddenly collapsed; and, as his rival Ethelric of Bernicia became supreme and entered Deira in triumph, the sons of Ella and their kinsmen fled for safety over the border. Thus the two states were united, and became the ancient kingdom of North-Humbria.

The story of young Edwin, the future king of Northumbria, and conqueror of Elmet, carried into exile by his brethren, a boy of three years, is one of the most interesting in the annals of Saxon history. Both as a fugitive, hiding from the enemies of his father's house, and afterwards as the successful monarch, his life is full of strange vicissitudes and incidents, and, as in the rule of Ethelfrith, his predecessor in power, closely in touch with the Celts of Elmet.

The great fear and jealousy of the exiled house of Ella, which Ethelfrith (who succeeded his father in 593) evinced all through his reign, and which ultimately proved his ruin, seems to have grown more acute year by year, and were the only difficulties which marred his triumph and ambition. During all the wanderings of the fugitive sons of Ella, this striking fact is impressed on the mind, for wherever they took refuge, the emissaries of Ethelfrith found out their hiding-place, and pursued them, with bitter malignity, from court to court.

For years they found an asylum with the north Welsh, and also with Cerdic, king of Elmet. The youthful Edwin spent some years at the court of Cadvan, the Celtic prince of Gwynedd (North Wales), who generously provided him with shelter and education. His companion during these years of exile would, most probably, be Cadwallon (or Cadwallader), son of his host, Cadvan, the afterwards famous prince, and Edwin's rival on the battlefield. As this friendship has a bearing on the fate of Elmet, more will be told.

Another place of refuge for the royal fugitive was with Cearl, king of Mercia, whose daughter, Quœnburga, he married while in exile. Here, Edwin would also become acquainted with the celebrated Penda, who, after the death of Cearl, became king of Mercia, and a rival to Edwin's supremacy. These are historical items which require noting.

Whoever gave shelter to the exiles were continually bribed with costly presents to murder or remove, in some way, the sons of Ella. Failing this, their protectors were menaced with the scourge of war. In this manner, two of the exiles seem to have been removed—Eadfrith, the only brother of Edwin, and several years his senior, disappeared out of history mysteriously; and his son, heir to the throne of Deira, Hereric, father to the saintly Hilda, was removed by poison, when receiving hospitality, and under the protection of Cerdic,* the king of Elmet, a dark deed which hastened the downfall of his kingdom.

In all these harryings, plottings, and murder, we can see behind the scene the malignant hand of Ethelfrith, unable to rest until the royal line of Ella had been extinguished.

On the death of Hereric, nephew to Edwin, the latter became sole representative to the throne of Deira, and the object of even greater hostility, being hunted like a wild beast from covert to covert. His last refuge was with Rædwald, king of the east Angles, whither he was probably accompanied in his flight by Hereric's widow and children, for a nephew of Rædwald's soon after married Hereswith, a daughter of Hereric. Hither, in quick succession, to the court of Rædwald, appeared three separate embassies from Ethelfrith, offering gold and costly presents for the murder or removal of Edwin, or the alternative of war if the Northumbrian's request was not complied with. Either the greed of gold or the fear of Ethelfrith made Rædwald's pledge of protection for some time waver in the balance, and it is said he even went so far as to promise the envoys either to slay the prince, or to place him a prisoner into their hands The following story is the outcome of the king's vacillation

One evening, some friend of the exile visited his chamber, and warned him of his impending danger, and offered him guidance to another hiding-place. The reply of Edwin shows the greatness and nobility of his soul—"I cannot do this thing," he said, "I cannot be the first to break the pledge which I have received from so great a king; if I am to die, it is better Rædwald should slay me than some meaner man, and I had rather perish with honour than continue to live a friendless fugitive." However, under the cover of darkness, he withdrew from his chamber, and, not knowing whither to fly, he sat on the stone bench at the door of the king's court, and there sank into a dreamy slumber; when, suddenly, a stranger of dark complexion appeared before him (probably Paulinus, of whom we shall

* The name Cerdic or Cereticus is the Latinisation of a Celtic original.

hear more anon), and thus addressed him: "Wherefore, at this hour of night, sit ye here, sorrowful and watching, while others rest in sleep?"

The exile replied: "Of what concern can it be to you where I spend my vigils?"

"I well know your distress," said the stranger: "what meed will you give, should I be the means of making Rædwald spurn the overtures of your enemy, and enable you to outshine in greatness the glory of every king who has gone before you?"

"Surely," answered Edwin, "would I listen to the counsel of him who would deliver me from the great dangers which surround me, and exalt me to be king over my own people, and do, in return, whatever lay in my power."

"And, if I foretold you this," said the stranger, "and could show thee better rede for life and soul than any of thy kin ever heard, would'st thou hearken?"

Edwin readily assented.

"Then remember the pledge," said the vision, as he laid his right hand on the head of Edwin, and vanished into the darkness, so that Edwin thought he had seen a vision.

Probably through the influence of his queen and Paulinus, Rædwald absolutely refused to betray the royal fugitive. Instead, quickly gathering his troops together, he led them to meet the army of Ethelfrith, which was already on the march south. The latter was taken by surprise, in the tangled forest and marsh land of the lower Trent. The battle was a desperate one, but ended in the death of Ethelfrith, and complete victory of Rædwald. The place where the engagement took place is on the banks of the little river Idle, and was the first great battle fought between Angles or Englishmen.

"Foul ran Idle with the blood of Englishmen,"

says an old song.

On the defeat and death of Ethelfrith, the fierce Deirans rose in arms against the house of Ida and called in Edwin, heir to the throne. Not content with the latter, he quickly overran Bernicia and ruled jointly over the two kingdoms. Making York his capital, the past glory of the old city was again revived under his rule. According to Ninnius, his conquest of Elmet seems to have immediately preceded his accession to the throne of Northumberland, probably on his triumphant march north. Green says, "The young king could see from any of the Roman towers of York, a few miles to the west, the woodland and moorland of a British realm, and to him the most pressing foes were the Celtic people of Elmet, and thus from the old city he marched to avenge the murder of his uncle Hereric when in exile with his family at the court of Cerdic, king of Elmet."

Connected as Edwin was with the royal family of Mercia, by his marriage with the daughter of Cearl, and with the assistance he would naturally obtain from Rædwald, king of the East Angles, his power would be quite sufficient to cope with and crush the resistance of Elmet, even supposing he accomplished the conquest previous to his accession in 617. We have no historical evidence of any battle having been fought; tradition of its conquest is also of the slightest.

Elmet of that day was vastly different from the Elmet of to-day, with its mammoth industries and teeming population. Then, and until centuries later, it was one of the loneliest parts of Yorkshire. Shut in by rivers whose very form tells of a chain-like series of lyns and almost impenetrable morasses, it was surrounded by forest swamp and dreary moorland. Even up to the eighteenth century Elmet was a region of desolate moorland. Bullerthorpe Common joined on to Swillington and Garforth Moor—to the east lay Whinmoor, Hook Moor, Bramham Moor, and Blackmoor; to the west, joining on to the latter, were Aldwoodley, Eccup, and Adel Moors.

An old tradition says that Edwin's army approached the stronghold of Barwick by way of the old York road, the ancient hollow way, still traceable in many places, which branches out of the Ermine Street, on Bramham Moor, and crosses the present York Road, near the four lane ends. Thence through the fields and plantations immediately behind Potterton Hall, and by the three lane ends, locally known as "Morgan's Cross," it led into a dark lane to the fortified enclosure at Barwick.

Another tradition states that on the night preceding the morrow of Edwin's probable assault on the capital, the British with all their movable property filed silently out in the darkness unobserved, although in the distance the light from the camp fires and innumerable sounds proceeding from an army proclaimed the presence of their enemy. Striking west up the valley of the Wharfe, they passed over the source of the river and joined their kinsmen of the northern Rheged and Cumbria, the first-named district stretching from Pendle Hill or the lower Ribble country to the inhospitable fells of Westmorland.

This tradition can be taken for what it is worth, the more probable supposition may be that the Britons found they were powerless against an enemy of Edwin's strength and ability, knowing the justness of his anger against their king, who had, out of great fear, by pressure brought to bear on him by the fierce Ethelfrith, slain the prince whom he had passed his plighted word to protect. It is also possible that Edwin's quarrel was more with Cerdic than the Britons, and the latter, after slight skirmishing, may have submitted to the overlordship of Edwin. Ninnius says, "Cerdic was expelled from his kingdom, which was occupied by Edwin," and the *Annales Cambriæ* record his death 616. On the downfall of Elmet, Edwin possessed an uninterrupted breadth of territory from sea to sea, even pushing his conquest into the territory of Cadwallader, son of his former benefactor. Numbers of the British who refused to live in subjection to Edwin's rule no doubt found their way to the Welsh kingdom of Cumbria, the northern Rheged and Gwynedd, only to return seventeen years later with the avenging army of Cadwallader, to be reinstated in their possessions. This reconquest by the Celts and death of Edwin will be told a few pages later.

THE STORY OF EDWIN'S CONVERSION AND THE DESTRUCTION OF THE HEATHEN TEMPLE AND GODS AT GODMUNDINGHAM.

In the first ten years of his reign, Edwin extended his power and influence over nearly the whole of Britain; his kingdom reached from central Britain to the Firth of Forth. He was, says Bede, Bretwalda, or overlord of every kingdom in England, save Kent, and his reason for non-intervention there is obvious. Bede says that "A weake woman might have walked with her new-borne babe over all the yland, even from sea to sea, without anie damagee or danger."

For his second wife he espoused Ethelburg, a Kentish princess, and with her came Paulinus, the stranger of Edwin's vision. For generations later this subtle churchman was well remembered in the north. Paulinus is described by Bede as being—

"In personne a taulle man, somewhat crooked back, and black of haire, lene in face, and having a hooked and thin nose; in countenance both dredful and reverent."

Several years had rolled past since Edwin's accession, and he still worshipped the idols of his people. Many and various were his excuses for not accepting Christianity. At last he promised his queen that should he return successful from war with the West Saxons, he would then forsake the pagan doctrine of his ancestors and worship her God. Yet, although victorious in this war, the king still delayed under one pretext or another to embrace Christianity. He was waiting for conviction, before taking this all-important decision, which was to change the worship of his people, and we cannot but admire his discretion on this momentous question.

During the following winter he spent most of his time in deep meditation. Two circumstances roused him from this lethargy—one was his attempted assassination, from which he escaped by only a hair's-breadth, the other circumstance was a conversation with Paulinus, during which that crafty churchman, placing his right hand on the head of the King, claimed the fulfilment of the pledge he had given to the stranger when in exile at the court of King Rædwald. Edwin was visibly impressed, added to which was the pleading of his Queen. After another long and anxious deliberation on the subject he arranged to receive baptism if the wise men of his kingdom should approve. So the wise men of Northumbria were gathered together to give their rede on the faith he was about to embrace.

The place where this memorable Witenagemot took place is supposed to have been at Londesborough. The record of the debate is of great interest as revealing the sides of Christianity which pressed most on our forefathers. To finer minds its charms lay, then as now, in the light it threw on the darkness which encompassed men's lives—the darkness of the future, as of the past.

Paulinus having pleaded in favour of Christianity, Coifi, the pagan high-priest, thus addressed the assembly of wise men: "It seems to me, O king, that our paternal gods are worthless, for no man's worship of them has been more devout than mine; yet my lot has been far less prosperous than that of many others not half so pious!"

A chieftain then spoke—"The life of man, O king, reminds me of a winter feast around your blazing fire, while the storm howls and the snow drives abroad. A distressed sparrow darts within the doorway: for a moment it is cheered by warmth and shelter from the blast; then, shooting through the other entrance, it is lost again. Such is man. He comes we know not whence, hastily snatches a scanty share of worldly pleasure, then goes we know not whither. If this new doctrine, therefore, will give us any clearer insight into things of so much interest, my feeling is to follow it."

Before such arguments, resembling strikingly those of Indian warriors, Northumbrian paganism fell. Coifi was foremost in making war upon the superstition which had so severely baulked his hopes. His priestly character obliged him to ride a mare, and forbade him to have a weapon. The people, therefore, thought him mad when he appeared upon Edwin's charger, and with lance in hand rode furiously to the famous temple at Godmudham, pierced the idol through and through, shattering it to pieces, and ordered the temple to be demolished and burnt to the ground. Soon afterwards, Paulinus kept a most impressive Easter by holding a public baptism at York, in which Edwin, his principal men, and multitudes of inferior people, were admitted into the Christian church.

Camden says: "In the Roman times, not far from its bank, upon the little river Foulness (where Whyton, a small town but well stocked with husbandmen, now stands), formerly stood Delgovitia. The word is said to signify the statues or images of the heathen gods. In a little village near to stood, in Saxon days, a celebrated idol temple. The name of the place is very significant of its use: 'Godmundingham,' now 'Godmudham'—the home of the gods."

This village is situated on the southern spur of the wold hills. The path which we follow from Market Weighton crosses for some little distance over meadow fields and into a winding lane. The country around is beautiful, fresh, and pleasant. A small limpid beck flowing from the wold edge winds and prattles under the hedgerow by the roadside at one's feet, the old church shows out finely on the high ground, forming with the winding road and village a most interesting picture. A gentle ascent conducts one up the sinuous road into the rural village; to the right, situated amongst the trees, lies the rectory. On our left, in a meadow we notice some slight irregularities in the earth. On inquiry we are told this spot is called the Hall Garth. A few yards onwards the clink of the anvil betokens the shop of the village blacksmith, which stands rural enough at the bend in the road, and there, before us, high above the village street, stands the historical church, lowly and reverent. Like ivy to stone, the romance of history seems to cling about its aged walls.

On our visit the structure was undergoing extensive alterations. Its appearance tells its story of antiquity, probably the edifice as it now stands

F. Bogg.]
PRE-NORMAN ARCH, GODMUDHAM.

is early Norman. The font and chancel arch may be earlier, and a few other fragments point to even a greater age. As we muse on the scenes connected with this spot, the impression is formed in our mind that a church has stood on this site since the downfall of paganism. It may stand on the very site of the heathen temple destroyed by Coifi, the high priest. On that point there is not any satisfactory evidence. The sexton tells of large quantities of human bones discovered when digging, but nothing pointing to the temple has hitherto been found. The building which sheltered the idols would, no doubt, be principally of wood, and soon perish. A young girl pointed out to us some elevations and depressions in the meadow a little distance from the village street and adjoining the south side of the Rectory. The peculiarity of the ground here is very significant, and our little guid assured us here formerly stood the pagan temple: the ordnance map also points to this spot. I also inquired of the farmer; to my question he replied, "Nea van knaws whear."

To our thinking the position of the church marks the site of the Angle pagan temple. Although not fully satisfied as to the site of the building whose destruction marks a great page in our history, the writer turned away with feelings of pleasure and interest, for around the village lies the charm of that sweet rural simplicity and breath of bygone ages, which cannot fail to impress and influence the mind of the visitor.

The sun of Edwin's splendour was now fast approaching its horizon. Green says—"This religious revolution gave a shock to the power which he had built up in Britain." Though Paulinus baptised among the Cheviots, as on the Swale and other rivers, it was only the men of Deira that followed the wish of their king. Storm clouds, presage of disaster and death, were fast brewing from the south and west, which were to eventually envelop him in their folds.

Penda, the famous warrior, about this date, 626, had risen to the Mercian throne. His first great object seems to have been to throw off the overlordship of Edwin. What other feelings of revenge may have rankled in his breast against Edwin, history does not say; although, as the son of Wibba, and grandson of Crida, the first Mercian king, his claims to the throne of Mercia seem to have been greater than Cearl's, the king who befriended Edwin when in exile, and who gave Edwin for his first wife his daughter, Quœnburga. Naturally, the sympathies of Edwin would be with the house of Cearl, in opposition to Penda. Thus, no doubt, a volcanic fire of revenge may have been smouldering in the mind of Penda, which, afterwards, was to burst with terrible fury on Edwin, and the Angles of North-Humberland.

Yet another king, whom misfortune, and the ingratitude of Edwin, rendered a more cruel and bitter enemy to the Angles than even the immortal Arthur, like a meteor flits across the history of Northumberland. His motive for revenge is more apparent than that of Penda's.

Edwin, a youth of tender years, a wanderer and fugitive from his native soil, as we have before mentioned, found protection with Cadvan, father of Cadwallader, at this time prince of the north Welsh. For years, he was carefully guarded and educated; and not only Edwin, but, as we have observed, all the royal house of Ella found shelter among the Welsh hills.

It was the outcome of this hospitality of Cadvan to the royal line of Ella that eventually brought on their heads the hostility of Ethelfrith, either from Cadvan's refusal to give up or oust the fugitives; or, peradventure, the apprehension of a league being formed between the Deirans and the Welsh, for the restoration of the sons of Ella was the cause of his anger and jealousy, which ended in the Angle king's famous march across the Pennines; and the battle of Chester, which followed, proved so disastrous to the Welsh that the city of Chester fell into the hands of Ethelfrith.

Amongst the slain, that day, were twelve hundred British monks, who had repaired to the field of battle to pray for the success of their countrymen, and, as they stood some distance from the fray, with arms upraised in prayer and supplication,—"Who are all these numbers of unarmed men?" the king inquired.

"Monks," was the reply, "come hither, after three days' fasting, to pray for the success of their countrymen."

The fierce pagan warrior ordered his soldiers to slay them in the coming fight: "Bear they arms, or no," said he, "they fight against us when they cry against us to their God."

This great disaster, which overtook the monks of Bangor, has generally been attributed to the intrigues of Augustine, who, however, was altogether guiltless. It was his violent antipathy and unwarrantable claims of jurisdiction over the Celtic Church, which caused this suspicion.

To return from our digression, which is only to prove that Cadwallader, who had just claims on the friendship of Edwin, received, instead, the yoke of a master and ambitious overlord, who not only made war on the son of his former host, but chased him out of his own kingdom, Gwynedd (north Wales), the fair district or region of quiet waters.

In the army of Cadwallader, doubtless, would be numbers of refugees from Elmet, who would fly hither for protection and assistance, recognising in this chieftain the only hope of regaining their kingdom. Thus came about, but from vastly different motives, the confederacy of the two kings, Penda, the pagan Mercian, and Cadwallader, the Christian,—the first thirsting with ambition and conquest, the other burning to avenge the wrongs of his countrymen against all the nation of Angles, besides the chance of winning back the land of Elmet, and the country to the west, which Ethelfrith and Edwin had wrested from the Britons. A strange compact, indeed, was this, but one which, for the time being, changed the face of the north.

The two kings met the Northumbrians, led by Edwin, at Hatfield or Heathfield Chase, just to the south of the Don, a region of river and morass, alive with fish and wild fowl, even down to the sixteenth century tenanted with deer, said to be as plentiful as sheep on a hill at this period.

Edwin, no doubt, held the only available gateway into Northumbria (the strip of land where, in former times, the Brigantes had defied the strong arm of Rome), and thus drew the combined force of Welsh and Mercians into the Fen land, hoping to crush his assailants more easily, as they struggled confusedly across the sopping, peaty, pathless moor, "which rose and fell,' so said the natives, " with the tidal waters of the rivers which ran through." Camden, in his time, speaks of this district as a collection of river islands, floating on wide stretches of water. Edwin, having drawn them on to the chase or fen, crossed the Don at Stainforth (the paved ford), somewhere near the present town of Hatfield. The two armies met, and a desperate battle ended in the defeat of the Northumbrians, and the death of Edwin.

The men of Powys so distinguished themselves by their valour on that field, that they obtained from Cadwallon* a boon of fourteen privileges.

On Hatfield Chase, slight evidences of the entrenchments are still to be seen.

The death of Edwin proved the ruin of his house; his queen, with her two children, accompanied by Paulinus, fled south to her brother in Kent, paganism and confusion again reigned supreme.

As prearranged between the two confederates, Cadwallon now marched his army north across the Aire valley, reinstating the Celts in their kingdom of Elmet, and, marching on York, drove out the defenders and made the old city his headquarters. Here Osric, who had ascended the throne of Deira, attempted to oust the Britons. In the battle which took place outside the

* Cadwallader or Cadwallon, variously spelt.

walls, the Deirans were routed and Osric slain. Eanfrid, king of Bernicia, suffered the same fate, he having come with only twelve soldiers to crave peace from the British king. Instead of peace, he and his little escort were put to death at the instigation of Cadwallader. The rule of these two kings, Osric and Eanfrid, and the story of the miserable year of 634, when Britons overran Northumbria, was not forgotten for generations later. The sword of Cadwallader seemed to be destined to drive out the Angle and reinstate the Celt, not only in Elmet but also in his beloved fatherland, Deifyr and Bryneich. Three kings had already been offered as a sacrifice, and the

RELICS, ADEL.

hopes of the Cymry revived in this chief. "Triumphant," says Turner, "with the fame of fourteen great battles and sixty skirmishes, this Celtic prince spread fear over all the north." Growing careless and intoxicated with success, he rashly gave battle to Oswald, the successor of Eanfrid, who had taken the field and secured a strong position on the north bank of the Tyne, and there calmly awaited the advance of his foes. The battle proved disastrous to the Celt. Cadwallader and the strength of his army perished, and with his fall the hopes of the Cymry to return to their homeland, Deifyr and Brynaic, districts which they regarded and loved above all others never again became possible.

This campaign marks the last great effort of the Celt to oust the Angle from Northumbria, and the determination and zeal of this last effort proves their tenacity and grip by keeping possession of the land between the Humber and Tyne for over a period of twelve months.

'Tis a strange and terrible story, that long struggle of rival races, but with the battle of 'Heavenfield' the strength of the Cymry was exhausted. From henceforth all their efforts were required to guard the Welsh border.

How long the Britons held unlimited sway over Elmet after this date we have no exact knowledge. It is possible they kept the Angles at bay along the frontier until the death of Penda, at the battle of Whinmoor, removed the last of the two great antagonists who had overshadowed and awed Northumbria for thirty years. Oswald of Northumbria, whose fame as a warrior and great king was only eclipsed by his religious fervour, met the same fate as Edwin. He was slain in the fight with Penda, at the battle of Maserfeld, 642, and again the grim old pagan carried war and desolation across the land of Northumbria, and generations later the young people shuddered when seated round the blazing hearth-fire, listening to their grandsire's story of the cruel pagan. If the victory of Cadwallader and Penda over Edwin at Heathfield resulted in the winning back of Elmet to the Celt, the battle of Whinmoor would result in a loss to a lesser or greater extent of their independence.

Hoary with the age of eighty winters, Penda again determined to invade Northumbria. The strife which then began between the two Angle kingdoms was for supremacy over East Anglia. Penda was the first to take the field and march north, plundering and destroying with fire and sword along the route. His army seems to have crossed the Aire by the Roman way which leads right into the heart of Elmet. This road, as we have previously mentioned crosses the river Cock between old Manston and Stanks and aims direct to Scholes, and thence on to Whinmoor, where the engagement is supposed to have been fought. There is ample space on this wide heath for the disposition of an army. In the *Annals of Cambria* we are told that king Oswy's headquarters were near to a place named Luden (Loidis—Leeds) and the battle was fought on the field of Giti or Witi, evidently Witi, afterwards receiving its terminal "kirk" when a church was added to the village, hence Whitkirk, and Whinmoor of that day would reach to beyond Whitkirk. No doubt the fight and chase of the Mercians would be continued as far as the river Aire, across which lay the only hope of escape to the vanquished.

The *Annals of Cambria* also says that Penda's army was encamped before the battle at Manu (now Manston), a name which speaks plainly enough of a Celtic 'maen'—a boundary stone. This shows us that Penda entered Elmet by the Roman road, and his headquarters, previous to the battle, were on the high ridge between Manston and Halton.

Thoresby mentions a Saxon fortification, visible in his time, at Gipton, which we may reasonably suppose to have been the encampment of Oswy, whose army was vastly inferior to Penda's, and who, on the approach of the Mercians, fell back to Potterton, where, in the event of defeat, his line of retreat by the Ermine Street to York, would be kept open. There are yet to be seen in a wood, known as Manor Wood, at Potterton, remains of a strong entrenched position, the fighting platform facing on to Whinmoor. These earthworks are very significant, and point strongly to an enemy approaching the moor by the Roman way. Here, also, by the entrenchments, is traditionally supposed to have stood the monastery of Thridwulf,[*] in the wood of Elmet, mentioned by Bede. Three stone coffins have been unearthed in the vicinity of Manor Garth Wood, one of which is still to be seen in the yard of a house adjoining the hall. Here are also several relics which point to the former existence of a religious house in this vicinity. In the wood, some years ago,

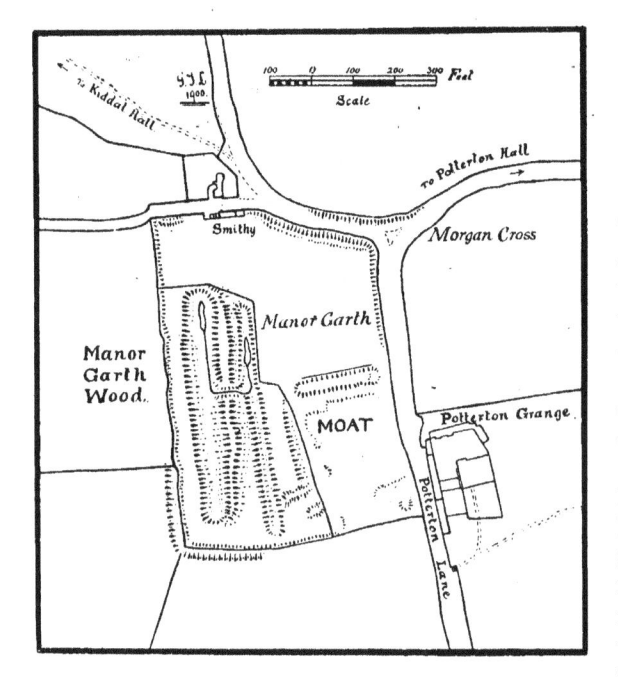

---

[*] "In the life of St. Gildas, who lived in the fifth century, it is said that his brother, Mailoc, after being instructed in sacred learning, came to Luihes, in the district of Elmail, and there built a monastery, in which, continually serving God with prayer, praise, and fasting, he rested at length in peace." Perhaps a mistake of one letter has been made in each of these names, and that for Luihes and Elmail we should read Luides and Elmad, *i.e.*, Leeds and Elmet.

there was found a beautifully finished axe, very sharp, formed out of a volcanic stone from the north of Scotland. This weapon was purchased by the late John Holmes, of Roundhay

But to return to our subject. In vain Oswy tried, by every means in his power, to conciliate the Mercian king by the offer of gold and silver ornaments, and other costly gifts. An old MS. of the tenth century says that "Osguid sent all the wealth which was with him to Penda, and Penda distributed it to the kings of the Britons." From this are we to understand that Oswin gave Penda the ransom, but still the old pagan refused to make peace?

Bede says that necessity compelled him so far as to promise to give greater gifts than can be imagined, to purchase peace, all of which Penda refused, having resolved to utterly destroy the kingdom of Northumbria, and exterminate the people.

Seeing the uselessness of his offers, Oswy cried, "If the pagans will not accept our gifts, let us offer them to one who will," vowing, at the same time, that if successful he would dedicate his daughter to God, and endow twelve monasteries in his realm. The Northumbrian army was only small compared with the hosts of the Mercians; but, putting their trust in God, they boldly prepared for battle. The dreadful fight took place on the 15th November, 655. In vain the Mercians tried to penetrate the ranks of Oswy's army.

The power of paganism received its death-blow when he, who for fifty years had been the cause of so much misery and bloodshed, lay with his commanders and thousands of his army a ghastly and confused heap of slain, their blood changing the waters of the little rivulet to crimson. The wreck of the Mercian army fled southward, and in their frantic rush from the battle many fell into the river Cock, and were trampled underfoot until their bodies formed a bridge for their flying comrades, who in their turn were swept away and drowned, in attempting to cross the swollen waters of the river Aire.

"In Winwidfield was amply avenged the blood of Anna, the blood of the kings, Egric, Oswald, and Edwin." Soon after his great victory, Oswy sent his little daughter Ethelfleda to the monastery over which presided the sainted Hild, whilst the lands and other goods he gave were the means by which the noble abbey was built on the summit of the cliff overlooking Whitby.

Towards the upper reaches of the Cock rivulet, the stream has furrowed out a deep channel through the moor, which is seen to advantage where the present York Road crosses the stream, still known as Grimes Dyke. The natives associate the word Grime with the discolouring of the stream by the blood and bodies of the slain from the Whinmoor fight. The name is obtained from the Anglo-Saxon "Grimes-dic" (a deep ditch forming a boundary), and from the same source we obtain "Grime"—a witch.

From thence, the beck curves its deeply furrowed way, like the bend of a bow, through the land. In the far-off times, its pent-up waters formed a chain of lakes, a natural boundary, as we find in its lower reaches unto this day. Thus we have, in this Grimesdyke, a name which has lasted through centuries, a boundary line of the Saxon.

It is traditionally supposed that the battle of Whinmoor took place on the high ground immediately to the east of Grimesdyke. In the rush from the field, the flying Mercians would have the deep hollow of the beck to cross, the Vinwæd or Winwæd of the historian (not the name of a river, but "the ford of the battle"). Here great numbers would perish in the water, or be trampled underfoot by their flying companions, who, in turn, would be swept away and perish in their attempt to cross the Aire.

In the garden adjoining a small cottage, a few hundred yards to the west of the beck, is an old disused well, known as Penda's Well. Local tradition says that the Mercians quenched their thirst at this well.

On the north side of Crossgates, and two miles from the battle-field, there is a spot known as Hell Dyke or Garth; here, it is said, according to an old tradition, numbers of the slain were buried. The Anglo-Saxon "hel" is indicative of the grave (the strand of the dead, the shadowy realm without sun, or the glory of war, feast, and revelry).

Hungerhills, to the west of Stanks, is the supposed site of Penda's encampment; and "Soldiers' Field," in this district, either points to this battle or some later engagement.

Places in Elmet suggesting the Name of a People—The Original Inhabitants of this Kingdom.

There are, at least, five place-names in this district, all derived from one source, pointing to the name of the aboriginal race, whose date of immigration into Elmet reaches beyond our earliest records, and which establish, beyond dispute, both the kingdom and the name of its people. The name of Leeds is a wide-spreading memorial of this ancient tribe, a name which, although slightly transitional, is to be traced over two thousand years. Fourteen hundred years ago, there existed in Elmet, as we find to-day (yet under strangely altered circumstances), at least five settlements, all suggesting the name of a people, namely, the Ludees—"Ledes" (now Leeds city), Ledely (now Leathley), Lede (now Lead), Lede (Ledsham); the affix 'ham' tacked on is a Saxon word denoting the ham (heim) of the Ledes; Ledes-ton bears the same meaning in its terminal, 'ton'; or it may be the Angles have settled on the former site of Celtic occupation.

Edwin Guest says—"The three early colonising races were known as the Cymbry, the Llœgyrings, and the Brythons." It is the men of Llœgyr that concerns our subject, a people originally dwelling in the basin of the Ebro and the Garonne, previous to their settlement in Britain. It is not a far cry from the Lœgrwys—Ligurians to Ligures—Ludees Loidis—Ledes Caer-Loid-Coit of the old historian, is simply the Caer of the Ludees or Loidis, a people dwelling in the wood of Elmet.

BASE OF KNEELING CROSS, RIPLEY CHURCHYARD.

I am here conscious of trespassing on debatable ground, but from actual survey of sites, and the consulting of many authorities, I have sketched out the kingdom and its people as realistically as imagination can depict. It may be that the true etymology of the word Loides or Leedes is lost in the mists of antiquity. Were the Ligures from the region of the later Gascony, a branch of the Brigantes, as we are led to suppose the Parisees of Holderness were; and were they the ancestors of the Leods, Loidis, or Ledes people, dwelling in Elmet in Bede's day?—are the questions which remain to be answered.

From whatever tribe or nation these ancient dwellers in Elmet may have originally sprung, they have left behind a name not likely to perish for ages to come; the name of a people given to the districts which were allotted to them, on their final subjection to the Anglian people; namely, Leeds, Ledely, Lead, Ledes-ham, and Ledes-ton.

The Name Elmet.

Kemble says the Elmedsetan (Setna)—that is, the people of Elmet, the ancient British Loidis—was an independent district in Yorkshire. We have before mentioned that the Celts of Elmet observed the forms of early Christianity from its first introduction into Britain. 'El' is one designation of the Supreme Being; "Metae" is the place of wisdom where the holy people assembled; the Holwara folk of the Riding; Hœlymete—land used for holy purposes.

Camden, speaking of this district, says—"The country for a little way about Winwidfield . . . was anciently called Elmet."

The Venerable Bede refers to it as the "Sylva Elmetæ"; he further says that "the monastery of the most revered Abbot and Priest, Thridwulf, stood in the wood of Elmete."

Thoresby says the word means frondulous—full of branches.*

The Cornish 'Dewedh' means an end or limit, 'Demetais' are the men of Demet, or Land's End. 'Ell'—a Saxon measure, 'Met'—an extremity or limit; Elmet, Elmy, El'mi—the boundary kingdom.

The right upon which the kingdom of Elmet claims its recognition is not that which belongs to its regality, for its kings in full strength were little more than chieftains, and its throne has never been more than the seat of a Regulus (a petty king). Its war force has, probably, been very significant, judging from the earthworks reaching from Lotherton and Hazelwood to that more stupendous creation in the meadows of Barwick. Yet, in the progress of nations, they count for but little. Its armies, in full strength, probably numbered not more than a thousand or fifteen hundred men; its victories and defeats were mere skirmishes; its wealth, the corn and cattle of a few hundred husbandmen; its greatest length two score miles, its breadth not more than one score; its soil varying from the fertility of a garden to vast reaches of desolate moorland and rugged hill and wild forest, or back to the east, into the adjacent plains, a region of lagoon and swamp, into which, sullenly, the rivers drained.

To Roman, Saxon, or Dane, in its greatest prosperity, it was hardly worth much consideration; hence the scarcity of Angle settlement. It was merely a retreat and place of refuge for the vanquished Celt. And yet it is possessed of a fame that must continue fresh and green. As long as the story of England's growth is worth telling, not only of the devotion of a

* *Frondosus*—full of leaves.

people clinging to their fatherland, but wherever the glorious records of Christian devotion stir the hearts of men, will the story of Elmet be told, for it is written deeply in the annals of the Cross—the one bright spot in the surrounding darkness of paganism and ignorance, which for three centuries overshadowed Northumbria.

Barwick may owe one of its ancient emblems to the pomp and custom of Edwin. This Anglian king, the conqueror of Elmet (Bede states), lived in suchs plendour, that he had not only standards carried in time of war, but also in times of peace; when he travelled in state through the provinces and the streets of his capital he had always a standard carried before him—the Roman Tufa—the English Toup. This kind of standard was made of feathers of various colours, a globe-like tuft, fixed on the end of a long pole. Barwick Feast is still one of the most celebrated of our ancient revels; its Maypole has long been one of its suggestive ornaments. Who shall say that King Edwin's Tufa has not graced the original Maypole, and that the sumptuous feast is not the direct survival of Edwin's rejoicings?

The conquest of England, by the Normans, gave the *coup de grace* to the kingdom of Elmet. By that tremendous overthrow Celt, Saxon, and Dane were in one " red burial blent," to live no more in their individuality, but in amalgamation to come forth a great people, full of a strength that has since shaken not only their oppressors, but the whole world beside. The Tufa is no longer borne through its streets, heralding the progress of an arbitrary monarch; but every child who plays there now is a monarch whose Tufa is Liberty, and for whom home is raised by unshackled energy.

Amid the storms of fifteen centuries, Wendell Hill ("Auld Howe") has reared its grassy head above time and tide. For nearly as many centuries the vesper bell has called the villagers to prayer, as well from the royal mansion, and the serf's cot in the woods, as from the happier hearths that know little of monarchs and serfs. The same church of All Hallows which received royal worshippers when Abbot Thrydwulf's little monastery held God-fearing men, still knows God's service and resounds with the hymn of praise. Like its equally celebrated sister church of Sherburn, that of Barwick has been prominent as a stately edifice in pre-conquest days. Long before Brunanburgh was fought, the former had a peal of bells and a sumptuous equipment. To Barwick we may safely ascribe an equally distinguished possession. It matters little whether the Celts received their Christianity from the Romans, or gave theirs to the legionaries, through the influence of the Empress Helena and Constantine. What appears to be indisputable is that the Elmet churches of All Hallows at Sherburn and Barwick register a Christianity at least coeval with, if not established before Rome could boast of a similar temple.*

KIRKSTALL ABBEY.

  This statement is not made haphazard. The church of St. John Lateran, the finest, and perhaps the oldest church in Rome, was built by Constantine the Great, a few years before A.D. 320, when it is more than probable that the Empress Helena and her son, Constantine, had countenanced and supported Christianity in Britain. Constantine was in York with his father, the Emperor Constantius Chlorus, when the latter died in 305. If we may push our speculation one step further, may we not say that under the shadow of Wendell Hill the Christian Empress Helena and her Christian son, as the guests of the Regulus, who paid them tribute, are very likely indeed to have witnessed the earliest of the Celebrations on the Altar that had supplanted the ministrations of the Druids. Constantine the Great was chosen Emperor in York, where his mother's name was revered, and especially by her British subjects.

CHAPTER IV.

HISTORY, ANTIQUITIES, AND GENERAL DESCRIPTION OF ELMET.

IN our brief description of Elmet as seen to-day, we commence our tour on the north bank of the Aire at Cookridge, and follow the watershed of the small stream known as Adel, Meanwood, or Lady Beck, which flows through an important valley, both historically and geographically. After a course of some seven miles the stream enters the river Aire, just to the south of the Leeds Parish Church.

Cookridge, Adel, and Breary, places of a very ancient population, are situated on the upper reaches of the watershed of this beck. All along the hill slopes, from Aldwoodley Moor to Bramhope and Cookridge, there are traces of Roman, Celtic, Anglian, and Norman people. The views from here, when the atmosphere is clear, are fine, bold, and sweeping. The wooded vale of Meanwood and the city of Leeds in one direction, and opposite, in the foreground, are dark patches of pine woods; and beyond, over the high brow of Bramhope, Almescliffe and the moors westward, to Great Whernside. To the north-east we look far away over the great plain of York, and obtain glimpses of the dim blue outline of Hambleton and the Wolds.

In our path to Cookridge, we pass through the woods formerly belonging to the abbey of Kirkstall, rich in foliage, dense undergrowth, and of romantic contour. Deep down in the vale, resting amid murky surroundings, stand the ruins of the once noble abbey of Kirkstall. But what a strange contrast this place presents to the time when the ancient churchmen trod the hallowed ground! At that period, the Aire, the most delightful of rivers (bright, shining water), did not, as now, belie its name. Around it were lush meadows and delightful vistas of river, glen, moor, and woodland, undefiled by the smoke of a thousand chimneys, factories, or the belching forth of black fumes from forges, such as we see to-day—strange contrast, indeed.

If we could but induce some of the old abbots to return from shadowland, what stories we might learn of the abbey's history. But those who are gone do not return from their bourn, even to tell us of the doings of the past; so we leave Alexander the Abbot, and his patron, Henry de Lacie, Parson Peter, Robert the Priest, and a host of other clerics and notables, who gave lands and goods to the upbuilding of this church for their souls' welfare, to rest in peace; and pass on to Cookridge.

Some two miles north from Kirkstall is Cookridge Convalescent Home, standing on a fine elevation in the woods. Though rather remote, the situation of Cookridge is the most salubrious and delightful in the borough of Leeds, and the Home is of great benefit to the poor of the city.

Cookridge Hall, once the home of Edward Sheffield, Duke of Buckingham, is a fine residence, built on an ancient foundation, with many Roman touches around it; also vestiges of a British settlement (foundation of hut dwellings) have been discovered in the woods hereabouts.

Simpson says Cookridge derives its name from the Saxon Geac-hrig or rig (the Geac-rig—a way). The old forms of spelling are Cuk-rig and Cueryc, the latter syllable implying the Saxon "ric" or government, which gives an individuality to this place which cannot be overlooked, however it may be explained. It was evidently a seat of power in Roman-Celtic times. Of this prominence strong evidence has been obtained from time to time.

S. W.

KIRKSTALL ABBEY.

During the 17th century, a great number of coins were turned up by the plough, chiefly of the reigns of Domitian Nerva, Trajan and Adrian, all in fair preservation. The Norman tenants (Cukryc) were a family which did not long preserve their identity hereabouts; Richard-de-Cukerigh appears about 1180. The monks of Kirkstall were not slow to lay their hands upon this fair domain, which became one of their closely preserved hunting grounds. An early charter says that " Roger Mustell gave to the house at Kirkstall, the Barony of Cokryge, with mill and all other appurtenances."

From Cookridge, we pass on to Breary and Echope. At the Domesday Survey, both places were included in the possession of one Alward, a Dane. In the Confessors' reign, the total value of these places was sixty shillings. Attached to the end of the brief Domesday record is the ominous word 'waste,' showing how severely the vengeance of the Norman king had fallen on these places. Breary, or Brerehayh, gave its name to a family who resided here for many centuries. In the reign of Edward III., a Robert Brerehaugh married Agnes, daughter and heiress of Richard Frank, possibly the ancestor of the Franks who afterwards became possessed of Aldwoodley.

In our walk to Blackhill we notice the fine length of old road which we traverse from the Willows to the upper dam, where the exquisite blending of wood and water is apparent to all. By the road side, opposite the wood at Blackhill, is an old time-worn milestone, which previously has been used for some other purpose.

MILESTONE, BLACKHILL, ADEL.

Hereabouts we are passing over sites of very ancient occupation. In the by-lane running from hence to Echope, we notice, built into the wall of a farm, the almost perfect base of a cross, which rests upon a stone of much larger dimension, the latter being below the level of the ground. The base of the cross is octagonal. From the situation and the careful manner in which the wall has been built over it, it is evident that this has been the original position of the cross. The socket of the shaft is still left open, and in rebuilding the wall care has evidently been taken to preserve the relic. Part of the farm has been rebuilt and other portions restored during the last century and numerous fragments of stone from some ancient building have been placed in the walls, and here probably might be found portions of the shaft of the above-named cross.

THE RAVINE, ECHOPE.

There are several traditions respecting Blackhill, one of which points to a settlement of the Brigantes on or near this spot, in the early Roman period, which required a camp and the imperial troop in this vicinity to overawe. Another story runs that a pre-Norman church stood on Blackhill.

Besides numerous Roman-Celtic relics, funereal urns and querns, etc., foundations of ancient walls unearthed in this vicinity, and fragments of Saxon wheel crosses, added to the remains of the base already alluded to, point significantly to a Christian temple having stood hereabouts. Thus it is quite possible that Norman Adel may have been constructed of material from the Roman camp and the settlement on Blackhill, both of which stood on the north side of a long and almost impassable swamp which cut the connection with the present site, Adel.

To the above evidences we learn that in the Confessors' reign the total value of Adel is described as only one-half that of the adjoining places of Cookridge and Burgdunum.

ALDWOODLEY.

Immediately north of Blackhill stands the obscure village of Echope or Eccup, resting on the edge of a narrow ravine, down which a small beck meanders to the bed of what was formerly a large mere, now formed into a Leeds reservoir. Echope means "the narrow valley on the eminence abounding with oaks." 'Ec' or 'ack'—oak, and 'hope'—up; *i.e.*, the oak-place on the up or higher position. The legendary name, as its root-word testifies, goes back to Celtic times.

The prospect from the commanding situation on a fine spring day is delightfully grand. Seen at twilight, when the moonbeams shimmer on the lake, the cottages fringing the edge of the little romantic gorge, with here and there a tree etched definitely against the silver sky, the picture presents a scene strangely weird, yet beautiful. An ancient "pillar stone" was found here, some time ago, about two feet six inches square, with a hole perforated in the centre.

Apart from the Norman church at Adel there is no building in the district between Cookridge and Echope of great interest, age, or of architectural importance. The farms and cottages are sparsely scattered, and in winter time the district has a solitary note and forbidding aspect which the dense, dark fir woods help to deepen. To the artist the chief interest centres in the upper dam at Adel down to Scotland Mill, near Meanwood. To the antiquary and historian every yard of ground speaks eloquently of past ages. One mile in the direction of Chapeltown, over pleasant field paths, brings us into the township of Aldwoodley, the undulating wold land. The old form of the name was Alwaldley, most likely "the old hill district," * an interpretation that may give the meaning hidden in the formation of a later military station at Adel.

Aldwoodley Hall was a place of consequence in the Plantagenet era, when it was inhabited by the responsible family of Franks, the "free," in contrast to the neighbouring serfs. They mated with the Gascoignes and helped largely to increase the wealth of that meritorious family. It was long the seat of an important family bearing the same name. Appended as witness to a deed of the Abbey of Kirkstall is the name of Henrico-de-Alwoldley and another bearing the name of Willo-de-Alwaldeleye.

The estate came into the hands of the Franks by the marriage of William Frank, son and heir of Robert Frank, with Alice, eldest daughter and heiress of Roger-de-Aldwoodly.

In 1638 this manor was sold by the Franks to Sir Gervase Clifton, a gentleman remarkable for having married seven wives. Hopkinson says of him—"He was a complete gentleman and darling of all men;" we might safely add—"and the beloved of many women." His first wife, whom he called his beautiful Penelope, is said to have been the greatest beauty of the age, not only in body, but also in mind. She died in 1613, at the early age of twenty-three.

The site of the old Hall is just to the north of the Roman road running over the moor to Brandon, and on the first ascent from the sheltered

---

* As referring to one of the changes of frontier and that sufficiently important we may take the case of Aldwoodley. The Domesday form of the word is Aluuoldelei, "the old wold district," the Angle Eald-wald-lega, presumably an indicated contrast with the "Herewod" which represented a change wherein the Angle soldiery and military government were recognised.

basin of the vale. The ancient Hall, was pulled down early in the last century. A few relics still remain, a pointed arch and triple window, also the site of the antique garden of Tudor period, with the wall, remains. The present Hall, partly built on the site of the old one, has begun to assume a dilapidated and neglected appearance.*

In our walk to the camp at Adel, we follow the line of the Roman vicinal, portions of which, of late years, have often been laid bare during the cultivation of the land over which it runs.

Of Adel as a Roman station we have unquestionable proofs, for on the roadside leading to Echope, and just beyond the mill, the camp can yet be clearly defined, and shows a double agger and the remains of an aqueduct. It has been larger than that of Ilkley, but probably not its equal in military importance. In breaking up the moor, east of the camp, many footprints of Roman occupation were unearthed, amongst others several monuments and fragments of urns, statues, coins, etc.†

The imperial garrison at this station seems to have kept an equal grip upon the vales of the Aire and Wharfe. The Roman name of

HOUSE AT THE MILL, NEAR SITE OF ROMAN CAMP.

---

* The Franks established a branch at Aldwardeley, between Leeds and Harewood, and through it became of territorial consequence. In the Selby Coucher Book, page 97, there is a long account of an inquest (26th August, 1441), touching the thefts of sixty two-year-old sheep, of the price of 20d. per head, the property of William Frank, *apud Almley juxta Harwode*. The inquest, which is well worth reading for sundry reasons, was taken before Henry Vavasour, then Escheator for Co. York.

† The relics found about Adel are to be seen in the small museum of antiquities, standing by the entrance to the churchyard.

NORMAN DOORWAY, ADEL.   *Percy Robinson.*

the station—Burgdunum, suggests a rather late origin, its last syllables, "dunum," being the latinisation of the Celtic "dun"—a hill.

From the many vestiges of British names still remaining hereabouts, we may venture to assume, as already mentioned, that the Brigantes held a strong position on the hill range over which this road passed to Calcaria. Anyone who will examine the site of the camp will at once notice how wise the selection has been. The situation is rising ground, on the north bend of a deep valley, which in the far-off days was, from appearances, probably an impassable swamp.

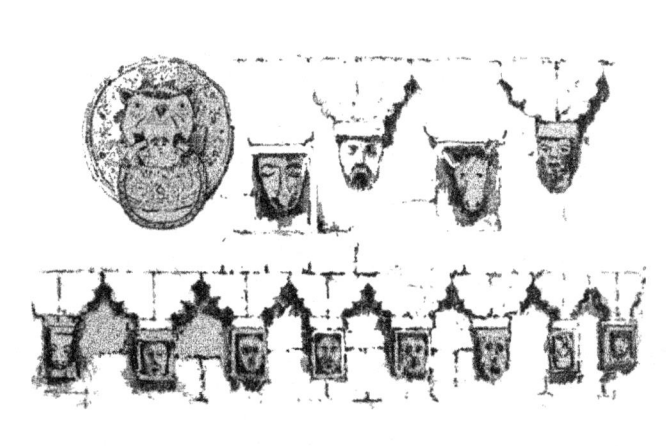

One of the objects of the garrison appears to have been to watch the undulating land lying between the Wharfe and the Aire, about where the Celtic tribesmen of Elmet were rather thickly located.

The Roman callis, or roadway, which some writers say ran from Adel to the ford over the Aire, at Leeds, is said to retain its identity in Call Lane.* Supposing this tradition to be correct, the roadway had not been of much importance during the imperial occupation, although the *débris* and remains of ironstone mines, found so plentifully about Call Lane, show that the mineral riches of the district were discovered and perhaps worked under Roman supervision.

DOOR KNOCKER AND HEADS ON CORBEL TABLE, ADEL.

Strange indeed are the changes which have taken place since the legions of the mighty Cæsars held sway here, and it requires some amount of fancy and imagination to picture the scene and repeople this camp with the activity, pomp, and circumstance of military life. Then would be heard

* The writer has not seen any vestiges of this, and doubts the existence of such a road.

the stately tramp of armies, the fluttering of eagle-crested banners, the passing to and fro of couriers and speeding of chariots, and ever and anon the sound of battle, the clash of arms, the despair of the vanquished and fierce exultant shouts of the victors.

Centuries ago the bodies of the legionaries returned to the dust from whence they sprang; but Adel still remains a silent testimony of the engineering skill of the Roman and his mastership in the art of war. It also points out the mockery of man's boasted strength, wherein can be read in plain and impressive characters: "The vanity of earth and all that rests thereon."

The church of St. John of Adel, just a few hundred yards to the southeast of the camp, stands on a high plateau amidst charming surroundings. It is one of the finest architectural structures that Norman genius has bequeathed to our time. This church and half the village of Adel are included among the possessions of Holy Trinity Priory, York, given to the Priory by Ralph Paganel and confirmed by Pope Alexander II. The Priory appointed its curates here from A.D. 1242 or earlier. To this day a pension of six pounds, thirteen shillings and fourpence—a fine, it is said, levied on some refractory rector, is annually paid by the Rector of Adel to the Dean and Chapter of Christ's Church, Oxford, who have succeeded to the property; the advowson has fallen into private hands.

It would be impossible to particularise in detail the artistic work, exquisite design, and symbolic grandeur which adorn this sacred edifice. The most striking object of the exterior is the magnificent doorway, consisting of five semicircular receding arches richly decorated with zigzag and beak-head moulding, enclosed by an ornately sculptural gabled pediment, from the apex of which the image of Satan scowls down—a picture of awful malignity and venom—on the good work he sees progressing but cannot hinder. Immediately below this head rests the Cross and the Lamb of God with banner triumphant, on either side of which are the sun and moon, underneath the figure of the Son of Man on His throne; the figures on either side represent the four evangelists, symbolised by an eagle for St. John, a bull for St. Luke, a lion for St. Mark, a human face with the wings of an angel for St. Matthew, and a lamb for our Saviour .Altogether it is one of the most treasured doorways in this country. The grotesque and repulsive heads sculptured on the corbel line are also very interesting. The door handle is of fine bronze and a rare piece of craftsmanship, worked around with artistic and elaborate tracery. The same demoniac image of

Satan, a compound of human and fiend, that we see on the apex of the gabled pediment, glares from the door handle as the worshippers enter the building. From the evidence of this unique handle, we are led to suppose this church has in olden times been a place of sanctuary, thus connecting this edifice with that story of Biblical days and the picture of the fugitives fleeing hither for refuge.*

ADEL CHURCH.

The carving of the interior is quite as interesting, symbolic and beautiful as the exterior, the admiration culminating in the magnificent Norman chancel arch. Simpson says:—"This magnificent structure strikes us unaware. Turning from the font eastwards, we deliberately survey it. We make our gradual approaches nearer and nearer, till we are enabled to decipher the beautiful symbolism with which it is embellished." It recedes, as the spectator will observe, in three orders. The outermost displays a fine course of the dog-tooth moulding, crowning the arch, as it were, with a graceful touch of delicacy.

* On the sun-dial in the churchyard is the following expressive motto:—"*Ut hora sic vita*" (As the hour, so is the life).

We have previously mentioned the existence of numerous relics found in this district, now contained in the little museum adjoining the churchyard, permission to inspect which can be obtained on application to the rector. These relics tell the story of the district a thousand years previous to the coming of the Norman, and point to the settlement of four distinct peoples—the Celt, Roman, Saxon, and Dane. Adding this to the testimony contained in the chaste and beautiful Norman fabric, we obtain a history of Adel for nigh twenty centuries.

The stone fences in this locality contain numerous stones which have evidently been quarried and prepared, in the first instance, for some other purpose. Existence of a supposed British village, *i.e.*, remains of pit hut dwellings, were to be seen just to the east of the church, until they were filled up recently; and on the moorland which has been reclaimed, around the reformatory, there have, at different times, been found scrapers, flint arrow heads, spears, stone hammers, and other pre-historic implements: of these the Philosophical Society possess about fifty specimens. A short distance from the church there is a spring of water dedicated to St. Helena, the mother of Constantine the Great, who is said to have discovered, at Jerusalem, the Sepulchre and Cross of Jesus Christ. Many wells, also churches, in the north of England, are dedicated to this saint

Aldwoodley Crag is a fine elevation of sandstone rock, from which may be studied the force of mighty waters which, in former

OLD MILESTONE, ALDWOODLEY.

ages, swept resistlessly through the valley, scooping out the deep hollow as we see it to-day; and on the higher ground are huge boulder-stones, vestiges, in their ice-scratched faces, of the glacial period.* The scenery of the moor, known as Adel Crags, stretching towards Moortown, although so near Leeds, still remains wild and picturesque; yet, in all probability, the time is not far distant when Adel will become a line-and-rule regulated portion of Leeds, and the evidences of Roman occupation will then be blotted out by the works of the children of men who survive him. At the present, the beauty of the vale of Adel is apparent to the least cultured, and the features of every stage of its past history can be still recognised. The heather still blooms there, for the moors have not yet been destroyed, the sniff of the keen wintry air, sweeping down from the Chevin, is still as pure and pungent as when the imperial legionaries dreaded its blast, of which fact a letter of that day, sent by a wit in Rome to his friend in Britain, testifies; the letter and the reply to it have fortunately been preserved.

A century ago, before the huge tanneries and other large industries were in such strong evidence, no fairer spot, teeming with natural beauty, can be imagined than the pleasant vale of Meanwood,† with its then crystal stream and murmuring woods, interspersed with cottage and mansion, and the bold line of ridge, from which far-reaching views can be obtained.

[Scrimshaw.
SANDY ROCK, ADEL BECK.

* The name Tingwald Hill—a natural eminence (Ton-wald-how)—midway between Adel and Moortown, carries the mind back to the customs and laws of a bygone people—our Teutonic forefathers.

† The root signification of the place-name 'Meanwood' is closely akin to that in which we use the word 'meaning,' *i.e.*, defining one thing from another. In Celtic, *maen* meant a measure or limit; 'mea,' in Scandinavian, the same. Meanwood, therefore, denotes boundary wood, and is, in fact, a forested tract well marked off from the Weetwood slope, immediately to the south, by Adel beck, which follows the valley bottom between them, as

F

66   THE OLD KINGDOM OF ELMET.

Turning towards Headingley, from Adel, there still remain delightful vistas of charming residences, gardens, meadows, and woodland, yet blurred to some extent, in the background, by the smoke and flame from forge and factory. At eventide the lurid flare, fitfully lighting up the smudgy atmosphere, gives a weird aspect to the scene.

OLD HOUSE, MEANWOOD, HILL TOP.

well as by the configuration of the land. But it is now impossible to say whether 'Mean,' here, was a Celtic or a Danish occupation term, most probably the latter. To a decrepit house, standing with its gable end to the old Pack Horse Road at Hill Top, local tradition ascribes the distinction of being the oldest in Meanwood. The illustration shows its sagging roof ridge, finialled gable, and angle-arch mouldings, in dressed stone, over doors and windows, to be of late Tudor or early Jacobean times. It was the first hostel in this district. Over the door the words "Tap, W. P." (a Proctor—one of Meanwood's oldest family names) and the date, 1630, may still be deciphered, flanked by the conventional 'bush'—a bushy-headed tree incised in the stone—which, in the 17th century, took the place of the living bough hung out as the sign of 'a place of entertainment for man and beast.'

HEADINGLEY.

One object which attracts and interests the antiquary and historian is the gigantic old oak, now in the last stage of decay, and from whence the Wapentake of Skyrack derives its name.

The place-name, Headingley, is of Angle coinage, and, as we have already observed, was the only clan station, in pre-Norman times, on the north bank of the Aire, between Swillington and Arthington; this place was probably one of the early divisions of conquered land which the Angles designated the "hundred," that is, the division of land shared by a hundred warriors and their families. "This way of dividing land," says Isaac Taylor, "would be rough, rather than exact, from the first, and would soon become only a historical survival." Thus, the "hundred court" was the early military and judicial organisation of the Angles. Under the rule of the Norse or sea kings, their military provisions included the formation of a strong federation and well-belted arms district (in his speech a Wapentak) making the Angle station of Headingley the headquarters, with the huge oak—then, in its full strength and beauty, the pride of the forest—a rendezvous and beacon point. Here the Norseman settled the present Wapentac of Seyre-ac, the Shire oak marking an allotted military and political division.*

The old Norse word, "vapna" or "vapn" means a weapon, and "taka" to grasp or touch: hence the Norse "vapnatak" means the touching of weapons. Tacitus says that in the assemblies of Teutonic warriors, when they wished to express their assent to any proposal, the armed warriors struck their spears together. The laws of Edward the Confessor also state that when a new chief of the Wapentake was appointed, the other chiefs or freemen met him at the usual place of assembly. Here the chief dismounted from his horse, and held his spear erect, while the other chiefs touched his spear with theirs, in token of fealty to the king whom the chief represented. Most of us, when children, have taken part in the game known as "tiggery, tiggery, touch wood,"—this child's game is a survival of the touching of weapons at the Wapentake, the magic touch or contact.

Perhaps there are those who will scoff at the idea of this venerable tree having been the place under which the Wapentake Court of Skyrack was held, but when we consider that in the sixteenth century the tree was in an

---

* This district was called a Wapentak, because, when called upon by the chief, the people took their weapons, and hastened to the appointed spot and touched their weapons, a ceremony which bound them in fealty to their chief. *A.S.:* "Scire"—a shire or county, from "sciran, scerau"—to shear, to divide; compare share, shear, etc.

advanced state of decay, and an engraving, published two hundred years ago, shows that, at that time, the sap of life was nearly exhausted, yet the tree still survives. At this rate of decay, we may be allowed to presume that at least six hundred years ago its prime of existence had only been reached, ere decay had begun. Allowing three to four hundred years for its full vigour and glory of life, thus a thousand years ago the tree would have reached its pride and luxuriance of grandeur, and therefore be a conspicuous and natural object for the Norseman to form his Wapentake of Seyre-ack —the shire oak. The old monarch has long survived the customs of the court to which it gave its name—a hoary memorial of times and manners long past. But how changed since the Norsemen met in conclave beneath the shade of its ample boughs, then in its fulness of sylvan majesty and loveliness![*]

[From a Drawing made two hundred years ago.]
THE SHIRE OAK, HEADINGLEY

> "Survivor sole, and hardly such, of all
> That once lived here—thy brethren;
> A shattered veteran, hollow trunk'd,
> And with excoriate forks deformed—
> Relic of ages."

* At the east end of Weetwood, by the path from Meanwood wood to Otley old road, is the largest living oak tree in Elmet. In the early fifties it went by the name of "Parliament Oak." Like the major oak of Sherwood, it had many wide-spreading arms, convenient, in the writer's early days, 'for hanging upon,' so low down did they come, and, like the Skyrack, may have many a time served as a gallows. The shade area of its thirty feet bole had a diameter of thirty or forty yards. It is hale yet, being enclosed in a garden.

Adjoining the tree is the old Oak Inn, standing on the site of a very ancient hostelry.

Opposite is the church of St. Michael's, forming a most handsome and conspicuous object. It has been rebuilt on the site of a very ancient chapelry dating its existence from Norman times.

The church of St. Chad's rests in pleasant surroundings, and with its tall, commanding spire, rising above the tree-tops, forms another pleasing and interesting object.

Although not nearly so delightful as a generation ago Headingley is still the most charming suburb of the great city. Beautiful residences, half hidden in umbrageous foliage and rich gardens, peep out here and there all along the route, and ever and again castle-like halls and towers stand forth stately and imposing in luxuriant grandeur, a veritable paradise for the homes of our city merchants.

[*From a Drawing by Owen Bowen.*
THE SHIRE OAK IN 1902.

The extreme contrast to the above is only too apparent yonder in the valley. One sees smoke, there are hideous noises, the creak, clang and shriek of machinery, and belching of fumes and flame from forge and factory, with grime, dirt, and the sky pregnant with evidence of the commercial enterprise of this great manufacturing centre, and the dark, turbid river of Hades rolling through.

It is not our purpose to describe this dismal side of the picture: the evils and transgressions which our city forefathers tolerated in the past are now fast being remedied. We shall soon have a purer atmosphere and consequently more sunlight; and the Stygian flood, wherein no creature can now exist, will again become a pure river, in whose liquid depths fish will sport and the contemplative angler ply his peaceful avocation as of yore.

BURLEY GROVE.

CHAPTER V

LEEDS.

IN the midst of the large forest, which, in Celto-Roman times, shadowed the kingdom of Elmet, the land of the Leogrys, Leoidi, Ludees, Ledes (the original Celtic people), was a clearing of timber on and around the brow of a small eminence near the river, and within this clearing stood a little settlement; or, as one old British writer* with vivid imagination describes it: "The Caer Loid Coit," which means, "The stronghold of the Leoidi, in the wood of Elmet." This situation was naturally strong; besides other advantages, it was well watered by river and stream, being in the angle of land between and contiguous to both.

Quarry Hill is the supposed site of the British Caer in the wood, and here, says Thoresby, in his time, a strong entrenched position could be clearly defined. The wild lonely heath and forest around abounded with game, and the larger animals were fairly numerous, whilst every stream and river swarmed with fish, and the low-lying fen-land was frequented by immense flocks of wild fowl. In the open glades around the forest clearing, the domestic animals found pasture; at that period the cultivation of land was not carried on to any great extent.

Here on the lonely moors of Elmet, and in the thick forest of oak, beech, and elm (which for many centuries later remained in almost primitive condition) the wild cattle, red deer, wolf, and boar roamed, down to the time of the Tudor kings.

What a marvellous transformation has taken place since the Leoidi or Ledes—the original founders of the city, whose name as a memorial it still bears—raised their Caer in the wood, between the bright stream (Sheepscar beck) and the crystal waters of the limpid Aire! Instead of the innumerable branches of a vast wood dancing on the sun-kissed waters of

* Nennius.

the Aire, all the varied undulation of a large forest waving in the breeze, river and stream still flow, but not bright and limpid as of yore, and all else is changed. A great city, whose foundations reach back to the dim vista of pre-historic time, has risen; and, instead of forest trees, we see a huge forest of chimneys, factories, forges, and warehouses, stately edifices, and scores of miles of streets: a great city, carrying the name of its original Celtic founders onward through time.

Although Leeds is referred to by no fewer than three historians, who wrote in the early Saxon period, very little which can be relied on as authentic is known about the place previous to the Norman era. Bede mentions it as "In regione quæ vocatur Loidis;" Nennius as the "Caer Loid Coit;" again, Mailoc or Madoc, brother to St. Gildas, is said "to have journeyed to Luihes, in the district of Elmail" (doubtless the reading should be Luides and Elmet) "and there built a monastery in which, continually serving God with prayer and fasting, he rested at length in peace." Did the monastery here referred to, and built of wood, stand on the same site as now occupied by the Parish Church, as the relic now remaining, and others now unfortunately lost, are very suggestive of an early origin?

TUDOR ROOF FRAMEWORK—A RELIC OF ROCKLEY HALL.

The above are, indeed, but brief notices, but what can we expect when, regarding Barwick (to which Leeds was greatly inferior and subordinate, both in military importance and population, the former with its huge entrenched position and long line of earthworks proving its superiority and importance), history is strangely silent? More can be learnt anent the earlier period from the earthworks still existing in the district, and others now obliterated, though mentioned by previous historians. The remains of

Roman roads and camps all point significantly to the strength and number of the Celtic people in the locality, who required careful watching.

The relics and evidences of pre-historic times found in the city itself are only scanty. If we take into consideration the lapse of time, and changes which have come to pass, and the lack of interest formerly taken in archæology, we may be thankful for what remains. In the vicinity of Briggate, in 1745, there was found, at a depth of two feet below the surface, a British urn of rude formation, containing ashes (calcined bones), and a stone axe, perforated for a shaft, and a few other stone implements and querns or handmills. Another implement, formed out of hard slate stone, evidently a hammer, was found by a navvy, when digging in the vicinity of the N.E. Station.* A British torc of pure flexible gold, value eighteen pounds sterling, was found at Rawdon, by a weaver, in 1780; and in the same vicinity was found a rude urn. A massive gold armlet, value eighteen pounds sterling, was offered for sale to the late Mr. Denny, curator of the Leeds Museum. The above are only a few instances of pre-historic finds, others might be added, but these are sufficient for our purpose.

Connecting Leeds to the Roman-Celtic period, scarcely any relics have been discovered; yet there are several vestiges of earthworks, just without the city boundaries, some of which still remain: for instance, those mentioned by Thoresby and Dr. Whitaker, at Gipton and Harlow Hill, and remains of defences, visible until very lately, in Batty Wood on the Ridge; others at Giant's Hill, Armley, Bramley, Beeston, and Killingbeck; also those further afield at Kippax, Barwick, Bardsey, etc.

Although several writers have described Leeds as the site of a Roman station, said to have stood near the line of a road running from Adel to Slack, there is not sufficient evidence to prove this. Thoresby makes mention of it, yet he brings no positive proof to support his idea. Supposing a station had existed, connected by a well-paved road of Roman construction, running between Adel, Leeds, and Slack, surely sufficient testimony to place the fact beyond dispute would have been forthcoming in Thoresby's time, two centuries ago. Fletcher, in his *Picturesque Yorkshire*, gives this rather bald statement: "It was a Roman station, but there is nothing left which shows the enquirer that its story goes so far back." Why these statements are repeated by most writers I fail to understand, considering there is no evidence forthcoming to demonstrate the existence of such a station here, and the nearest point to the actual line of Roman road is fully

* Just without the boundary.

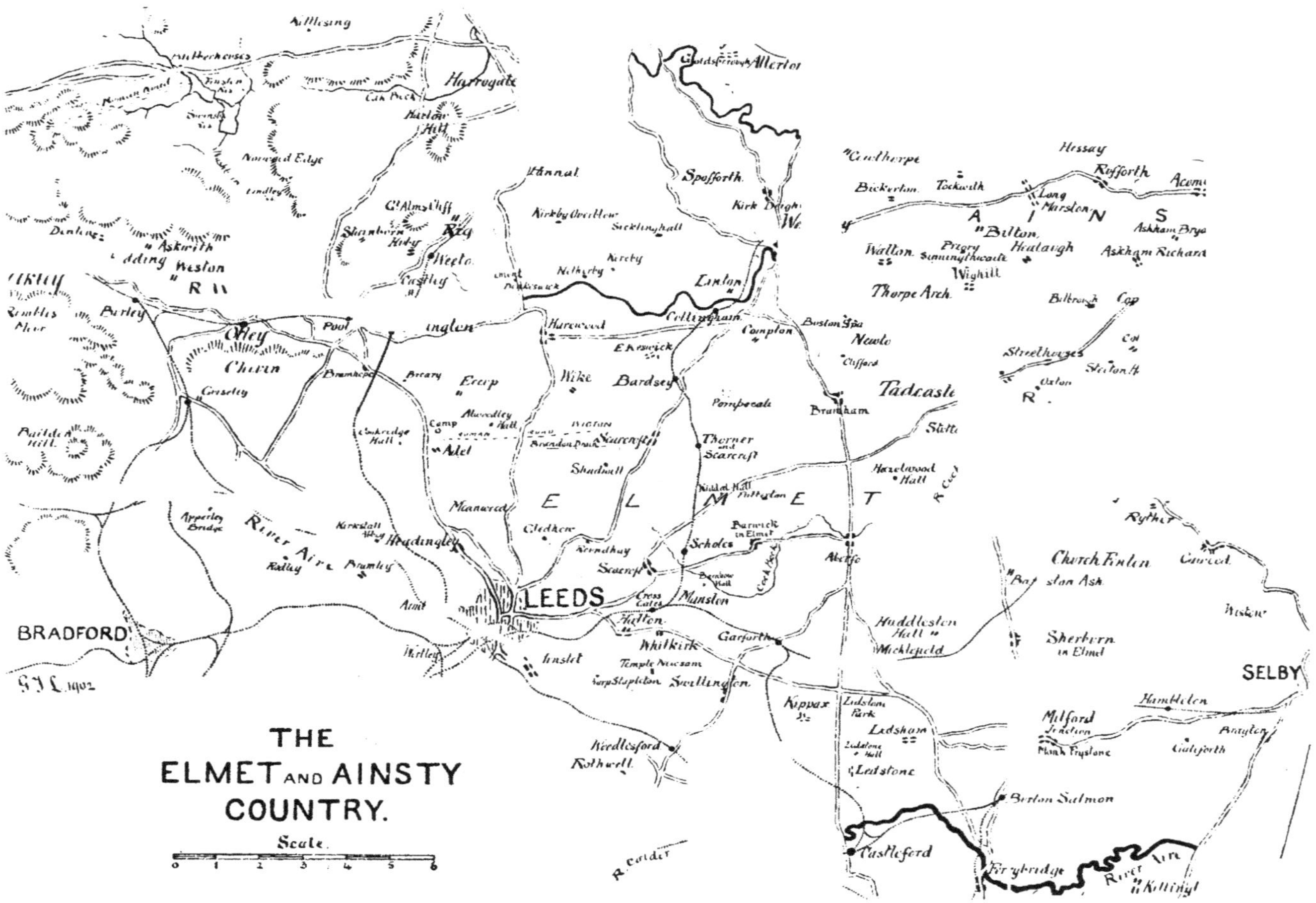

THE
ELMET AND AINSTY
COUNTRY.

six miles away on either side. That a paved ford existed just below the site of the present bridge, and a road or path led hither from the Calls and Church, there is ample proof; yet this does not necessarily imply it was Roman.*

That Leeds would be well known to the Romans, the stations in the vicinity (Adel and Castleford) are sufficiently conclusive; and it is also probable that these people quarried the district for ironstone; evidences of such quarries are always found when digging foundations between Briggate and Call Lane; but by whom the industry was worked is a matter of conjecture. The Rev. J. G. Simpson, in his work on the Leeds Parish Church, says that in all probability Leeds was the seat of the Royal Court of the Scandinavian kings of Northumbria. Another writer says it was a residence of Angle kings; but, like the supposed Roman castrum on Quarry Hill, and the Roman road running through the Calls, and the ford over the Aire, all are mythical, resting on the imagination only, without any foundation of fact to rely upon.

Supposing Leeds had once been the residence of either Angle or Danish kings, its name would have surely found a place in the Saxon chronicle. Bede certainly touches upon it, but only as a people or district, not as a town or city.

In point of antiquity, apart from its name (Leeds—a memorial of its founders), comes the Parish Church, dedicated to St. Peter. Its foundations carry us back in imagination down the shadowy aisles of time for, at least, fifteen centuries; but as to the precise date the first Church was erected on this site, history is again silent. One writer says five structures have stood on this spot. Supposing this to be the case, the first would be a British Church of timber construction, with roof of thatch, superseded, in the seventh century, by one of more durable material, which lasted through the Angle and Danish dynasties, say from the eighth to the eleventh century.

Remains of crosses and carved stones of this ancient edifice were found in the walls, during the last restoration. According to a statement by Robert Dennis Chantrill, the architect of the present Church, and to whom, in some measure, we owe the existence of the runic cross, now to be seen by the Altar,† great numbers of carved stones, portions of pillars, shafts,

* *Callis*—a beaten path.

† This stone is supposed to have been raised to the memory of Aulaff, the Norse leader, in the invasion which culminated in the battle of Brunanburgh. In our opinion, the work on the stone is of much later date—eleventh century.

capitals and fragments of crosses, etc., were carted away with the debris. If we reconcile ourselves to this statement, we can only regret the utter lack of the sentiment of veneration, and a strange apathy shown for past relics amongst the clergy of that period, and those in charge of the demolition of the structure. Leeds, with few relics of her past career, can ill afford this loss.

Of the third Church, supposed to have been erected about the end of the eleventh, or early years of the twelfth century, its architecture, naturally, would be pure Norman. The original structure appears to have consisted of nave, transept, and choir, additions being made in the thirteenth, fourteenth, and fifteenth centuries.

During some alterations, in 1809, many fragments of a more ancient structure were discovered,

LEEDS PARISH CHURCH, KIRKGATE.

amongst which was a stone coffin, hewn out of a solid block of stone, supposed to be at least seven hundred years old.* From evidences, this church seems to have been partly destroyed by fire: hence its diversity of architecture.

* *Leeds Mercury*, 1809:—STONE COFFIN FOUND AT LEEDS PARISH CHURCH. The issue of July 29th records that—On Wednesday last the workmen employed in repairing the Parish Church in this town found a stone coffin containing a complete skeleton and the bones of two other human subjects under the foundation of the church, near the entrance

The fourth church was demolished in 1838, and the fifth church erected on the lines of the old foundation, completed and duly consecrated on Thursday, 2nd of September, 1841, under the vicariate of Dean Hook, whose earnest zeal performed such wonders in Leeds, both temporally and spiritually. What Thoresby said of the former church—"Black, but comely" —can be partly said of the present structure, which is certainly very black, although, perhaps, not quite so comely as the previous one. From an architectural standpoint there is much to be desired. Its appearance does not greatly impress the onlooker, nor does the dingy squalor of its situation and surroundings add any charm to the fabric.

ARMS OF MOWBRAY AND HOWARD, QUARTERLY, FROM AN OAKEN BEAM IN AN OLD HOUSE IN SWINEGATE, LEEDS.

Whatever may be its shortcomings in architectural grace and grandeur of outline and design, it was around this early religious foundation that, for centuries, Leeds of the Celtic and Anglo-Danish periods existed, with a population which, in pre-Norman times, never exceeded four hundred souls. Leeds had not then spread west even so far afield as Briggate, the beginning of this now important thoroughfare being called into existence by the slow but gradual growth of the town during the early rule of the Norman lords.

---

to the bell-chamber. The coffin has the appearance of having been cut out of a solid block about seven feet long by a foot and a half deep; its interior dimensions are six feet three inches in length, about twelve inches deep, and of width sufficient to hold a tolerably large figure. From the situation in which it was found, it must have lain in that place ever since the church was erected, possibly above 700 years.

78   THE OLD KINGDOM OF ELMET.

Of mediæval Leeds there are few traces, and space compels us to touch lightly. When the Norman William succeeded to the patrimony of Harold the Saxon, momentous changes took place. Characteristic of the Norman

TEMPLAR STREET   VICAR LANE   LOWERHEAD ROW

BRIDGE STREET   LOWERHEAD ROW   OLD GEORGE BRIGGATE   TEMPLAR STREET

TEMPLAR STREET   LADY LANE   TEMPLAR STREET   TEMPLAR. ST

TEMPLAR CROSSES IN LEEDS.

S. Harrison

was his despotic rule and strict enforcement of law and order. All went by rule, from king to slave. We have charters from the king to the baron, from the barons to the knights, and from the latter to the soldiers, landholders, and even cotters and borderers. A most remarkable charter was given to Leeds by Maurice Paganel, 1207-8; it presents an interesting and singular picture of mediæval Leeds. The charter is fully translated in Whitaker's *Loidis in Elmet.*

The Domesday records tell us Leeds and surrounding district were bestowed by the king on that powerful Norman, Ilbert de Laci, the founder of Kirkstall, who consolidated all its estates under his great Barony of Pontefract, where the skeleton of his once huge castle still remains to be seen; and to fully understand the vast extent of this lord's territory, it is said he could ride three days on horseback, continuously, and see nothing but his own property. From De Laci the land in and around Leeds was subinfeuded to Ralph Paganel or Paynel, and by him the advowson of the Church of Leeds, with the Chapel of Holbeck, was given to the Priory of Holy Trinity, York.

In the early Norman period, a bridge was built over the river, and the street bearing its name, Bridge-gate (Briggate), began gradually to assume its outline and importance, until, as centuries rolled past, it reached to the confines of Kirkgate; still growing upwards it joined the Head Rows, which began to take something like definite shape by the end of the sixteenth century.*

Wheater says, "Cloth was made in Leeds before the reign of Edward the First, for in 1275, Alexander Fuller, a cloth maker of Leedes 'makes cloth not of the right breadth;'" and in 1201, one Simon the dyer is fined 100/- for selling adulterated wine, and so we find that short measures and adulteration were practised even in the old days of Leeds; and we also find that two of its principal industries, cloth making and dyeing, have had their origin in early Norman times.

The feudal rights exercised by the occupiers of the king's mills compelled the inhabitants of the manor of Leeds to grind their corn at the said mills. From this restraint, however, those houses which are situated within the manor of Whitkirk were exempt. The origin of this custom is very remote. In ancient times each family ground its corn in hand-mills. When water-mills were invented their introduction was eagerly desired; few, however,

* It was about the old bridge that the cloth market was held. "And here," says Thoresby, "several thousand pounds have been known to pass hands in a few hours" (mark the sequel), "and in comparative silence surprising to strangers." Here, also, stood the famous "Bridg-end Shots," "where the clothier may, together with his pot of ale, have a noggin o' porrage and a trencher of either boiled or roast meat for twopence." Good old times and customs! Briggate of that day, 1700, had very few shops: there were flower gardens to the front, and orchards and paddocks to the backs of the houses.

were able to build them. In some poor districts the king was petitioned to erect mills, to which he consented, on condition that the inhabitants would bind themselves and their heirs for ever (mark the word) to grind at such mills, on the terms then agreed to. During the Holy Wars, many privileges and immunities were granted to the Knights Templar, and among these was the exemption of their lands from certain taxes, and free of the obligation to grind at the Soke Mill of Leeds manor. The houses thus exempt are marked with crosses; there are several different styles of forming this cross—single, double, and also the Maltese cross. The "Court Leet" of the manor of Whitkirk and Templenewsam are yet held, and an annual gathering of the constable and assistants takes place. In Templar Street (which takes its name from the Knights of the Temple) the crosses are to be seen in abundance and variety; also in Templar Court and St. John's Square (named after the Knights of St. John). Less than a century ago, this Square was the residence of well-to-do trades people, and it still bears evidences of better days. Other objects worthy of note in this district belonging to the manor of Templenewsam, are the many antique door knockers.

[F. Bogg.
A BIT OF OLD BRIGGATE.

Timble Bridge, over which the road ran, leading from Leeds to Templenewsam, is said by Thoresby to be a corruption of Temple Bridge. In the fourteenth century, this was one of the most important parts of the town. In 1379, one John of Tymbill Smith dwelt here, and is said by Wheater to have been one of the four richest tradesmen in the town.

The stringent laws of the Plantagenet kings, which compelled the people, under severe fines, to wear clothes suitable to their order and position, from cloth of gold down to coarse black serge, made the cloth manufactured in Leeds a necessity. Width, weight, quality, colour, and price, were all regulated by the Government, in accordance with the decision of the Guilds, chartered to conduct the trade and manufacture.

We have already indicated that the Leeds of the Normans spread from the bridge to Kirkgate, and of the Tudor dynasty up to the Head Row; under the Jacobean kings the town grew west to Albion Street, and during the reign of the Georges to Park Lane and the west end, and at the same rate of progress also north and east.

Of mediæval Leeds scarcely a vestige remains. Swinegate and King's Mills, however, retain the memory of those days;* Swinegate being the approach from the bridge and town to the mills and the manor house, which stood on Mill Hill, erroneously described as a castle, doubtless a myth, like the supposed Roman camp, that never existed; and from the garnish of this baronial and imperial robe Leeds must, perforce, be divested, being in the same plight as an individual of humble parentage who, having suddenly acquired great wealth, must needs manufacture a crest and an ancient ancestry. Thoresby was evidently led astray by the existence of Leeds Castle in Kent.

The moat which surrounded the manor house is said to have been visible in Thoresby's time, and it is from the description of the place by this antiquary, that the legend of a castle grew into shape.

A BIT OF OLD LANDS LANE.

* Within the last half century several very quaint houses, of the Tudor period, or even earlier, have been demolished in Swinegate. A piece of timber, bearing the arms of Mowbray, taken from one of those old houses, is now to be seen in the Philosophical Hall.

Of Leeds of the Tudor period, very little remains. Of the Jacobean there are several examples, notably, two or three quaint gabled shops in Briggate; one dated 1615, the old Pack Horse Inn (formerly the Nag's Head), and the inn yards between Briggate and Lands Lane,* exhibit several quaint examples of seventeenth century architecture. The Leopard Inn and yard, containing both Tudor and Jacobean architecture, wear quite a Flemish aspect.

The last relics of the Butter Cross, in the shape of columns, have lately been removed owing to extensive alterations required for the new street known as New Bond Street, which has also caused the removal of the shambles and its necessary appendages—a most creditable improvement.

Some part of Ralph Thoresby's house in Kirkgate is still in evidence, it is the one now occupied by Fourness, druggist; portions of the framework of the observatory still exist above the passage leading into the yard where Thoresby's museum was also situated. From his study window, which was immediately over the shop, the antiquary could see across Briggate, and just beyond to the green fields of the country, the Aire flowing bright and limpid, the hills above Kirkstall and Bramley filling the background of the picture.

"PACK HORSE," BRIGGATE.

There are other ancient features in Kirkgate: the Golden Cock Inn and block of houses with antique gables, near to the Parish Church; Cherry Tree Yard, opposite to the church, with low, narrow entrance, is a type of those folds, peculiar, quaint, but dirty relics of old Leeds. The widening of Call Lane has been the means of sweeping away much old property.

In Lowerhead Row a few relics of Rockley Hall are yet in evidence. This Hall was formerly the finest in the town, it occupied all the high

The lane formerly leading to cultivated patches of land—hence Lands Lane.

ground immediately above top of Lady Lane, extending to Wood Street, with gardens and grounds reaching down to Lady Beck. The Rockleys, of ancient lineage, were the only family in the parish of Leeds who were honoured with a chapel or queere in the Parish Church. A portion of the old Hall, on the north side of the Row, was converted into cottages, about a century ago, and formed part of what was Cryers Yard. These have been recently demolished, and a few fragments of the old Hall were met with, and still exist. On the south side of the Row, portions remain in the foundations of the old shop of Oates',

OLD GREEN DRAGON HOTEL, GUILDFORD STREET.

the saddlers, Three Legs Yard, and Proctor's, tobacconists, at the corner just undergone alterations; and one in Malt Shovel Yard, dating from Tudor times, have no doubt done duty as out-offices to the Hall. Other antique bits of property still exist in this street.

The Moot Hall,* which stood in the middle of Briggate, has long since been demolished, so have the several Chantries: one stood at the Bridge, one in Kirkgate, one in Lady Lane, and one to the west of Briggate,

* "The Moot Hall in Leeds (a building which served the purpose of a Town Hall) stood in front of what was called the Middle Row, and faced down Briggate, at a point a few yards above Kirkgate. Apart from the obstruction in the leading thoroughfare of the borough caused by the Middle Row, the Moot Hall had proved wholly inadequate for its purpose long before it was demolished. The agitation for the removal of the whole Middle Row began about the year 1820. The first definite step with this object was not taken, however, until 1822. In July of that year a meeting for the purpose was held in the Parish Church, of all places, and by a large majority it was resolved to proceed with the much-needed improvement. The demolition was completed on May 30th, 1825. The pillory and stocks were in prominent positions in front of the old Moot Hall. When the Court House (afterwards the Post Office) was built in Park Row, the stocks were transferred to one side of that building, and no doubt there are old Leeds residents able to say that they remember having seen them in use."

in Upperhead Row, removed by Mr. Legg in 1869. The walls of this Chantry were very thick, with beams of black oak. There were fragments of mediæval pottery, ancient candlesticks, and a deep draw-well with steps leading down to the water. This Chantry belonged to Kirkstall Abbey. Connected with it is the legend of the subterranean passage leading to the abbey.

The names of old hostelries, Pack Horse and Nag's Head, King's Arms, Golden Cock, Cock and Bottle, Malt Shovel, Black Bull, Three Legs, Old Malt Mill, The Royal, Bull and Mouth, etc., hereabouts, remind us of the old market days of the early years of last century. The first calls up the time when much of the manufacture and produce was carried on the backs of pack horses, which followed the old hollow roads; vestiges of the ancient road between Leeds and York still remain.

What a charming picture the memory relimns, shall we say, of the 'good old days,' when the travellers, with their string of pack horses, to the accompaniment of jingling bells, drew up to the hostelry—Pack Horse, the Nag's Head, King's Arms, Black Bull, etc., to bait their horses, and refresh themselves with bread and cheese and tankards of brown sparkling ale, relating to Boniface the scandal and gossip of the countryside. These were the days of highwaymen, when scores of waggons and coaches rumbled along the 'hightoby,' and through the quaint crooked streets and narrow alleys of Jacobean Leeds; carriers' carts and rickety old vehicles of a past age carrying the farmer and his wife and daughter; others mounted on the dappled grey,' or heavy cart horse, wended their way through the streets, presenting a jostling, bustling, and 'motley' crew.

Leeds did not suffer greatly from the miseries of the Civil War. This arose, no doubt, from its situation—being located some distance from the highways, and partly from its insignificance as a town of any great historical importance, in those early troublous times, never having had a castle, wall, or any works of defence.

During the civil wars of the Cavaliers and Roundheads, the greater part of the inhabitants seem to have been in favour with the latter; this doubtless arising from their sense of freedom and independence. The town was stormed and taken by the Roundheads, after a two hours' fight, January 23rd, 1643.

* "Leedes was taken by Sir Thomas Fairfax, eleven soldiers slain, buried 24th; five more slain two or three days after; six more died of their wounds. Buried 1st April, 1643, Captain Boswell, slain at Seacroft battel, and six soldiers. A gentleman and two common soldiers, slain in Robert Williamson's house, of Hunslet, buried 13th of April, 1643. Five

During the rebellion of 1745, Leeds was thrown into a state of feverish excitement on hearing the news that the Pretender, with a large army, was marching south. This excitement somewhat abated when John Wesley rode into the town from the north, on the 5th of November, bringing the news that the Pretender's army was steering towards Preston and Manchester.

It was on this occasion that Marshal Wade, with an army of thirteen thousand men, encamped in the vicinity of Sheepscar and Woodhouse, and from which circumstance Wade Lane received its name. Wade Hall still remains at the corner of Kelsall Street, and the above lane is said to have been the headquarters of the gallant Marshal.

OLD HALL HOTEL.

In 1753, a very serious riot took place, and to properly understand the reason of this disturbance, and the stupid ignorance of the people or ringleaders of the mob, we may say that up to this period Leeds had never been properly connected by good roads with the chief centres in the county; for instance, the old, deep, hollow road, which led from Leeds to York, and which, in many places, can still be distinctly traced, was only wide enough for the passage of a single vehicle, drawn by horses in single row. The inconvenience arising from such a narrow way must necessarily have been

soldiers n ore slain. Nine n ore in May, 1643. Sixteen n ore in June, under Captain Lascelles, Major Gifford, Sir George Wentworth, Captain Thornton, and the Earl of Newcastle. Twelve n ore in July, under General King, Sir Ingran Hopton, and Sir William Widdrington; twenty-six soldiers buried in July and August, 1644. A soldier buried in the old School Garth."

great. The attempt to improve the then existing state of things, by the formation of good constructed roads, and the erection of turnpike bars, was the cause of the riot. The people of Leeds strongly objected to the payment of tolls, and a large mob marched to Halton Dial on the York Road, demolished the toll bar there, and from thence came to Beeston, and destroyed the bar, and also the one on the Leeds and Bradford Road. In the attempt to destroy the bar at Harewood Bridge, they were successfully resisted and driven back towards Leeds by Mr. Lascelles, who had armed his tenants and workmen. Three of the instigators were arrested, and on the following day brought before the magistrates. This proceeding aroused the fury of the mob to a greater pitch, and a rescue was attempted. The military were called out, the Riot Act read, which being of no avail, a volley of powder was fired; this not having the desired effect, and the fury of the mob passing all bounds of restraint, the soldiers again fired, this time with ball. The effect was electrical: the mob suddenly fled in all directions; upwards of thirty people were wounded, several fatally.

Thus ended the great turnpike riots. Since that time, Leeds has witnessed many innovations in her rapid stride upward to wealth, and the position of the chief commercial and manufacturing centre of Yorkshire. In point of antiquity and interest to St. Peter's follows that of St. John, built by John Harrison, a native of Leeds, who, having acquired a considerable fortune by trade, and being childless, determined to erect and endow a chapel. It was completed and consecrated September 26th, 1634. Its exterior walls do not by any means present a fine example of church architecture. It is of the debased order, sixteenth century, when the art and expression of church building was at its lowest ebb. The interior is contrary to all rule and consists of two aisles only, with a row of columns up the middle, and a heavy dark oak screen completely obscuring the choir. Yet the question of beauty in point of architecture is counterbalanced by the richness of the carving, which is most lavish and elaborate, presenting the most complete carved interior of the Jacobean order in the county.

John Harrison was first buried in his own orchard in Kirkgate, but his body was afterwards removed into the choir of St. John's, and over his tomb is a monument of black marble.

Thoresby says of this church:—"So noble and stately a structure is scarcely to be paralleled in England."

Whitaker, on the other hand, says:—"St. John's Church has all the gloom and all the obstruction of an ancient church, without one vestige of its dignity and grace."

The church was restored in 1867 under the supervision of Norman Shaw, when the galleries were removed. Up to that time, all the pews had beautifully carved doors; these with other rare carved work at that time disappeared. Where? That is the question. Probably worked into unique specimens of Jacobean carving and now adorning some private residence in the city.

Apart from the church, John Harrison built the Free Grammar School* and founded the Hospital adjoining, for the relief of indigent persons of good conversation and formerly industrious.

Adjoining the church to the west is a row of antique cottages known as St. John's Court. A little beyond, also built by John Harrison, is Wade Hall. The only building which stood between this and Red Hall in the seventeenth century was a cloth warehouse; portions of which have recently been exposed, owing to the alterations for the widening of Woodhouse Lane and Wade Lane.† Red

ST. JOHN'S CHURCH.

* The Grammar School was first founded by Sir William Sheaffield, Priest, and stood on the site now occupied by the Old Pinfold in Edward Street. It was removed to the West side of North Street, near top of Lady Lane, by John Harrison in 1624 where it remained until taken down for street improvements some three or four years ago.

† The last remnant of Lydgate has just been demolished. Just beyond in Woodhouse Lane stood a Tower, hence the names, "Tower Hill" and "Tower Buildings."

Hall, red from the former colour of the bricks of which it is built, is a large gabled structure facing Guildford Street. Seventy years ago large poplar trees adorned the front, and a garden, reaching down to the Music Hall and Theatre, now called King Charles' Croft. At the time of its erection, by Thomas Metcalf, merchant and alderman of Leeds, it would present an imposing appearance, and doubtless ranked with the finest structures in the town.

It was here that Charles Stuart, a prisoner in the hands of the Roundheads, rested on the journey south, and, whilst here, a maid at the Hall offered to assist the King to escape, entreating him to put on her clothes to escape detection, and she would escort him in the dark through the garden into a back alley to Lands Lane, thence to a friend's house. The King declined the offer, but presented her with a token of service; this she afterwards brought before the notice of Charles II., and told him the story, who, out of gratitude, made her husband chief bailiff in Yorkshire, and it was he who afterwards built Crosby House in the Head Row. The story also says that John Harrison, by permission, sent the King a tankard of excellent ale. Hid in the depths of the tankard were a quantity of gold pieces, which the King is said to have dexterously hid about his person.

There is one striking fact in connection with journalism and the growth of Leeds, namely, the career of the *Leeds Mercury*, which commenced nearly two centuries ago—May, 1718. In 1801 it was sold to the late Mr. Edward Baines, whose family last year celebrated their century of ownership. Thus, to Leeds belongs the credit of producing the first

Yorkshire newspaper. On its appearance in 1718, Leeds was then a small town of less than ten thousand people. To-day the *Mercury*, growing with the requirements of the inhabitants, circulates in a city of over four hundred thousand people.

The *Leeds Intelligencer*, which has ultimately grown into the wide-famed *Yorkshire Post*, began its career as far back as July 2nd, 1754. The copy now before me bears the date 1767, printed by Griffith Wright, at New Street end. Thus we find that the two most important newspapers in the north of England to-day began, one in the early years, and the other in the middle of the eighteenth century.

Of rare and striking examples of architecture Leeds can boast but few; one noble example—the Town Hall—alone relieves it from mediocrity. Suppose we stand by the Queen's Hotel and look up Park Row. To the left is the new Post Office, the interior arrangements of which are, no doubt, excellent; but the site, the best and most commanding in the city, is worthy of a far greater type, in fact it is the poorest example in the square to which it has given its name—Post Office Square.

The Standard Office, built in crescent form, has a much better effect. Between the latter and the Post Office rises forth in the background, above the roofs of warehouses, etc., noble and impressive, the dome of the Town Hall. The two buildings on our right, the Exchange and Mill Hill Chapel, are the best examples of pointed Gothic in the city, uniform in style and ornamental work, and redeem, in some measure, the paucity of the city's architecture.

The Banks and Insurance Offices, which line either side of Park Row, in some instances, rise above the average standard of street architecture, and give a stately effect to this row. The Philosophical Hall, a severe, classic structure, and the Mechanics' Institute, now given over to science and art for a very different class to that originally intended, are worthy of their object. The Infirmary and the Yorkshire College can only be classed as a series of good buildings.

Leeds, however, possesses one magnificent structure which does not fail to arrest the attention of the citizen or stranger. Seen down the vista of streets, in the miasma of evening, the stately dome of the Town Hall reminds one of some ancient Grecian temple, at the waning of the light, when the sharp outlines of intervening buildings are softened and subdued, and the noble dome towers high over all, dreamlike as a vision of olden time.

We cannot, in our brief sketch of Leeds' architectural adornments, omit mention of the carving on the façade of the Queen's Hotel. The work is, perhaps, the most artistic of its class in Leeds, and deserving of great care in its preservation. It was done by Messrs. Burstall and Taylor. The first-named sculptor built himself a house in Lofthouse Place, and enriched the front by some of his own carving; he was an admirable man, both as a citizen and artist. Taylor, although perhaps not quite so proficient a sculptor as his partner, was a fair musician, and somewhat of a cynic.

Amongst the citizens whose memories are held in honour and respect, are John Harrison, the benefactor and founder of St. John's Church and the hospital adjoining, and who also performed many other good works; Ralph Thoresby, the historian and antiquary; John Smeaton, the architect and civil engineer, the builder of Eddystone Lighthouse; Joseph Priestly, theologian and scientist, some time minister of Mill Hill Chapel.

Among artists, Leeds produced C. H. Swanfelder, Joseph Rhodes, J. N. Rhodes, Edward Armitage, R.A., W. Cope, R.A. (the latter presented

THE TOWN HALL AND ST. ANN'S CATHEDRAL, FROM GUILDFORD STREET.

the beautiful altar picture of the Ascension to St. George's Church); Richard Waller, portrait artist ; Thomas Sutcliffe, member of the Water Colour Society; Atkinson Grimshaw, noted for his wonderful moonlight effects; James Roberts, for lake and mountain scenery ; and Henry Inchbold, the poet, friend of A. C. Swinburne, and the interpreter, both by brush and pen, of Wharfedale's Priory and the white faunch of Rylstone.

The chief interest of Leeds centres round its great number of industries.

In historic evidence and antiquities Leeds is notably deficient, never having possessed a castle or fortification, like Pontefract, Knaresborough, or York. Unlike the latter city, it was not a centre of great municipal life, and never the scene of mediæval pageantry.

The wonderful growth of the town, from a population of less than a thousand people, in the fourteenth, and even the early years of the fifteenth century (then only the tenth town in point of wealth in the riding), to the greatest city in the county to-day, presents a striking example of industrial development.

In the past, Leeds stood too far away from the great highways of communication to properly develop her resources. With the introduction of steam, and opening out of new roads, river-way, and railway lines of communication, the advantage of her situation was apparent. Blessed with many industries and great enterprise, Leeds has advanced by mighty strides, and now become one of the most prosperous cities in the world.

Potternewton, Gipton, and Chapeltown, on the highway to Harewood and Harrogate, are most pleasant suburbs. The former, according to Thoresby, received its prefix "potter" from the ashes of an adjacent Roman pottery.* The same antiquary also informs us that the place had been known by its present name in his day:—"These four hundred years, that ancient family of the Mauliverers, who took part in the fight and conquest at Hastings, had a seat here for generations, and in the fifteenth and sixteenth centuries, a branch of the family of Lindley, of Lindley, dwelt here."

Allerton Hall was of old the seat of the Kitchingmans. It was a custom of theirs, when any member of the family died, the body was borne hence to the church of St. Peter's, Leeds, in weird and solemn procession at night,

*Potternewton, known by its present name for at least six hundred years. Its prefix "potter" may have been given it from the many fragments of pottery strewn around, a former occupation, and on the rebuilding, the terminal "Newton" given to it to mark the former significance of the old pottery, hence—Potternewton.

by torchlight, and deposited near the altar. The story says that it was only on these occasions that the great chandelier of the the house, which contains thirty-six branches, was lighted.

The Domesday Survey says:—
"Newton Alward had three carucates of land to be taxed, and there may be two ploughs there. Ilbert now has it, and Hunfrid of him. In the demesne, one plough and two villanes, and one border with one plough, and five acres of meadow. Value in King Edward's time twenty shillings, now twenty shillings."

CHAPELTOWN.

The same record states, in Alreton (Allerton Chapel)
"Glunier had six carucates of land to be taxed, and there may be three ploughs there. Ilbert now has it, and it is waste. Value in King Edward's time forty shillings, now two shillings. There is a church there and wood pasture half a mile long and half broad."

Here, the thirteenth century chapel gave place to the present structure, erected during the eighteenth century. The ancient parsonage house, destroyed in 1870, had walls of immense thickness, and is supposed to have been used by the monks of Kirkstall, who served this chapel.

The church is in the Corinthian style, and the spire a commanding feature in the suburban landscape. A grant of land made to this church by the lord of the manor, in 1736, specifies its tenure to be the presentation of "one red rose, in time of roses, if the same shall be lawfully demanded." The Roman altar discovered in this churchyard is now in the museum, Park Row.*

About a mile beyond Chapeltown, and separated from the latter place by a deep valley, is the Moortown, of old standing on a solitary moor, and even to-day resting on the fringe of it. Hereabouts rise the streams which supply the lake at Roundhay, variously known as Roundhay, Killingbeck, and Wyke Beck, which empties into the Aire between Thorp-Stapleton and Templenewsam.

In Street Lane, evidently a byway of old which ran out of the military road passing from Adel over Bramham Moor to the 'Ermine Street,' we are again treading in the footsteps of the Roman. About Elmet Hall and Roundhay Park relics, both of Roman and Celtic people, have been found. As late as February, 1901 (*see illustration*), three well-preserved bronze axe heads were unearthed, when digging foundations just off Street Lane. We should surmise that a small outpost of the Romans was located in the vicinity of Elmet Hall, to overawe the Celts dwelling hereabouts in the heart of Elmet. Other indications of bygone occupation remain in the vestiges of trenches and fortified sites. Just to the east, and abutting on to the Wetherby Road, near Elmet Lane, are the outlines of such a site; the position, strong by nature, and well adapted for defence.

ROUNDHAY PARK AND ITS ENVIRONS.

This beautiful domain, acquired by the Leeds Corporation in 1872, and transformed into a free park for the benefit of the Leeds people, contains about eight hundred acres of wood, lake, gardens, and meadow. There is a charming variety of both cultivated and natural scenery. The view from the Mansion, south and eastward, across the park, is all that can be desired by the mind that loves to linger on the rich and ever-changing hues of scenery. The landscape recedes and melts into dim perspective, enriched by hill, wood, valley, meadow, and cornland, with spires and towers of adjacent village churches.

The historic significance of its surroundings reaches back to Anglo Celtic times. It formed a principal outpost for the latter, when Celtic influence was paramount at Barwick, hence the vigilance of the Roman in this district.

Roundhay is in the parish of Barwick. Round-haig—round enclosure set apart for hunting purposes; the terminal "haig" is Saxon for a hedge.

* Near to this spot a stone coffin has recently been found.

The manor of Roundhay comprises Seacroft and Shadwell; and in olden times, when the forest of Elmet cast its sombre hue over the secluded dells, this district appears to have formed a royal chase for the Anglo-Danish and Norman kings and lords. Hither, in September, 1272, came King John to hunt in this forest; following in his train would be many of the lords and barons of the north country. It was part of the great 'Laci' barony of Pontefract, and from this family, the founder of Kirkstall, the grange or granary in this district would doubtless be given to the monks; part of the

LOOKING TOWARDS WHITKIRK FROM ROUNDHAY PARK.

great barn still exists, and stands on the extreme watershed of one of the tributaries of the Wyke Beck. Except the interesting old barn at the Grange there is nothing of much antiquity or importance remaining above ground. A few old by-lanes are some indication of past occupation. Cobble Hall, standing high above the east bank of the upper lake, has no particular interest or history attached to it.

Gipton in the Domesday Survey is called "Ciptune," and between this name and Kippax, the latter in Domesday, "Chipesh," is a great similarity; the prefix "chipe" no doubt has the same meaning—the cheap—a market,

indicating spots where trading could be transacted between Celt and Saxon.*
Thoresby, however, concludes the place obtained its name from "Cip," a
tent or personal name—and "Tun," an enclosure. The Norman record
shews it to have been fairly prosperous just previous to the Conquest.
After the raid of the Norman king through Yorkshire, it was left desolate
and waste.

> "In Cipeton and Coletun (Gipton and Coletun) Gospatric had four carucates of land and a half to be taxed, and there may be three ploughs there, Ilbert now has it, and it is waste. Value in King Edward's time, forty shillings; now two shillings. There is a church there, and wood pasture half a mile long and half broad."

Thoresby also records, in his survey of this parish, the remains of an
entrenched enclosure:—"Here amongst the thicket I found an ancient
fortification, the out trench whereof is 18 feet broad. The first camp about

---

* From the Anglo Saxon "ceap," a market—hence we obtain "Cheapside" and "Eastcheap."

INGRAM'S HALL
or HILL HOUSE, BANK

PERCY ROBINSON

100 feet long and 60 feet broad; and the second about 165 feet square. Both are surrounded by deep trench and rampire." This he supposed to have been the camp of Prince Odiwald, sub-King of Deira, who, previous to the fight on Whinmoor, had ranged on the side of Penda. Probably fearing the battle would go against the Mercians he remained neutral in camp until he learnt the turn in the tide of battle and then joined his forces with those of the victor. This hesitation of Odiwald contributed largely to the disaster which overtook the Mercians at the great battle of Winwæd.

NEAR FOUNDRY MILL.

The remains of these entrenchments were very faint in Whitaker's time and are now completely obliterated. Gipton Well was formerly noted for its mineral properties.

In our description of Elmet we shall endeavour to follow, when convenient, the natural lines of the various important waterways, as by so doing it will be much easier for the reader to follow. Besides in olden times the waterways often constituted a boundary.

Starting from Roundhay we keep to the valley; a mile downward and at some little distance from the beck is Foundry Mill, the waterwheel here being a construction of Smeaton's genius

Of the old forge, not much precise record has remained green; even the lane perpetuating in its name the early foundry—one of, if not *the* most ancient in the vicinage of the Templars' Newsame—shows little trace, save in its sinuosities and the few decrepit but significant bushes of spindle tree, cat oak, and cornelwood, of the bird-haunted hagg in which the charcoal was burnt and the iron smelted for ploughshare and sword, lance-head and halberd, through the late, if not the early middle ages of Elmet's 'frondulous' forest. Men were alternatively too 'throng' fashioning the implements of peace and war, to dot the i's and tail the y's of written history. Even the bits of gnarled wryed greenery are going the way that quite lately the four-square hypæthral tower of the foundry—brick-built—has gone. The onward-thrust furrow of civil industry turns up each of earth's sites in turn, like a Nemesis—even the graveyards of great towns such as that of Leeds Parish Church disappear in time, though sentiment, preferring Nature's crematory to that of the Greeks, makes a sooty poplar grove of them for a few decades. But that anvil and hammer, wielded by brawny arms that wrought with sweat, alike rang to the uses of seed-time, harvestry, and conflict, cannot be doubted.

[E. Bogg.
WYKE BECK.

Seacroft, situated on the very extremity of the watershed of the Aire valley, is about half-a-mile beyond. The village rests in a small dip in the land which, in past ages, was covered by a mere. The situation is on the eastern edge of the great coal beds. Two hundred yards east begins the watershed of the Wharfe. Seacroft Hall, a seventeenth century building, is now the residence of the Wilsons. Seacroft was filched by the Earl of Lincoln about 1250, and evidently made a member of his barony. In the terminal "croft" of Seacroft we have distinctly an Anglian adjunct probably to a more important farmstead.

The village contains a few antique features. The most picturesque is seen just at the entrance from Leeds. On the other side of the village is a good Jacobean house, the residence of Dr. Pogson. A mile beyond in the direction of York is the battlefield of Whinmoor, the story of which will be told more fully in a later chapter.

According to the Norman record there is a great discrepancy in the value of this place in King Edward's time, and that at the compiling of the Domesday :—

"In Sacroft (Seacroft), Ode, and Niueling, Ulnar, Stainuef, Ragenild had seven carucates* of land to be taxed, and there may be four ploughs there. One Robert now has it of Ilbert, and it is waste wood pasture, four quarentens long and three broad. Value in King Edward's time four pounds, now twenty pence."

Crossgates, now a residential place rapidly extending, consisted, a century ago, of a little more than a dozen cottages, which stood near a crossing shut off by gates to keep the cattle, pasturing on the adjacent common, from straying. There is a small plot of land still known as "Crossgates Green."

In this vicinity Soldiers' Field and Hell Dyke are suggestive of the adjacent battlefield of Whinmoor. The first name probably points to the encampment before the battle and the latter to the burial of the dead after the conflict. From Crossgates the land falls sharply down to Wyke beck.

[Scrimshaw.
WYKE BRIDGE HOUSE.

Killingbeck Hall, to the east of the stream, is on a commanding situation among exceedingly fine trees, the park gently shelving down to the lake, a most picturesque sheet of water. The Brooks resided here from 1638-1788.

* Each carucate of land was as much as a team of oxen could plough in a year. That area would be the standard measurement, there would be three carucates of wood, pasture and waste land that would be less taxed than the ploughed land. From the Latin *carruca* —a plough.

Situated between the Leeds and Selby Railway and the York. Road at Wyke Bridge is Wykebridge House, a very interesting half-timbered structure, sixteenth century period, with an addition probably a generation later; in the south wall is a good example of a Tudor door thickly studded with rivets. The interior contains Jacobean panelling and bits of antique furniture and the 'ingle neuk' with seat complete. In an upper room, formerly the large room of the house, is a plaster coat-of-arms—on the shield are three bucks, supported by winged goats rampant, and surmounted by a crest bearing a goat's head between two wings. The worthy people who now inhabit the house are tenants of the Hon. Mrs. Meynell-Ingram, and on the wife's side are descendants of the Thompsons, who resided there early in the seventeenth century.

The hamlet of Killingbeck, considering its close proximity to Leeds, contains features which are simply charming, and which even the railway does not tend to destroy; the steep embankment has been planted with trees, giving it the appearance of a long wooded hill.

Less than a mile hence, on the south of the railway and commanding the edge of a fine plateau, is the village of Halton. The antiquity of this place has long been the theme of various comment. Philologists account for its derivation thus :—Hal, Hœlig, *i.e.*, Holy; ton from the Angle tun—an enclosure ; hence "holy town." Thoresby mentions the tradition of a

---

* Whereas the highewaie leading fron Leedes to Wikebrigg and so to Seacrofte and so to Kiddall towards Yorke hath been heretofore p'sented by Jury to be in great decay for want of amendm^t So that travellres cann verie hardly passe to the great hynderance of all her ma^{is} subjects that have occasion to travile that way. Dated, Wakefield, 13th July, 40, Elizabeth (1598).—"West Riding Sessions Rolls," Yorkshire Arch. Assoc. Record Series, v. iii., p. 104.

religious house having existed here, and he seems to have concluded this village was the site of the monastery in the wood of Elmet, mentioned by Bede. Following in Thoresby's footsteps, other writers relate that King Edwin's palace and church burnt by Cadwallader after the fatal fight and death of the former at Heathfield, stood at Ossethorp, now Osmondthorpe, and the stone altar, the only vestige of the church which escaped the fire, was removed to the monastery in the wood of Elmet, which, according to their theory, stood at Halton.

The evidences in support of these statements are very faint indeed. The stone altar referred to by Bede, and the only relic of Edwin's church which seems

[W. G. Foster.
LOOKING TOWARDS LEEDS FROM HALTON.

to have escaped the flames, came from Campodonum (not the Camboduuum of the Romans), Saxon "Dona-felda," that is Doncaster, and the latter town was also the "Villa Regia" of King Edwin. Bede says, A.D. 627, Paulinus built a church at Campodonum, where there was a royal villa, "in regione Loidis," which afterwards the Pagans (by whom King Edwin was slain) burnt, together with all the town, and we learn in addition, from Bede, that the stone altar from this church was long preserved in the monastery of Thridwulf which lies in the wood of Elmet. From this plain statement of Bede's we gather that the "Villa Regia" of Edwin and the church built by

Paulinus were not at Osmondthorpe,' but where Bede expressly states, viz.: Campodonum—Doncaster.

Turning to the supposed site of the monastery the evidences in favour of Halton are very slight indeed, resting chiefly on the derivation of its name, "Hœlig"—holy town, which is certainly very suggestive.

The name of the adjoining hamlet of Killingbeck probably locates Celtic Christianity in its prefix "Kil," a Celtic chapel. Built in the length of wall by the road side from Leeds to Halton and near the latter place are many fine shapely stones, which at some date have been used in the walls of a church, but of a much later period than the monastery of Thridwulf, which, in the writer's opinion, stood at, or near to, Barwick-in-Elmet, the capital of the ancient kingdom.*

Halton Feast (locally Horton), old pronunciation "Autun Feast," half a century ago, was the largest feast in Yorkshire. Open house was kept for all who came hither, abundance of roast beef, pickled cabbage and onions, not only at Halton, but even as far afield as Leeds, revelry and riot running rampant. York Road from Marsh Lane towards Halton for nearly a mile was lined with stalls on either side. The Golden Cock in Kirkgate is supposed to have been the limit of the feast westward, and it included the north side of Kirkgate, but not the south. Its origin seems to point to some remote Christian or Pagan festival, or from a notable event in the history of the Templars of Newsam.

Leeds, seen in the dusk of a winter's afternoon from the high ridge of Halton reminds one of some spectral phantasmagoria, the fitful gleam and flare of furnaces lighting up the murky surroundings, and ever and anon the fading light creating sombre shadows and dark, weird masses. The distant sound of machinery, the whirr and shriek of many trains, the glow of innumerable lamps and lights glittering from cars moving swiftly to and fro, with all the discordant hum and the varied throb and pulsation of a vast hive of human beings, combine to make up the strange picture of a great city by night.

* In Bede's time and long after, churches were of stooppen construction, or of timber, with stone slab for altar table, hence so easily fired when pillaged. What have come down to us as reliable stone work of Saxon period were of later time, and the vestiges are rare. Stone crosses are the earliest examples of the mason's craft.

"In Halletune (Halton), Morkare had six carucates of land to be taxed, where there may be three ploughs. Ilbert now has it, and it is waste. Value in King Edward's time, twenty shillings; it now pays two shillings."

There are few ancient features in Halton. The Irwin Arms, a hostel, seventeenth century period, is perhaps the most picturesque, but other survivals point to a remote past.

One charming picture is to be seen from the outskirts of the village near the "water tower," just in the silver shadowing grey of evening, between day and night, the tower of Whitkirk church rising amongst the surrounding trees, the moon glinting over all, forms a picture full of pathos and rare pastoral beauty.

WHITKIRK IN THE GREY OF EVENING.

It will be well to precede our description of Whitkirk and Templenewsam by a few remarks on the vestiges of antiquity at Osmondthorpe, the mediæval remains at Thorpe-Stapleton, and the unique specimen of early Jacobean work at Knowesthorpe.

The suffix "thorpe" attached to the above-mentioned places is sufficiently indicative of Norse or Danish origin and permanent settlement. In

Lincolnshire, chiefly colonized by the Danes, the word Thorpe—meaning a settlement of people, a village, is attached to more than sixty places.

The Domesday mention of Osmondthorpe is very brief: "In Ossetorp four carucates to be taxed."

Besides Thoresby and Whitaker, many later antiquaries have fixed on this place as a royal residence of Saxon kings, the Villa Regia of Bede, " in regione Loides," and we cannot but admit there are a few evidences in favour of this idea. The fine situation and remains of trenches, foundations of buildings, etc., discovered in the levelling and ploughing are all indicative of its antiquity. A small piece of painted glass was found here bearing the arms of Redwald, king of the East Angles (the Prince who so hospitably befriended Edwin and reinstated him into his birthright (the kingdom of Deira). Probably the relic is not earlier than the fifteenth century, yet it appears to illustrate a tradition, connecting by its presence King Edwin and Osmondthorpe, and bearing on its face the story of Redwald and Edwin. The question naturally arises: Was this piece of glass specially designed and painted for Osmonds at Osmondthorpe, or was it filched at the dissolution of monasteries, or during the Commonwealth era from Kirkstall, or from any of the surrounding parish churches? The last conjecture is the most feasible, yet the singular circumstance of its discovery here, perpetuates one of the most notable events in early Saxon history—the hospitality of Redwald and deliverance of Edwin from exile, and the foundation of Angle Christianity in Northumberland. To this relic principally

[Scrimshaw.

OLD HOUSE, OSMONDTHORPE.

we owe the legend (doubtless only a legend) connecting Osmondthorpe into a royal residence of the Saxon Kings, Edwin and Oswy.*

Neither the Ossetorp of the Domesday, nor the Osmund of the later Norman period lend freely to Thoresby's conjecture that the place received its name from its connection with King Oswy. In addition to the suffix thorp,' which establishes its Danish foundation, the two names attached to

IVY HOUSE, YORK ROAD.

this place are supposed to denote a certain regal dignity, namely, the prefix in Coneyshaw and Coneygarth—'shaw' from the Norse, 'skogr' means a shady place; 'coney,' rabbit—and the position of the land here, shelving gently towards the Wyke beck (wandering through rich alluvial soil to the main valley), fully bears out this suggestion. The terminal, garth, purely Norse, means an inclosure, the 'garth' and 'shaw' establishing beyond a doubt its Scandinavian foundation. In 'shrog,' a bush or thicket, we have the Norse word almost unaltered.

* NOTE.—Singularly enough, Dr. Lees, our living authority on Leeds botany, informs me that the *Osmunda Regalis*, whose English name is Royal Fern or King Fern, grew in the low-lying land towards Killingbeck, as late as the Georgian thirties: this is upon faith of a dried specimen of the late Dr. Heaton's, which came into his possession. The name is, of course, a coincidence only: the fern grew in boggy thickets on Adel Moor as well.

After the Norman conquest a family named Osmunds settled here. "By deed, dated 1376, Thomas of Osmundthorpe gave to the chaplains of St. Mary's, an acre and a half of land in Osmundthorpe." From the Osmunds it passed by purchase into the hands of Sir James Ibbetson, Bart.

The old Norman hall of the Osmunds is said to have been pulled down in the early years of Charles I., and the second one partly demolished in the year 1814; and a large mansion erected near its site about the same date, now often tenantless, wears a rather melancholy and neglected appearance.

The situation of Osmondthorpe in the past would be charming indeed, standing on a commanding brow, a magnificent landscape all round.

There still remains a late Tudor house of great interest, probably part of the old hall—now used as cottages, mullioned windows, stone courses, and door lintel being of artistic and unusual character, the finish of the mouldings rendered effective by a choice, but simple ornament. In connection with this place is a very extensive barn, in appearance much like a tithe barn, in length thirty-one yards.

OLD HALL, KNOWESTHORP.

Knowesthorp, locally known as Knostrop, a mile and a half west from the latter place—in olden times a more pleasant hamlet, luxuriant in trees

* To our query one of the residents replied:—"All at ah can tell ya that's t'owd hall."

and flowers, was not to be found by the limpid Aire. Its place-name Thorp tells also of a Danish founding. The decorations at Knostrop Old Hall, early Jacobean, are considered unique. Whitaker says: "The great hall contains perhaps the latest specimen of a dais or raised step, for the high table, which is to be found in England." On either side of the gateway entrance, with its massive 'piers' finely decorated, are two quaint arm-chairs wrought in stone. There is a raised garden on the south side of the house and a pleasance adorned with stone figures. The house has undergone several alterations, the lower portion of the great hall has been converted into an entrance hall, and during the tenancy of the late Atkinson Grimshaw, this fine hall was in its pristine condition, and the decaying hand of time had dealt leniently, and in keeping with its age was decorated with antique furniture, old armour, and bric-a-brac of olden time. One panelled oak room, beautifully carved and decorated, and the old oak staircase, still remain to prove the artistic quality of old-time craftsmen.

THE PLEASANCE.

In the days of Stuart kings, this was the hall of the Baynes family, of ancient lineage, an ancestor of whom was standard-bearer to the king, at the taking of Boulogne, in the early years of the fourteenth century. One Captain Adam Baynes represented Leeds in parliament, during the Commonwealth period—"He purchased the royal manor of Holdenby in Nottinghamshire from the parliament for £29,000, but was obliged to refund the same at the restoration." He afterwards returned to Knostrop, where he died in 1670. A family named Stables seem to have lived at the Hall some time during the sixteenth century. Thoresby says they became tainted with

Quakerism, and turned part of the orchard into a burying ground, a proceeding common enough with the Quakers, in the seventeenth and eighteenth centuries. At no time during its long career did the old Hall witness such an array of talented men, in art, letters, and music, as were from time to time seen here during the tenancy of the late Atkinson Grimshaw, and they always found a cordial welcome in this kindred spirit. Its unique decorated gateway, and old-time gables and mullions, inspired him with many a theme, and laid the foundation of that dreamy representation of the shadowy realm of the past which lives in his work, of which he was famed as a master of unquestionable ability.

A mile and a half down the river, and adjoining Templenewsam Park, are the ruins of a mediæval house (Thorp Stapleton). Thorpe again denotes Danish origin ; Stapleton, the name of an ancient family who resided here during the Norman and Plantagenet era : a name which still survives. Whether this family gave or took their name from this place we cannot determine.

Here, and at Killingbeck, Osmondthorpe, Knostrop, Skelton, and Thwaite (over the river Aire), we have names unquestionably of Norse or Danish origin—places not in evidence until the latter part of the eighth or early years of the ninth century.

At different periods during these centuries, the sea kings entered the Humber, and, following the course of the riverway in their war keels, found here a congenial site for a series of settlements.

In a place-name the word " staple," of common Teutonic usage, means a barter place or market—to put into a heap for exchange of product—a custom which still prevails in the semi-civilized parts of the world, remote from large centres, the Far West, and interior parts of Africa, etc. " The word 'staple,'" says Isaac Taylor, " denotes a place where merchants were wont to stow their goods." At this day the word is chiefly used to denote the leading trade of a town : for instance, steel is the staple trade of Sheffield, woolcombing the staple of Bradford, and lace of Nottingham. In Staple towns, courts were held for determining all mercantile disputes, and punishing offenders.

It was a fair region which the Stapletons, and, in later centuries, the Scargills owned. On one hand, a beautiful stream—the Wyke beck, came wildering in many a turn from the moors beyond Roundhay, passing, in its course, through rich alluvial soil (in pre-historic times the bed of a lake), and entered the Aire near to the Hall. Hereabouts, in its sylvan reaches and varied windings, the river passed through a delightful vale of undulating forest and fair meadow land. To-day, the hand of blight and death is only too apparent on the trees, caused by the poisonous fumes belched forth into the atmosphere from chemical works and factories.

Thorpe Hall—a semi-castellated structure of the early fourteenth century—is now in a ruinous condition. It stands on the north-east bank of the Aire, about four miles below Leeds. By a deed, witnessed near the end of the twelfth century, Sir Robert de Stapleton had license from the Templars, at their chapter in London, to build a chapel in Thorp Stapleton and to establish a chantry there, swearing fealty to the Templars and reserving all offerings to the mother church at Whitechurche (Whitkirk). From the Stapletons Thorpe passed to the family of Scargill, of Scargill Castle, a border peel, which stood by the bank of the beautiful Greta, about two miles above Mortham

THORP STAPLETON. [A. Bottomley.]

* Arnold Lees says:—Beyond Hunslet and Knostrop, on the way to Woodlesford, was (half a century ago) a nearly level, low-lying tract of marshland and pasture turf; a pleasant Oval was there, and races were annually held. Hereaway, in the boundary dikes, grew the water violet, the serried ranks of its lovely blossoming stems piercing the clear dike water's emerald and bronze counterpane of two sorts of duckweed; and by the river (still batheable in then) grew the orris-scented sweet flag with flower-de-luce, and the handsome great water dock. All these have vanished, but the doubtfully odoriferous flats of a sewage farm, gay with yellow rocket in late spring, and later with the unfamiliar faces of alien weeds, brought in sewage, and the scourings of foreign wool, are poor compensations. Still, as a whole, this tract is only a little drier and more treeless than it was in 1835. Even yet a little of the spindle tree, "that in our winter woodland looks a flower," as said Tennyson, referring to its pink-winged fruit with scarlet seeds showing as they open when ripe, drags on a miserable begrimed existence in the stubbed hedge by the river road.

To the north and east of the tract already described, off the York Road, beyond the old and uncomely Dog and Gun public house, branched a charming and truly rural lane, named from its ancient foundry, where, from late in the fifteenth century to nearly within living memories, swords and ploughshares and coarser castings were manufactured. This lane, with its foundry pools and its "honey well" in a field, nurtured several rare and

Tower (the latter structure still remains near the junction of the Greta and Tees). The Scargills were a notable family in North Yorkshire (which the chapel on the south side of the altar in Whitkirk Church plainly demonstrates), founded by William Scargill, of Thorpe Hall, 1488. Within this chapel is an alabaster altar tomb bearing two effigies to the memory of Sir Robert Scargill, son of the founder, and Lady Scargill, his wife.

Standing away from the main road the castellated ruin of Thorp Stapleton (the only remnant of the Edwardian period remaining in the vicinity of Leeds) appears to be comparatively unknown, even people dwelling in the immediate vicinity have no idea of its former significance, and in some instances do not even know the place by its old name.

TEMPLENEWSAM AND WHITKIRK.

Less than half a mile to the south we enter the magnificent domain of Templenewsam, with its beautiful avenues of venerable and majestic trees and long sweeping vistas, here and there obtaining glimpses of fallow deer browsing on the undulating green sward, glade, lawn, valley,

---

striking flowers, the stately yellow loosestrife amongst them. This plant grins through the iron railings of Mount Preston gardens still, just possibly brought in, years and years ago, from this very foundry pool, as being plot-worthy. Wild plants were very largely so imported a generation or two ago. By the pool it can no more be admired for its fearless wild beauty. Long ago must it have been crowded out by an assertive plant, a very Titan, yclept the reed mace, more commonly called the bulrush, that in early autumn is sold in Briggate— a penny a stick—for the admirable use to which its massive brown clubs and swordy leaves can be put in chamber decoration. Fifty years ago this club-reed did not grow there, nor at Adel Dam, where now its thickset canes turn pond mud into dry land in the course of a few years; then themselves, in their turn, passing to that bourne whence no individual thing returns. A parallel between animal and vegetable holds, and in many a way runs unseen through all life.

To continue: From Seacroft, in a circling belt, two or three miles broad, across Whinmoor (then, as not now, a furze and ling clad waste), and round by Shadwell to Adel and Cookridge, all was moor or "moss," heathery for the most parts, fleece-white in acres with the waving plumes of hare's tail cotton grass, and with much wet, sandy peat about Moortown and Alwoodley "black moor." The place-names describe it in brief. The scant remains of these "haggs" at far Adel to-day convey no idea of what lovely and uncommon wild flowers flourished thereabout then. There was waxen-fringed bog-bean for one, the unique grass of Parnassus for another, and where they grew red-copper butterflies and azure gauze-winged demoiselles (dragon flies) hovered above, amid "a world of heather," though not "an empty sky" by any means. All these treasures, and fifty more, were to be had as rewards for the long tramp from Queen Anne, in her niche at the top of Briggate to the Four Lane Ends at Alwoodley "gates." A long mile further, to the first plantation marking the commencement of the Harewood demesne, both Jacob's ladder and the flaunting sunflower-like Leopard's bane, with blue geranium and spot-leaved lungwort, could be had for a stoop to gather. The Leopard's bane onlingers still; the others "are not," through transplantation into gardens, I believe.

upland, and sequestered pool—a situation teeming with objects of natural beauty. Here, with the seclusion and the classic sanctity of quiet rural groves, the contemplative mind can revel in story and on the magic of romance which lingers here, and feast on the loveliness around; peradventure in imagination hear the jingle of armour and obtain a glimpse of a goodly company of soldier priests, the Templars or Knights of St. John, sweeping down the distant forest glade. Here of old the tired wayfarer was never turned hungry from the Hall. 'Hospitallers' they were, not only in name, but by nature.

[W. G. Foster.

TEMPLENEWSAM.

At Templenewsam, we cannot omit mention of the Templars and Knights of St. John, but our citation must be brief. In Yorkshire the most potent benefactors to the two orders of Christian warriors were Robert de Brus, Roger de Mowbray, Robert de Stutville, Ilbert de Laci, the De Roos, and to some extent William de Viliers; from the latter the Templars, either by gift or purchase, received the lands of Whitkirk, Skelton, and Newhusum or Nehus (Templenewsam). Viliers held the above of De Laci, Lord of Pontefract, a great benefactor, and a member of the order.*

* The Paynes family were ardent Templars, more than three hundred knights were in the train of Hugo de Paynes in the first Crusade. John de Lacy was the greatest of all Christian warriors, and his name was a terror to the pagan at the siege of Danietta, and he was there surrounded by a court of Pontefract grandees, amongst the rest Master Roger, the Physician, parson of Kippax, his neighbour and fellow-parson, Robert of Aberford, and a good many notables and others, whose descendants still remain on the land, followed their Lord John de Lacy into Palestine.

The rules for the guidance of the Templars were, at the formation, most exacting and rigid, and one cannot feel surprised they were not religiously observed. Only an ascetic could have contemplated a strong man, with all the fervour of life glowing in his veins to enable him to mingle in the conflict and clash of arms, preserving strictly such rigorous devotion and excessive self-denial. Probably St. Bernard's ideal of a Knight Templar never existed. The statutes and rules of the order are too long for insertion here. There is a curious incongruity in this attempt to combine the monastic and military life.*

In the wars of the Crusades the Templars were the chief strength of the Christian army. It was their privilege to carry the true Cross before the army when in battle, also the banner with the red cross inscribed upon it. On the march they formed the advance guard and the rear in retreat. The original banner was black and white and was called "Beauseant," which word became their war cry. The bones of thousands of these gallant knights were left to bleach on the plains of Palestine.

Apart from the immense estates bestowed upon the Templars, they njoyed great privileges and immunities, such as:

The right of holding markets, advowsons of churches, and medieties of rectories, multure from wind and water mills, tributes of poultry, eggs, and swine, services of so many days in the year for ploughing, harrowing, hay making, sheep washing and shearing, mending ditches, and leading stones, rights of free warren, fisheries, and turbaries, and the manorial or baronial prerogatives of sac and soc, and tol and thean, and infangethef and utfangethef. A charter of Henry III. grants them exemption from aids, danegeld, and horngeld, from stallage and pontage, from all forced labour on royal parks, castles, or palaces, and allows them to take timber freely from their woods, without impeachment of waste, and to essart (clear) those which they possessed within the limits of the royal forests, without leave of the royal bailiffs. The same charter gives them all waifs and strays on their lands, not followed and claimed, and the goods and chattels which any of their men might have forfeited by crime, and allows them, in case of any of their tenants forfeiting his fee, to take immediate seisin of it, although the King had a right to keep it in his hands for a year and a day.

Certainly, a strange array of rights and privileges! Who can feel surprised that such rapid rise to wealth and prosperity should in the end have caused their ruin?

A record still extant proves their aim at even higher ambition. It is a bond by which Peter Middleton, of Nesfield, near Ilkley, who had dispute

---

* St. Bernard says of these knights: "They detest cards and dice, and abominate all shows, songs, and discourse of a loose nature. When they enter into a battle, they arm themselves with faith within and steel without; having no ornament either upon themselves or their horses. Their arms are their only finery, and they make use of them with courage, not being daunted either at the number or force of the barbarians."

with the tenants of the Templars in Wharfedale, undertakes, under a penalty of twenty shillings, to be paid towards the fabric of St. Peter's at York, that neither he nor any of his tenants should take proceedings against the Templars in any court, canonical or civil, that he would not avail himself of any right of appeal that might be prejudicial to them, and that if he was injured by any of their tenants he would bring his cause before their court at Whitkirk. This was a usurpation which might well excite the jealousy of the courts of law, says Kenrick.

The dress of the Templars was a white robe with patriarchal cross, enamelled red and edged with gold, worn at the breast pendant. There was a slight distinction between the dress and cross of the Knights Hospitallers and that of the Templars, although the system of the two orders was nearly the same. The former, who were also known as the Knights of Malta* and later the Knights of Rhodes, wore a black robe with a cross of eight points in waxed cloth on the left side of their cloak. In battle with the Turks, they wore, over all, a red cassock, with a large white cross before and behind without points. On the suppression of the Templars much of

* About the time of the first crusade some Neapolitan merchants built a house on the island of Malta for the use of their countrymen who came hither on pilgrimage. Afterwards they built a church and dedicated it to St. John, and also a hospital for the sick, hence the name of Hospitallers. In 1104 when the order became military they adopted the title of Knight Hospitallers. In 1310, when they captured Rhodes, the name changed to the Knights of Rhodes, and two centuries later, when they were expelled from Rhodes and took up their abode on the island of Malta, became known as the Knights of Malta.

their property was transferred to the Hospitallers, who had upheld their martial fame in conflict with the Turks, in their gallant seizure and grip of the island of Rhodes, but the transference was, in many instances, only in name.

Templenewsam was granted by agreement with the Hospitallers to the Countess of Pembroke for life, from thence it passed into the hands of the D'Arcys, of Temple Hurst, for the share of this family in the Pilgrimage of Grace. The head of the house was executed on Tower Hill, 1537. Falling to the Crown it was granted to the Earl of Lennox, and here was born Lord Darnley, the ill-fated husband of Mary, Queen of Scots. Again reverting to the Crown it was granted by James I. to his cousin, Duke of Lennox. From the latter it passed by purchase to Sir Arthur Ingram, a farmer of customs in the city of London. He married the daughter of Lord Fairfax, of Gilling, and his son took to wife a daughter of Lord Fauconberg, and thus the family became allied with the aristocracy of the north.

The mansion, as it now stands, was built by Sir Arthur Ingram. It is a red brick structure composed of a centre and two wings, and forms a stately specimen of Jacobean work. One singular and effective feature of the house is the battlement composed of capital letters in stone work, forming the following inscription :—"All glory and praise be given to God the Father, the Son, and the Holy Ghost on High. Peace upon earth; goodwill towards men. Honour and true allegiance to our Gracious King. Loving affection among his subjects. Health and prosperity within this House." The interior contains a fine collection of rare pictures, besides many other interesting objects and works of art. The chapel attached to the house is a perfect study as a work of art.

The ancient mansion does not appear to have been completely demolished, for Thoresby mentions that the very room in which Lord Darnley was born remained intact in his day, and was known by the distinctive name of the "King's Chamber." During alterations made of late years positive proof of the existence of this ancient room has placed Thoresby's statement beyond doubt. There is no certain testimony where the preceptory of the Templars stood at Newsam, yet there is a tradition of a building known as the Old Temple having stood near to Wyke beck, north-east of the park.

COLTON.

A small hamlet resting on the fringe of the park has a foundation reaching far down the aisles of history. The place is mentioned in Domesday book in connection with Gipton (Cipetun and Coletun), and the record says there is a church there. The question here arises as to where this church stood, there being no evidence of such a church in after centuries. Morkhill, in his history of Whitkirk, supposes the edifice mentioned to have stood on the site of the present one at Whitkirk, and this conjecture we think is the correct one.

[*W. G. Foster.*]
A PEEP OF WHITKIRK CHURCH FROM COLTON.

Cipetun of the Saxon era stood more to the south than the Gipton of to-day and consequently nearer to the White-kirk, a name received, we should imagine, on its conversion from a dark wooden to a white stone structure; its conspicuousness on the ridge of hill being as great as it is to-day, hence the White-kirk, Whitkirk.*

From Colton fine views of Templenewsam and Whitkirk can be obtained. Less than a mile we reach the latter place, whose situation and surroundings are most charming. The present church, built about 1450, is perpendicular, the interior containing tombs and effigies to the memory of

* Whitkirk.—The Kirk of the White-robed Templars, or else one dedicated at Pentecost, Whitsuntide.

the Scargills,* mural tablets and memorial monuments to the memory of the Irwin family, and on the north wall, a memorial of John Smeaton, the celebrated architect of Eddystone. The stained glass windows are only poor examples of art.

The history of Whitkirk is largely mixed up with Templenewsam, its old manorial rights and customs, and the prerogatives still exercised are very interesting. The Templars' crosses affixed to the buildings, both here and in Leeds, telling of former privileges and immunities, afford ample scope for the imagination.† The court for the two manors was formerly held at the old Manor House at Whitkirk (a late Tudor structure still existing). Both courts are now held at the Brown Cow Inn in the village. A modest gift of a penny apiece to thirteen 'pure folk' of Whitkirk parish is contained in a codicil to the will of Robert Colyson, of York, mercer. The quaint and somewhat touching bequest runs as follows:—" That thare be deltt and geven to xiij pure folke in ilke parisshyn underwretyn xiijd; praying thame hertly the hole parishyns to for gefe hym if he hadde ever any gude of thayres be bying or selling or any other wyse, and if any of thame hade evir any grete losse by him thay sall have amendis and asseth for thare losse and thaie will aske it, and if noon aske it, he prayes thame for Goddis lufe hertly to forgefe hym and pray for hym at the reverance of Gode. The whilke parisshins are thes [there follow the names of twenty-two parishes]." Printed in " Test. Ebor," p. 217. This document is dated 9th April, 1436, and was proved as a codicil to a Will of later date, 3rd October, 1458.

Fine views eastwards can be obtained from the immediate vicinity of Whitkirk. In the distance the plain of Whinmoor, where the great battle, celebrated in early Saxon history, took place. A short distance from hence is Austhorpe Lodge, a red brick structure built in 1698 by John Smeaton, of Leeds, whose grandson and namesake, the celebrated engineer, was also

---

* The tomb was erected in accordance to the wishes of Jane Ladie Scargill, of Leade Hall. "That is to saie, firste and principallie, I yelde and bequeathe my soul to Almyghte God, my Creator and Redeener, to that most glorious immaculate virgine, our ladie Sainte Marie and to all the Copanyne in heven, and my bodie to bee buried in the psh church of Whitkirke, within the chauntrie quere there besides my saide late husbande, where I will that myne executores within three years nexte and immediately ensuenge my decease shall cause a tomb of albaster to be maide and sette over the boannes of my saide laite husbande, and me withe such arms and scuptures as to my saide executors shall seme moste convenient, the same to be in facion like to one erected within the Colledge at Macclesfield." Will proved at York, 24th Jan., 1546.

† See sketch of crosses (page 78).

born here in 1724. Near to the latter place is Austhorpe Hall, erected in 1694 by John More. It is a good specimen of a Jacobean mansion; over the front door a plate bears the date 1694 and the initial letters of the builder so arranged, forming the name John More in full. Wilson's MS. says that the last of the Mores of Austhorpe was murdered in London in 1720.

WHITKIRK CHURCH.

A little to the south, in the parish of Austhorpe, stands Barrowby Hall, the site of an early Danish foundation, of which the terminal "by" is sufficient testimony. The word "barrow" seems to suggest a burial place. During the seventeenth and eighteenth centuries it was the residence of a younger branch of the Ingrams, who purchased it from the Laytons.

In our journey by way of Bullerthorpe Lane to Swillington church, we noticed the line of a Roman vicinal, which can be traced for some distance northward from Swillington, and pointing, when lost near Scholes, in the direction of Bramham Moor. Between Swillington and Bullerthorpe it is marked on the Ordnance map' as "Street Lane," thence it can be clearly marked running parallel with the road over the fields to the Selby road. At one place it is localised by the name of Roman-rig field. North of the Selby highway it is visible running down into the Cock valley. Near the beck, half a mile east of Stanks, it is very conspicuous; beyond the stream it is traceable over two fields, pointing in the direction of Scholes, Thorner, and Bramham Park. This road is supposed to have been traversed by Penda's army, composed of Angles and Celts, the former bent on crushing the growing power of the Angles dwelling in the North-Humberland, and utterly extirpating Christianity, which had already taken deep root among the members of his own family. We can easily understand the object of the Briton in joining Penda's army in this campaign. The greatest danger to Elmet had always come from the north-east, and already the nationality of the Celt in Elmet was nearly exhausted. The ford in the vicinity of Swillington Bridge is the place where this army of invaders crossed the Aire. The story of that great disaster which overtook Penda in his final fight will not be told here. Nearly all who escaped the sword on the field of battle met their death by drowning whilst attempting to cross the swollen waters of the Aire.

OLD BARROWBY. [*Jones.*]

Turning to the left out of the Bullerthorpe Lane, through field-path and wood-glade, notable for the old thorn and bullace trees, we reach Swillington church (early English); situated on a gentle eminence, with most beautiful surroundings. At the east end of either aisle is a private chapel; on the south the Lowther Chapel, in which are inscribed slabs and memorial tablets, also a canopied recess, containing a wooden effigy, probably to the memory of a Lowther. The burying vault of the

Lowthers was beneath this chapel, from which, at the last restoration, were taken the ashes of fifteen bodies, including those of Sir John Henry Lowther, and which were reburied at the east end of the churchyard. The chancel contains ancient piscina and sedilia. There is a quaint inscription on the wall of the north aisle. The north chapel formerly belonged to the Greens, of Leventhorpe, now to the Leathers. That grand mediæval display of heraldry formerly in the windows, which Dodsworth speaks of, has now disappeared.

[W. G. Foster.
SWILLINGTON.

In Swillington we find the first clan station planted by the Anglian in the seventh century north of the Aire. Leaving the park, beautifully tree-clad, and the hall with its associations of many centuries, we pass forward to Preston and Kippax.

In our tramp to Great Preston we obtain fine views of Oulton, Rothwell, and Woodlesford. Down in the valley to the east is Garforth Bridge. A certain dignity of old time exists in the farms and cottages around. On the crest of the hill beyond the cliff the spire of Garforth church forms an interesting landmark.

Great Preston, judging from the testimony around, is a place of considerable antiquity. The old hall has undergone varying fortune of late, having done duty as the poorhouse, and is now a farmhouse! It stands on sloping ground at the foot of a hill, which rises immediately behind to the height of its roof, so that one can step from the ground into its upper rooms easily. The precursor of this hall was more pretentious, and stood on the hill overlooking the Aire valley, the latter being the hall of the Prestons, a family of very ancient lineage, whose names are found thickly strewn in the records of Swillington.*

A most beautiful and artistic picture of Kippax town can be obtained from here. A deep valley runs between the two places, and on the hill side and crest of the ridge the town clusters finely, the church tower presiding, high above the roofs, the *tout ensemble* being most charming. From our commanding elevation we look over the broad Aire valley, and note, even at this day, how beautiful it is, though blurred and contaminated by the existence of many manufactories and coal mines. In the past, few fairer scenes of a lowland river and landscape existed in Yorkshire.

GARFORTH CLIFF. [*P. Teasdale.*

* Thoresby says:—"I rode by Halghton and Whitkirk to Preston-super-le-Hill, most courteously received by Sir William Lowther, whose house is pleasantly but very strangely situated. They go upstairs to the cellars and downstairs to the garrets."

The valley separating Kippax from Preston has undergone a certain transformation during the last half century. We note the impressure left in the earth denoting the former existence of a large pool of water and the long outline of a mill goit, suggestive of the old soke mill* of Kippax, which formerly stood hereabouts. These are the only evidences now remaining, yet there are aged people who remember corn being ground at the mill, and even the name of the miller (Robert Fowler).

The entrance to the town from the south, with the rich colour on the roofs of the cottages, and the trees overhanging throwing long shadows over the road, added to the general contour, forms a picture of more than ordinary merit.

Kippax is in the Skyrack Wapentake and situated in a district of great natural wealth, and stands on the summit of a limestone ridge, a fine elevation, overlooking a magnificent sweep of the lower Aire country, which, as we have already observed, is blurred to some extent by the many evidences of the industry of man. Still the beauty of the vale is apparent, and the wonderful panoramic vistas, reaching south to the Peak of Derbyshire, seen finely (when the atmosphere is clear) are simply charming. If we compare the Domesday 'Appraise' of Leeds with Kippax, we find the latter nearly three times the value of the former.†

There are various conjectures accounting for the orthography of the name Kippax. Dr. Whitaker and other writers suppose the word to be a mere corruption of the Keep-Esh, the first a large mound still existing near the church called a Kip, Keep, and the latter a huge memorial ash, which grew near, hence Keep-Ash (to protect or guard), Kipas or Kippas as it is still pronounced by the natives. Another authority says "Chipe" is

---

* SOC AND MULTURE. Soc.—The holding as tenant of real estate under certain considerations, condition, or service to his superior, which would be equivalent to rent. A soc mill claimed with it the privilege of grinding all the grain in the district. The miller's fee for grinding the corn was called multure (grinding). Some called it mouthing, taking his multure fee out of the mouth of the sack. They were suspected of taking more than was just. The people had a saying that honest millers had hairy palms. The old-time custom of tenure by soc lingers faintly at Harewood, where the farmers have to lead coal for Harewood house (one condition on taking a farm). We have observed them day by day for two or three weeks bringing coal from the other side of Leeds to Harewood.

† "In Chipesch (Kippax) and Ledestune (Ledstone), Earl Edwin had eighteen carucates to be taxed, and there may be ten ploughs there. Land properly called Berewit (Berwick) belongs to this manor, in which there are eight carucates to be taxed, and there may be four ploughs there. Ilbert de Laci has now this land where he has twelve ploughs in the demesne; and forty-eight villanes, and twelve bordars with sixteen ploughs, and three churches and three priests, and three mills of ten shillings. Wood pasture two miles long and one broad. The whole manor five miles long and two broad. Value in King Edward's time sixteen pounds, the same now."

from "cheap," meaning a market—held near a prominent ash tree selected for the purpose. Coupled with Ledstone it was the centre of a Power to which most of the surrounding places were subordinate. One feature of the old mercantile importance of Kypis remains in the fact that the Lacies never subinfeuded Kippax (as they did Leeds), but always held it in their own grip and so had the power of transferring any of its market rights to Pontefract as the latter place grew into greater prominence. The vestiges of the past existing at Kippax fully demonstrate its antiquity.

KIPPAX AS SEEN FROM GREAT PRESTON. [W. G. Foster.

To a student of architecture the church tells its story of Saxon origin, and in the immediate proximity stands the old keep, a circular hill of artificial construction; round its base are remaining portions of what has formerly been a trench. It is situated on the highest point of land in the parish As at Barwick, a deep valley intersects it on three sides. As a place of defence its value can be easily grasped. The centre of the mound is·

122   THE OLD KINGDOM OF ELMET.

hollow, the sides of which form an elevated rim, thus giving the appearance of a basin: hence the answer we received from a villager to our question anent its name—" Why, we allus call it 'cheeny basin'" (china basin). Nowhere, says Edwin Hick, is this local name mentioned in book or history, but is said to have been handed down traditionally by the people, for centuries. The keep is no doubt of British construction, and used by those people as a place of security and defence, being situated only a few hundred paces from the great north road of the Roman—the Ermine Street—and also near to where the road penetrated the western flank of Elmet. The keep has evidently been the site of a manor house, in the feudal era, as the place is still known as Manor Garth, although not a vestige of such a house remains.

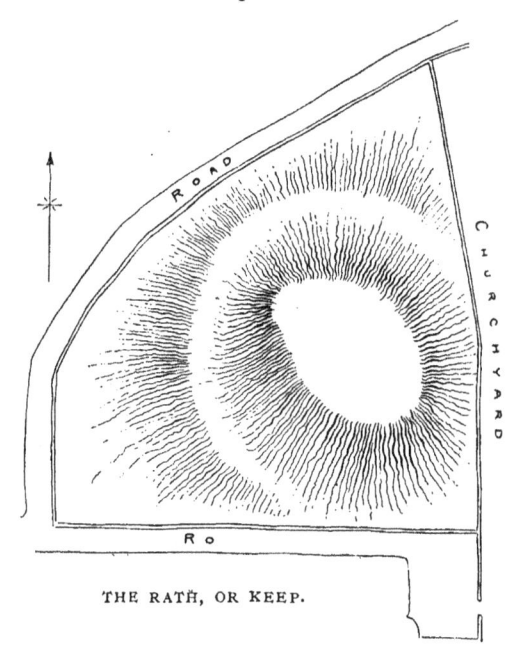

Down in the hollow, between Kippax and Garforth Cliff, is an old farm—Roach or Roche Grange—the impression around it clearly proves its antiquity; it has evidently been moated. Here is to be seen all that picturesqueness and flavour peculiar to old-time places. Hellas, a monk of Roche Abbey, was abbot of Kirkstall in 1209; probably he built the Grange, and named it after his former residence. Tab or T'abbey lands, here is said to be only a corruption of "the abbey lands." 'Roche' is Norman, meaning rock or stony cliff; a word commoner in place-names near Sheffield than hereabout.

Amongst others who paid the tax at Kippax, assessed in the reign of Edward III., are two names very significant of the above Grange, namely John of the Roche, who paid six shillings; and Roger of the Roche, who paid three shillings.

The approach to Kippax from the north, although distinct in character, is as full of charm as the one to the south.

The Parish Church of St. Mary is a most interesting structure, part of the tower showing the Saxon herringbone work, and the north wall with the deeply-splayed windows, are undoubtedly part of the original structure dating from Athelston's reign, if not earlier. It has been partly rebuilt in the twelfth, with alterations in later centuries, and was thoroughly restored in 1875-6. Some years ago, part of a Saxon cross was found built into the twelfth-century tower; it is now in the vestry. Carved on the stone is a rude representation of a human figure, beneath is a rough ornamentation of interlaced work which is surrounded by a cable border. This antiquated relic of art work in stone, symbolical of early Christianity, is very typical of stones lately found at Barwick, and probably dates from the eighth century, when the conflict of Angle and Briton had, to a certain extent, subsided in Elmet; when a season of peace spread over the land, and Christianity took deeper root in the soil. Part of a stone coffin, now in the vestry, was found underneath the floor of the church. From marks of fire apparent on many of the stones, the fabric is traditionally supposed to have been partly destroyed, by fire, at some early period. The few memorials in the church are chiefly to the Blands and Medhursts.

REMAINS OF CROSS, KIPPAX.

On the east windows, previous to the restoration, appeared the following inscription, now lost :—

"Guildford Slingsby, sonne of Francis Slingsby, Knight at the Coronation of King James, 1603. He was often Connander of His Majesty's shippes at sea, and is now controller of the navie, 1631."

The yellow-washed almshouses at the east end of the churchyard, with their quaint mullions, are characteristic of bygone days.

A new mansion now stands on the site of the old manorial hall of Kippax. The old house was pulled down in 1875; it was the home, in succession, of the Baildons,* Slingsbys, and Medhursts. This house is connected with the story of a sad domestic tragedy, committed by one William Wheler Medhurst about a century ago.

On either side of the market cross stand two very old inns, and hereabouts the buildings are cobwebbed and crumbling in decay, bearing on their face furrows of age. There are several quaint features and picturesque bits worthy of mention, which space forbids us to dilate upon.

Just on the outskirts of the village is Kippax Park, the residence of the Blands. The original mansion was erected by Sir Thomas Bland in the reign of Elizabeth. It has been considerably enlarged and altered, and only a part of the original structure remains. The mansion is nearly embowered in trees and stands on a slight ascent in a well-timbered and undulating park, with glimpses of browsing deer. It is still a most beautiful demesne, though not so delightful as of old, before the huge industries of the Aire valley were in such strong evidence. Midway between Kippax and Ledstone ran the great Roman military road known as the Ermine or Ermyn Street, described in our chapter on Roman roads.

[E. Bogg.
THE ALMSHOUSES.—"AN AFTERNOON CHAT."

This great 'street' came from the south by way of Lindum (Lincoln) to Danum (Doncaster) and so on to Lageolium or Lagecium (Castleford); from the latter it makes an angle and thence runs direct to Aberford. Near

A branch of the Bayldons, of Baildon.

Headley Bar a branch road bears away to the right, crosses the Wharfe at Calcaria (Tadcaster) and forward to York. The lapse of fifteen centuries and the cultivation of land has not yet removed the traces of this great military road. Between Doncaster and Castleford the ridge line is still traceable in many places, and if further proof is wanted it is to be found in the distinctive name of Roman Rigg given to certain lengths of it.

De Foe, in his journeyings North, says: "We turned aside out of our way in order to see the great Roman causeway which runs across the moor from Doncaster to Castleford. The causeway in many places is entirely perfect, and in other places, where it is broken up, the courses appear to be of different materials, that is clay or earth, upon that is chalk, then gravel, upon the gravel is stone, and then gravel upon that. It is very easy to trace its course over moors and open grounds which have not been cultivated." The district around Doncaster, the key and gateway to the north (lying between the wild peak and forest region on one hand and the inhospitable wastes of swamp and fen on the other), is a focus of vast antiquity. De Foe's account, too, is circumstantial evidence that the dry Permian limestone tract so definitely fixed was, in his day (about 1695), unenclosed common.

The ford over the river was defended by a strong castrum, the 'danum' of the Roman itinerary and the 'campo-donum' of Bede; and according to our theory the Don, in pre-Roman data, formed the southern border of the Brigantes. It was also the boundary of Elmet, on this side, until the latter kingdom was curtailed by the incoming wave of Teutonic invaders, ascending the Humber in their war keels, and from thence, using the principal waterways, the Trent, Don, and Aire, for highways into Yorkshire. Gradually by repeated invasions of fresh war bands, not by one great swoop, but slowly, year by year and mile after mile, did their keels and flat-bottomed boats glide upward into river and creek. All the while they were ousting the Briton and settling on the most favoured positions, until by the middle of the sixth century a great wedge of Engle colonisation had been thrust in between the valley of the Don and the Aire, and westward to the upper reaches of the Calder. Thus they separated the Britons of Elmet (who fell back to their inner line of defence) from their kinsfolk, the North Welsh.

This is no mere conjecture: the place-names, for those who care to examine, fully demonstrate this theory. Without placing too much reliance on the statements of Geoffry of Monmouth and several other ancient writers, who describe this region of the Don as a great theatre of war, the battling ground of rival races during the fifty years following the withdrawal of the Romans from Britain, the hapless struggle of the Celt to oust the Teutonic invaders, slowly but surely encircling them in a grip of iron, is evident until the kingdom of Elmet, which had risen out of the chaos and dismembered fragments of Roman power, became shorn and wedged into narrow compass.

On the south the Aire valley formed its boundary; on the east the broad Ouse river and, of old, that dismal wilderness, a vast extent of swamp, morass, and peaty fen land, where the mists hung low and the wild fowl piped and wailed in countless numbers. On the north, the boundary in all probability, according to the testimony of place-names, was the forest region and trackless moorland between the Wharfe and the Nidd. Westward the frontier stretched back to the great natural barrier, the wild, sterile hill land of Craven.

Here, and here only, had the Britons of Elmet, at the end of the sixth century, kept a connection with their brethren of Cumbria and Cambria, and this connection was sharply sundered early in the seventh century by that brilliant coup of Ethelfrith, the Engle king of Bernicia and Deira. Marching his army across the trackless moors of North Yorkshire, he swept resistlessly over the Pennines (the border line of three Celtic kingdoms), defeating the 'wild Welsh' and capturing Chester.

That this border line of Elmet was in many places almost naturally impregnable at that period, a glance at the map will show, and the Britons appear to have held to it in a strong grip, with almost the terror of despair. A thorough examination of the place-names on either side of the boundary indicated sufficiently proves this hypothesis.

The Parish Church of Castleford occupies the site of the Roman 'castrum,' and is located a few hundred yards below the confluence of the Aire and Calder. From all appearances it has been a Celtic fort, previous to its occupation by the Romans. It is on a fine elevation near to, and guarding the passage of the river.

The foundations of the ford were quite distinct half a century ago. Tesselated pavement, Altar querns, Roman lamps, and other relics have, from time to time, been discovered here. Inscribed on an altar, dredged up from the bed of the Aire, at Castleford (now in the Philosophical Hall, Leeds), appears the name "Brigant," in capitals. Perhaps there is nothing strange in this inscription, seeing that the stone has been planted by the

Roman in the land conquered of the ꞌBrigantes. Other altars found in Yorkshire have the word Brigant and Brigantia, in varied forms of spelling, inscribed thereon.*

The evidences of industry are so startling, and the hand of improvement so slow to beautify, that one need not be surprised that Castleford possesses little that can be called interesting or very picturesque. The church, built in form of a cross, is perhaps the most interesting feature. The adjacent collieries, glass bottle and earthenware manufactories, provide work for several thousand people. Thomas de Castleford, a Benedictine monk of the fourteenth century, author of a history of Pontefract, was a native of this place.

CASTLEFORD PARISH CHURCH, BEFORE LAST RESTORATION.

Anyone standing on the bold limestone elevation near Ledstone, looking south towards the Don country, and following mentally the course of the old road ascending from the Aire valley to the fringe of Elmet, will be forcibly impressed by the large number of Anglian place-names in the wide sweep of district before him, and will at once grasp the meaning of our last delimitation of the frontier of this British kingdom. The high ridge, rising boldly from what at that period would be marsh and fen by the low-lying land of the Aire (in itself a natural and outer rampart), runs like a frontier wall until it falls beyond Ferrybridge into the of-old impassable forest and waste of waters, stretching for miles around the banks of the lower Aire country.

It was here, in his furious work of retribution and revenge, that the indomitable will-power of the Norman conqueror was brought to bay. For weeks, his large army was imprisoned, as it were, on the south bank of the Aire, not so much because of the strength or boldness of the enemy, as of the impassable state of the river, then at flood. Here the Norman king fretted and

* See sketch of Roman altar and milestone, found in Castleford, in previous chapter on Roman roads.

128   THE OLD KINGDOM OF ELMET.

fumed, and swore by the splendour of God, for several weeks, ere he could find a passage for his army over the river. If the difficulties of crossing this line of frontier were of such magnitude as to curb his fiery spirit and hold in restraint the great army led by the Norman king, in the eleventh century, we surely can better understand the physical aspect of the district, and the difficulties which beset the army of invaders during the early centuries of Engle invasion. Here, in the tenth century, between Aberford and Castleford, a smart engagement was fought by Danes and Saxons, the former being defeated and chased back along the old highway to York, the capital at that date of the Danish kingdom, but which, from this time, was changed from a kingdom to an earldom.

Close by the road, in the Ledstone wood, is still to be seen the site of a dwelling adjoining the hill known as Mary Pannell hill. This woman was supposed by the people to be a witch. She was tried and convicted as such at York, for having be-

LEDSTONE HALL.

[E. Bogg.

witched to death one William Witham, of Ledstone Hall, who was buried on the eighth of May, 1593. Her place of execution was on the crest of the hill, near Ledstone, still bearing her name. There are old persons in Ledstone who claim that their great grandparents remembered this unfortunate woman, but how that can be is more than I can understand.

Ledstone and Ledsham still retain, in the prefix, 'Lede,' the memory of the original Celtic people, the Lloegyr Ligures, from southern Europe, variously spelt Ludees, Loides, Leedes; the 'ham' and 'ton' being grafted on in after centuries by Saxon settlers. The derivation assigned these places by Thoresby is rather curious, and, perhaps, in one sense, not so wide of the mark.

Ledstone and its surroundings are, indeed, most enchanting. The village has a picturesque and old-world look, peaceful and slumbering. Sheltered from the north winds by the lofty ridge of Peckfield, the red-tiled roofs, and white-walled cottages and farms are all suggestive of repose. Built in the walls of a farm, adjoining the street, is a fragment of what appears to have been a Saxon cross. The Domesday book records that there was, in the manor of Kippax and Ledstone, three churches and three priests. Two of the three churches mentioned have disappeared, thus it is quite possible one of the above may have stood at Ledstone, and, if so, may account for the interesting relic still preserved in the farm walls.

Ledstone Hall, the residence of the Whelers, stands in a most romantic situation on the edge of a grand elevation. It is a large Elizabethan mansion with picturesque gables, surrounded by magnificent trees, where the rooks nest, and in spring-time add a pleasing feature of interest to the house. Rather more than a mile, by a most pleasant footpath, over fields and through intervening woodland, we suddenly descend into a most rural and delightful little village (Ledsham). As we have already observed, the name speaks of a people, the Ledes, a tribe of Celts, who in after centuries accepted the suzerainty of the Angles.

This is indeed a charming village, nestling in a secluded dell. Here no sound of manufacture or rough traffic disturbs the pastoral sweetness. Undulating slopes rise about it, pretty nooks of wood fringe its borders. Here the birds seem to pour out a richer volume of song. The lowing of cattle wandering from pasture at milking time, the bleating of ewes and lambs in the meadows, mingled with the merry prattle of children at play, add pleasure and charm to this Arcadian spot. Down the village street a little wimpling stream wanders and empties into a small pond, where the ducks and geese disport, and where the lanes converge at the village is a tiny green. Near to is the ancient inn, "The Chequers," where the political and social life of the village is keenly discussed, and here the tired wayfarer can obtain suitable refreshment and a smile of welcome from the genial hostess. All around are quaint and picturesque lichened walls always proof of a pure atmosphere—and old trees, a medley of antique cottage, orchard, garden, and meadow croft, with their varied profusion of colour and bloom; and the scent of old garden flowers is wafted on the breeze through the half-open casement, on which the sunshine so delightfully lingers. Hard by at the east end of the street, on a beautiful woodland slope, almost hidden in frondage, stands the church of Ledsham. Its spire springing from a Norman tower, artistically rising above the intervening branches, and adding a finish to a delightful village picture.

NORMAN DOORWAY AND FONT, LEDSHAM. [*E. Bogg.*

The charities of Lady Betty Hastings and Sir John Lewis are very prominent in the vicinity of the church, and the kindly deeds performed generations ago still bear good fruit, and form a far nobler monument than marble to their name, and peradventure one that will live longer.

The interior of the church contains a Norman nave and tower; north aisle and chancel are transitional. The Lady Chapel is specially interesting, from the tomb and monument it holds to the memory of Lady Betty Hastings. The south side of the tower contains a low quaint doorway, typical of Saxon work and often erroneously described as such; doubtless it is only a part of the twelfth century Norman structure; here also is to be seen the original Norman font.

The vicinity of the churchyard is replete with interesting pictures, one of which is to watch the orphan girls, picturesquely dressed in old English costume, pass under the trees to and from service. Or, anon, to listen to the soft tones of the ring-dove, and the inspired harmony of the thrush and blackbird, or observe the halo of light flicker and fade away at sunset through intervening trees, transforming all commonplace objects into ethereal loveliness. At this hour Nature is so restful one hears the buzz of a belated bee, and sees the whirl of bats on the wing. The golden light has gradually changed to a silver hue, the church spire stands finely silhouetted against the light dying down in the west; as we turn away, the lines of Bryant appeal to the memory :—

"My heart is awed within me, when I think
Of Thy creation, finished, yet renewed for ever."

Ledsham includes in its parish the hamlet of Newton and township of Fairburn. A little to the east of the latter and about a mile from Ferrybridge is Brotherton, a straggling place standing on the frontier of our delimitation of Elmet and overlooking a fine sweep of the lower Aire country. The church, inns, and a few quaint houses are very interesting. Here the slain from the Ferrybridge fight* in 1461 (the prelude to the carnage on Towton Field) were interred. Here also, in a house adjoining the church, Margaret of France, second wife of Edward I.—(during a royal hunting tour in this vicinity, and when journeying to the Archbishop's castle at Cawood) — was delivered of a son,

SPRING-TIME, LEDSHAM.

* In coaching days the Old House at Ferrybridge was considered the largest and most luxurious posting-house on the great North Road.

afterwards known in history as Thomas-de-Brotherton. The king was at Selby and the news of the event so delighted him that he made large benefactions to the various religious Brotherhoods in the vicinity. The Archbishop of York had an ancient manor house here.

At Brotherton, on two occasions, the infamous Isabella, Queen of Edward II., took refuge during the unfortunate campaign of her Consort against the Scots. In the great foray of Randolph and Douglas through Yorkshire, she fled to the city of York to escape being captured by the raiders.

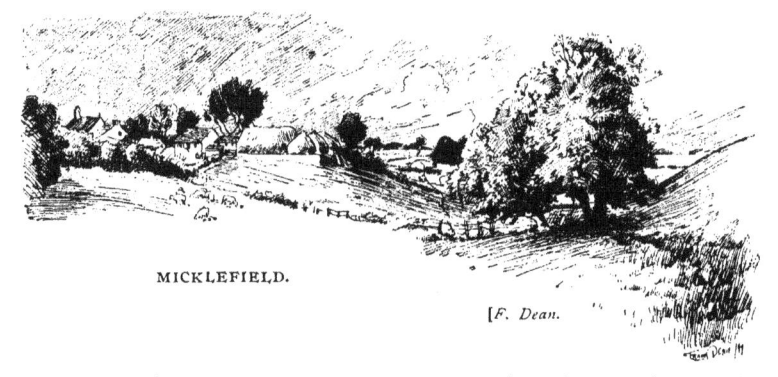

MICKLEFIELD.

[F. Dean.

Byram Hall is a most pleasant county mansion situated in a delightful and spacious park, long the seat of Lord Houghton (Monckton Milnes), the poet and biographer of Keats, who is said to have written his famous and best-known song—' I wandered by the brookside, I wandered by the mill"—by the very stream running under Ledstone from Kippax, which empties itself into the Aire at Bull Holme Clough.

Returning from Ledsham by way of Peckfield ridge (a bold elevation of woodland stretching from Kippax to Micklefield, a remnant of the older forest of Elmet), we descend by the Boot and Shoe Inn, standing at the fork of the Leeds and Selby road and formerly a resort of highwaymen, to Old Micklefield, situated on the fringe of the great coal beds. It still possesses, in its old cottages, farmstead and garth, etc., much to charm the antiquary.*
On the great Roman road between Micklefield and Stourton Grange is a spot known as Soldiers' Hill, but from what circumstance it received this name we cannot say.

* Micklefield was the home of Samuel Hick, the blacksmith preacher. It appears to have been the seat of a notable family. Hall garth and Castle hills are nomenal proof of past greatness.

Stourton Grange, a moated site to the west of the North Road, is of Anglian origin, and has been a goodly residence in Norman times, as the evidences around it fully testify.

Garforth stands on the high ridge of land dividing the watershed of the Aire and Wharfe. Of late years the place has grown considerably. The precincts of the church are most pleasant and picturesque. The old church, demolished in 1845, was an interesting fabric dedicated to St. Mary and given by Ilbert-de-Lacy to the Abbey of St. Marv. At the compiling of the Domesday book, a church existed here, thus proving the antiquity of Garforth. The new church is a beautiful building, and its spire a commanding landmark.

From Garforth cliff, a bold eminence, splendid views of Airedale and the valley of the Cock can be obtained. Round about the Old George at Garforth Bridge on the Selby road are to be found many charming bits of landscape and antique features of bygone days.

GARFORTH.

CHAPTER VI.

The Valley of the Cock.

IN the renewal of our journey, we follow the course of the above diminutive river, describing its features, historical reminiscences, ancient houses, notable battles, and incidents which have happened in this watershed.

The Cock rivulet rises in the vicinity of Red Hall, the residence of Sagar Musgrave, on high table-land between Shadwell and Seacroft. After passing underneath the Wetherby road, its bed gradually assumes the appearance of a well-defined valley, curving in the form of a full-strung bow, whose extremities are not more than seven miles across, whilst the curve of the stream is at least fourteen miles. Grimes Dyke and the battlefield of Whinmoor lie on its upper reaches. From thence it flows between the villages of Scholes and Seacroft, leaving Old Stanks and Manston Hall to the right.

Crossing the Roman vicinal, the stream bends in its course opposite Garforth, flows between the site of old Barnbow and Parlington Park, passes under the Barwick and Aberford highway at Ass Bridge, and just below is joined by its main tributaries, Eastdale and Guy-syke Becks, now forming a broad and deep valley, with the long series of earthworks in the woods of Becca Grange fringing the north bank. At Aberford, the river crosses the great 'Ermine Street,' and, immediately below, the earthworks line both sides of the stream. Further on is the old chapel of Lede or Lead, and beyond on the south bank are the villages of Saxton and Towton, also the site of the famous battlefield.

High up on the left bank, in a most commanding and picturesque position, its grey walls showing out finely from surrounding woods, is Hazelwood, the feudal home of the Vavasours. Now in sinuous windings, the river, under the shadow of dense woods, sombre and melancholy as if reflecting the sad story and carnage of Towton, winds through willow-garth, and osier-holt, and finally enters the Wharfe at Grimstone Grange, a mile below Tadcaster. Near its margin were fought, in the years 655 and 1461, two of the most fearful battles on record. The object of these battles was, however, widely different. The first was fought in defence of country and Christianity, and for the overthrowing of Penda, the champion of paganism. The last was the struggle of Princely ambition, and for the lust of power, pushed to an extremity that almost involved the ruin of the nation.

The first object of interest on Whinmoor is Grimes Dyke, a deep picturesque hollow in the bend of the beck, near to where it crosses the Leeds and York highroad. There are several dykes in Great Britain bearing the above name; for instance, Grimsditch to the south of Salisbury, the Grimesdyke, near Streatley. The wall of Antonius is still known as the grime or Graemesdyke, and there is a Grimsdale, near Netherby, from whence the great border family of Graemes possibly received their name. The Saxon 'dik' meant a deep ditch or boundary: 'dike'—grisly, horrid, is the same word; 'grime'—a witch, and 'grim'—fury or to rave.

Tradition assigns this portion of the valley to the battlefield of Whinmoor, and probably it is safest to follow the testimony of tradition in this instance. The most illiterate person will tell one of a great battle having been fought on the moor, near this spot, and the word 'grime'—to blacken or befoul—locally associates this stream with the bloody plain. The monks have not made the circumstance of the battle more clear by their testimony, perverting their knowledge in favour of the victors, of whom they were the chosen, thus adding a certain amount of exaggeration and confusion to the story.

That the action was fought in the kingdom of Elmet and near Barwick, the chief stronghold, there is no reason to doubt; and that Whinmoor was the actual field cannot, perhaps, be disputed. Yet, since the time of Camden down to the end of the nineteenth century, historians have floundered, vainly trying to fix the scene of action elsewhere. From the river Went, near Doncaster, to Barwick the ground has been searched without definite result. According to our knowledge there is no river known as Winwæd. The name is probably derived from Wien, a brook, and Wæd, a ford. Bede, the first historian of the battle, says that it was fought near the river Vinwæd, in the country of the Loides. There is every reason to suppose that the battle took place on Whinmoor, not far distant from the Roman road which crossed the Cock a little below Stanks. The thirty legions led by Penda in this campaign would require a good road for their progress north, and here they would find such a road leading straight on to the battlefield, the high moor in the district between Bramley Grange, Morwick Hall, and Potterton. The invaders had the River Cock in their rear, which heavy rains had greatly swollen. Oswald's army was greatly inferior in numbers to Penda's, but, putting trust in God, the battle ended in the rout and slaughter of the Mercians. Of the thirty Ealdormen who marched on to the scene of battle, commanding as many legions, few were left to tell the story of ruin and disaster. From the scene of fight, the victors chased the vanquished back over the road they had come, and Bede says:—"More of them were drowned, as they fled, in the River Winwæd, then overflowing its banks, than fell by the edge of the sword." Thus the River Cock formed a grave for the Mercian army as it did for the Lancastrians eight hundred years later. Those who escaped the first scene of disaster would probably find the same end in the swollen waters of the Aire at Woodlesford.

Supposing the Mercians fled by the Roman road, the scene of carnage and drowning in the Cock valley may have taken place between Scholes, Old Manston, and Stanks, the latter name signifying pools of stagnant water, and thirteen hundred years ago would be a dangerous morass for an army in confused flight to cross. In addition to our knowledge of the ground is the story told by Bede, who says:—"The river was in flood," surely sufficient testimony for us to understand that the Cock swallowed up the vanquished in this fight, as it did those on that wretched Palm Sunday in 1461. It must not be forgotten by those who incline to think Bede would not write of the Cock beck as a 'river,' that the volume of water was much greater then, than now, when there is much less wood and more tile drainage of the open fields, and less obstruction to the course of water. The Cock within its hollow channel, judging by the eroded banks, must at one time have run six or seven feet deep.

Morwick Hall, the residence of the Grays, situated on Whinmoor, half a mile east of the beck, is a plain-looking structure built towards the close of the last century. The late E. T. Gray was the last male representative of this family, connected with Scholes from the sixteenth century. The family trace their descent from the Barons Gray of Rotherfield, 'Scrutators' in the port of London during the reign of Elizabeth. The Grays were long resident at Kippax, and their coat-of-arms can be seen in the house now occupied by a Mr. Wilkinson. The name of Gray frequently appears in the parish register there between the sixteenth and eighteenth centuries. One

Edward Gray, of Kippax, was Mayor of Leeds in 1749 and again in 1768. He built Morwick Hall and was buried at Barwick.

In our journey down the valley, a little to the south of the York road is Penwell Farm and Pen or Penda's Well, which tradition avers is the spot where Penda and his army quenched their thirst previous to the fight. On the left bank lies the village of Scholes, of Norse origin (the Skali, a hut shelter). Scholes Hall, a seventeenth century structure, was long the residence of the Vevers. Potterton seems to have been the earlier home of this family. The will of Richard Vevers of the above place was proven at York in 1611, and one Richard Vevers, his nephew, settled down at Scholes Hall soon after this date. Traces of the gardens are to be found in the meadows, and a little to the east the Barwick road runs over the remains of a moated site, where an old feudal mansion (the predecessor of the present structure) formerly stood. Apart from the hall there is not much to interest one in Scholes. Old Stanks on the opposite bank of the Cock is quaint with antiquity and crumbling with age.

A mile down the valley on the south bank is Old Manston. Manston Hall, an antiquated brick structure, sixteenth century, is not the original one. The Manstons were a family of note in Elmet in the olden time; they intermarried with the Gascoignes and resided here from the thirteenth to the sixteenth century. The position, a fine plateau, commanding the valley of the Cock. To the south a small ravine separates this mansion from Lasincroft*; the prefix (Manu) is of Celtic coinage, Mani, Manston, the same in Mancunium (Manchester), Le-Mans on the Loire, Menaw—the Isle of Man.

MANSTON HALL.

* Lesincroft: Leys—meadows; ings—low fields; croft farn field, *i.e.*, the Croft house in the low meadows. A good instance of the duplication of equivalent terms, meaning the same thing, such as we have in any instances of all over the country, *i.e.*, Semerwater; Sea-mere-water; Seamer—Seamere, near Scarborough.

Lasincroft, a few hundred yards to the south, still retains in its farm buildings, garden, and also in the vestiges of a dried-up lake slight memorials of its former significance. Lasincroft and Shippen came into the possession of the Gascoignes by purchase from Geoffrey of Lasincroft, 1391, and their descendants eventually became established at Barnbow and Parlington.

As already observed, few vestiges remain. The house has been completely rebuilt, part of the ancient garden wall still stands, and a beautiful tree of immense growth and not a native to this soil flourishes—a silent witness of scenes long past. This many-armed tree is the *Quercus Ilex* of southern Europe, from Greece to Spain, and is known as the 'live oak,' because of its evergreen character and tenacity of life. From its great size, in spite of its continued vigour, this specimen must be nearly 400 years old, possibly dating from the later Tudor era, when foreign tree-planting came into vogue with continental fashions of garden-craft. An old stone paved footway leads from hence to Shippen (a farmhouse), its name indicative of Danish origin, and meaning a shelter for cattle, a very uncommon name in the district of the lower Wharfe; in the Craven country every cowshed is called a Shippon.

Barnbow, another old home of the Gascoignes, stood a little distance away on the opposite bank of the Cock to the north. Little of the hall remains except the mounds marking the site of the foundations. Within memory of man several cottages, occupied by the attendants, were standing here; now only one remains.

The site of Barnbow is a fine plateau, and commands the country for miles. The Cock rivulet winds round its base in half a circle. The deep woods of Parlington spread to the east, Barwick church to the north

---

* Rogerus de Quincy comes Winton Constabularius Scotiæ et jure uxoris suæ; did by his deed, under a great seal of his arms, give Lasingcroft and Schippen, in the reign of King H., 3., unto Robert Walcott, paying unto him and his heyres a pound of pepper, or xij^d. at Pentecost, which said Robert granted Lasingcroft and Schippen aforesaid, by severall deeds without date, unto Robert Walcott, his nephew, sonne of John Walcotte, his brother, which said Robert, the nephew, granted Lasingcroft and Schippen aforesaid, unto Geoffrey Walcott, his nephew, which Geoffrey, having no sons, but 3 daughters, one named Alice, married to Willian de Baroby, als Willian de Lasingcroft, another called Margaret, being single and unmarried; and the third married to the Lord of Parlington. The said Margaret dying without issue, gave her third part in Lasingcroft and Schippen, descended unto her from the said Geoffrey Walcott, her father, unto her sister Alice, of Baroby, als Lasingcrofte which said Willian of Lasingcrofte and Alice, his wife, had issue, John, of Lasingcroft; which said John had issue Geoffrey, of Lasingcroft, which said Geoffrey sould Lasingcroft, Schippen, and diverse other lands, in the 15th yeare of the reigne of King R., 2, A.D., 1391, unto Nicholas Gascoigne, second son of Willian Gascoigne, of Gawthorp.—Har. MSS.

peeps forth from the beautiful hill-and-dale landscape : further on are the woods of Potterton and Beckhey.* Bog Lane leads from Scholes hither, its name and position indicate the existence of a former swamp; of old this lane was a great resort of gypsies. The situation of Barnbow is well adapted for defence, probably it may only have been a domestic structure, but with very little strategy might easily have been made defensible. The becks on three sides of the house could soon have been rendered impassable. All is strangely changed at Barnbow; the old-time draw-well, with its hawthorn shade, still remains; and indications of former buildings everywhere present themselves. Terraced walks, gardens, and trench are still visible, and hid in nettles and undergrowth are the foundations of retainers' cottages; yet apart from these its past history is rather shadowy. The Gascoignes were evidently staunch Catholics of the old order, and did not fall in with the Articles of the Reformed church at the Reformation.

The following is a transcript from the original MS. in the Bodleian Library, by Edward Peacock, F.S.A., and will doubtless prove of interest, as it tells to some extent the story of Barnbow and the Gascoignes, and also the names of several old families once resident hereabouts :—

BARWICK PARISH.

"John Gascoigne, Esq., of Barnebow, Anne, his wief, Robert Lambert, his serving man. Laurence Wilson, master of his colemyns (coal mines), Edward Bennett, his milner at Hillome, Elizabeth Harrison, a servant, Ellene Ellys, a servant, Katheren . . . . . am a servant, Elizabeth Wortley. an antient servant there, she is thought to be a dangerous recusant in persuading; her surname is not certainly known: recusants reteynd, Mary Ellis, wief of John Ellys, Esq., a recusant.

Thomas Thompson, Mr. John Gascoigne, his shepparde, Joan, his wife, Mawd Feild, wife to Robert Feild, labourer, Barbury, wief of John Robinson, servant to Mr. Gascoigne, Nicholas Harrison, a young man, a weaver, Isabell Massie, an old woman, Margaret Massie wief of Cuthbert Massie, Ellyne Vevers, wief to Richard Vevers, Mr. Gascoyne, servant, John Slater, an old poore man, Elizabeth Gilson, a poor wedow, recusants for j yere, Mawde Gascoigne, mother to Jo. Gascoigne, Esq., a recusant, secret baptism, Mr. John Gascoigne, his children weare all secretlye baptised, and none of them came to ye church, nether is it knowne where they were baptised."

A mile to the east is the delightful domain of Parlington, ancestral and illustrious. It has been the home of Thane or Baron since the incoming of the Angle, and it is still the home of one of the best of county families, and

* In the old meadows, off the old hollow Car Lane, north of the site of Barnbow Old Hall, now marked only by uneven ground, and an old well shadowed by a gnarled thorn tree, great beds of pink-spiked bistort (formerly used as a pot-herb, and not a native plant) betoken with great certainty the existence of former settlements, such as accompanied the seat of the Gascoigne squires, in the days when the population of the Barwick region exceeded that of Leeds.

never in its long career of a thousand years has it been more worthily represented than at present. Parlington is the residence of Colonel Gascoigne, the soldier son of a soldier family, whose banner has waved in the earliest and best of the ranks of English chivalry.*

The men commanded by Major, now Colonel, Gascoigne of the Yeomanry, state how he upheld the honour and tradition of the old name in the last Boer war. Not only in feats of arms, but in the far greater chivalrous deeds—great qualities not over common in leaders of men—sharing in the privations, labour, fatigue, hunger, thirst, and watching with almost paternal care over the interests of those under his charge.

The Parlington Gascoignes are descended from Thomas, son of William Gascoigne, who in 1363 purchased land in Harewood of Robert de Insula, of Rougemont, and his wife Agnes or Anne, daughter and co-heiress of Nicholas Frank. This William was the grandson

STREET SCENE, BARWICK.

* Barnbow and Shippon was the scene of the supposed Popish plot, where Sir Thomas Gascoigne and others assembled to devise means to overthrow the Government and re-establish the Roman Catholic faith. Regarding this plot there is a printed pamphlet, now very scarce, entitled "The narrative of Robert Bolron, of Shippon Hall, Gent., concerning the late Popish plot and conspiracy for the destruction of His Majesty and the Protestant Religion." Bolron, the accuser, was steward at Sir Thomas Gascoigne's coal mines, and dwelt at Shippon Hall. He had been brought up in the reformed faith, but, on taking service under the squire of Barnbow, he became a Roman Catholic, and he seems to have changed his faith as easily as his coat.

of the William who married the daughter and heiress of John de Gawkethorpe, with whom he had the manor of Gawthorpe.

The first residents at Parlington with whom we are acquainted assumed the name of the place, and are known as De Parlyngton, occupying the mansion at the time Falkes de Brecante was at Harewood. They were succeeded by the Despensers.

In 1336 Philip, son of Philip, son of Hugh le Despenser, *le père*, shows that Hugh was in possession of Parlington. Philip, the son, married Margaret, daughter and heiress of Ralph de Gowshill; holding the manor of Parlington, of the King, as of the crown by the fourth part of a knight's fee—(a tenure of lands held by knights on condition of military service). In 1404 a Philip Despenser held the manor by the seizin of half a knight's fee. These Despensers are the men who brought such trouble upon England in the reign of Edward II. In 1424 Roger Wentworth, Esqr., and Margaret his wife, heiress of Sir Philip Despenser and Elizabeth his late wife, held the manor of Parlington.

Before the end of the century the Gascoignes were in possession and intermarried with the Vavasours, of Hazelwood. Dame Ivan Vavasour, widow of Sir Henry, died the 17th of September, 1462. The arms were Gascoigne, *or, in a pale sable, a demi-luce nest couped or.** In the chapel of Hazelwood "by the door lyes a blue marble, about two and half yards long, escutcheoned at corners," beneath which she and her husband are buried.

* *Or*, gold. *Sable*, black. *Demi-luce*, a pike's head. The fourth stage in the life of a pike fish, first a jack, second a pickerel, third a pike, and last a luce, hence the lucys or luces, pikeys. *Couped*, cut off smooth and even.

CHAPTER VII.

Barwick and Aberford Districts.

BY lane or field path, intersected with pleasant little vales falling sharply to the main stream, we reach Barwick, the ancient capital of Elmet.

The town stands in the angle—or, more properly speaking, tongue—of land formed by the meeting of Eastdale and the Cock beck. Its situation is naturally strong, being almost surrounded by water—forming a peninsula, the neck of which is only about half a mile across. Thus in the past it was practically encircled by a marsh-forest, which, even in dry seasons, could soon be flooded by damming back the flow of waters. Even at this day the valley on the north side is, in wet seasons, a dangerous morass to traverse, as the late rector, Canon Hope, demonstrated on one occasion in crossing; he floundered deeply and required assistance to be extricated.

High above and commanding the country around, is the 'Barrach' or 'Barugh' (bar and heugh, a prominence in modern north English and Scotch) see Great and Little Barugh near Malton—a high mound, the stronghold of the Celtic kings of Elmet.* Tradition asserts that this place was also a royal residence of Edwin, the first Anglian king to partly subdue the Britons inhabiting this district. That it is of great antiquity cannot for a moment be disputed. The inner or centre of the system of entrenchments was of old known as the 'Auld How,' now Hall Tower Hill, and is a conical mound enclosed by double trench and rampart. The inner trench closely encircles the base of the mound, which stands about seventy feet above the level; the outer edge of the ditch measures two hundred and seventy yards

---

* A British city or stronghold was not what is usually understood by that term. In the first instance, the spot chosen was one difficult of access by nature, river, forest, and swamp intervening, and the large space which took the name of city, surrounded by rampart and ditch, the edge of the latter, strengthened by pointed stakes and a wall timber paling surrounding it. Such was known as an oppidun,—the Latin name for a fortified wood enclosure of the Britons; the Saxon term being a wick, as in Berwick and Barwick—and formed the chief centre of a British tribe.

round; there is a flat three-sided space outside the inner trench, but the rim of the circle is broken on the south, where it comes abruptly in contact with the outer rampart. To the west and north the ground shelves sharply down to Eastdale Beck, or the 'Rakes.' The mound is supposed to have been enclosed by a wall. The outer rampart, when first raised, would be

HALL TOWER HILL AND WENDAL, FROM RAIKES BECK.

twice its present height, and to all intents would have the appearance of a high earthen wall, its exterior defended by a deep trench or hollow way, which encircled the outer edge of the fortifications, still to be distinctly traced. The primary object of this high mound is not fully evident. It has not the appearance of having at any time supported buildings. The space between the inner and outer rampart is ample for the accommodation of a large host. Thus, originally, the mound may have served as a gathering place for spectacular demonstration, either religious, civil, or military.

Professor Phillips supposes the name of the village is derived from the Gaelic word 'barrach'—a high mound, and the centre of an ancient population: thus we have 'bearruc' and the 'bearruc wudu'—a forest, from which name Berkshire has come, and 'bibroci'—a people, from either of which the word may be derived, or Irish and Celtic, 'barrackad'—hut or booth, in places a hut or house for soldiers. Again, Hall Tower or Castle Hill points to an ancient tradition, assigning the spot to a royal, or at least a chieftain's residence. And again, its ancient name, 'The Auld Howe,' seems to suggest a tumulus—the burying-place of an ancient race, 'the mighty chiefs of old.' Many similar mounds, though perhaps of less dimensions, have given up their dead, on being excavated.

There is a tradition in Barwick that the earth needed for the construction of Hall Tower Hill was carried hither in sacks, formed from skins of wild beasts.

THE OUTER TRENCH, SOUTH SIDE OF HALL TOWER HILL. [*E. Bogg.*]

Just to the north of the hill, and joining on to the same system of earthworks is Wendel Hill, quite as interesting, and of a much larger area, oval in shape. The trench, in many places, is still sixteen feet in depth, enclosing several acres. On the north it runs sheer along the high bank, and over two hundred feet below is a deep, marshy hollow—'The Rakes'—erosion by water on this side having formed an almost impassable barrier.

Thoresby quaintly observes, in his description of the place: "I came in quest of the Roman way from Bramham Moor to Barwick, where I found, on the north side of the town, a considerable agger, which is very high and steep on both sides. I traversed about three hundred paces upon the height of it, but there found obstructions that I could not easily surmount in my boots. The high bank, which is somewhat circular and winding, is called the Wendal Hill."*

Within and without the enclosure many relics of the far past have been found, and considerable quantities of human bones, from time to time, have been discovered. The plot of land recently added to the churchyard is thickly strewn with human bones—a funeral barrow of our departed ancestors. Altogether, the prehistoric fortifications existing at, and stretching eastward miles from Barwick, prove this ground to be one of the most remarkable places of antiquity to be found in England. There is a sanctity and veneration that still hovers around these prehistoric foundations stamped with the impress of long ages.

BARWICK, SHOWING REMAINS OF CROSS.

* Query: to what obstruction does the antiquary refer? Thoresby prejudges, and perhaps misleads, by using the Roman word 'agger' (an artificial heap) so frequent in Cæsar's Histories, whereas the original bank is one of natural formation, added and adapted to purposes of defence by the Brito-Celts.

Lingering here, one tries to pierce the shadows and mysteries of other times and learn something of that struggle which took place between rival races, the Briton and his Teutonic adversaries. From the landing of the latter and their settling along the Yorkshire coast, to the partial subjugation of Elmet, at least two hundred years elapsed, proving how long and bitterly the war was waged.

Barwick still retains its Maypole and customs associated therewith; it is renewed every third year. The rearing of the pole is made the scene of great rejoicing and festivity; from city, town, and village, crowds of people pour in and help to swell the tumult and babel. The echoes of the past are reawakened, and Barwick, as of old, is, on these occasions, truly the capital of Elmet. Midway between the high mound and the stately church, the Maypole is upreared; in close proximity stands the base and portion of shaft of the market cross.

A very suggestive superstition clings to this Maypole, though, perhaps, to those in other places as well; this is, during the uprearing, the timber mast (spirally striped in colours symbolic of red blood and white may—the renewal of life) has a baleful quality about it, as it were, the personified evil of a Pagan idol; and whoever is struck by it in the process (needing quite two hundred willing arms) is worse than lamed for life. As a Keswick rustic phrased it, to a friend of the writer, explanatory of an imbecile son, and gravely as of an indisputable truth, "He got knocked at Barwick" (*i.e.*, with the Maypole) "and was silly ever after." "Knocked at Barwick" is a saying for miles around when speaking of a person with weak intellect.

The village is remarkable for its character and charm, yet, strange to say, the writer has met with several intelligent persons who, although no strangers to Barwick, are altogether ignorant of its high mound entrenchments, and the great antiquity pervading it, and even the name of Elmet sounds as foreign and unmeaning to them as far-off Timbuctoo.

The two great churches of Elmet, Barwick and Sherburn, are alike dedicated to All Hallows, thus marking their Pagan source and also the Christianity the Angles received from the Celts upon their first becoming possessors of the old kingdom. Two other churches dedicated to All Hallows are those of Harewood and Otley, which to some extent goes to prove the communal boundaries of the little kingdom.

The church is a commanding perpendicular structure, with massive tower, dominating the village. It is built of two kinds of stone, limestone and sandstone; in the west face are two canopied niches, one containing the statue of a Vavasour, who gave the stone for building the tower. The inscription reads: "Orate pro Henrico Vavasour, Anno Domini, 1414." The other niche contained the statue of Richard Burnham, a former rector of Barwick, and benefactor, who besides contributing towards the tower also built the Tithe Barn. An inscription on a door lintel in the rectory grounds bears out this. The church underwent a complete renovation in 1856 under the supervision of Geo. Fowler Jones, of York, but in some previous restoration vandalism has evidently run riot, and many objects of archæological interest have been swept away. Only lately the writer, whilst inspecting a small private museum, was shown a "holy water basin" said to have been removed from Barwick Church at the last restoration, probably belonging to one of the side chapels

BARWICK-IN-ELMET CHURCH
(Taken before the last restoration—nearly fifty years ago).
The figures in the foreground are those of the late Rector (the Rev. Canon Hope) and his Curate.

there. The Gascoigne was on the north and the Ellis chapel on the south, the former contains an emblazoned window with the Gascoigne arms, also those of the Vavasours and Ellises.

The chancel is the most ancient part of the fabric, and doubtless contains Saxon masonry, bearing a close resemblance to the architecture of that period, particularly to the chancel of the church at Jarrow-on-Tyne. It certainly contains examples of the original pre-Norman church, but the objects which

148   THE OLD KINGDOM OF ELMET.

testify to the antiquity of the fabric are the Runic sculptured stones, which have been removed from the walls under the supervision of the present rector. Who shall say that these venerable relics are not a portion of Thridwulf's Monastery, formerly situated in the wood of Elmet? Two historians, Simeon of Durham, and Roger de Hovedon, state that Eanbald, Archbishop of York, died at this monastery in 796. Burton's Monasticon Eboracense relates that of ten monasteries founded by Scottish monks (of Iona or Culdee training) in Yorkshire, the last of them was founded at Barwick-in-Elmet in 730.

EARLY SCULPTURED STONES IN BARWICK CHURCH.

The carving of the figures on the stones is grotesque and rude, and not by any means the work of an artist who has been taught the ordinary rudiments of sculpture, or attained any knowledge in the Ligurian or continental schools, such knowledge as even the Italian artists of the seventh and eighth centuries possessed, for they were in direct touch with classic masterpieces—thus the carving on the stones is the work of a person who has received no art training, hence the uncouth modelling of the figures.

To definitely locate the site of 'the Monastery is beyond our power. The site probably rests between Barwick and Potterton. The former has the stronger claim. At the latter place, however, many vestiges found during the nineteenth century point strongly to a religious edifice having formerly existed there.*

The churchyard contains the body of Billy Dawson, the celebrated preacher and a native of Barnbow. Barwick teems with association to, and memories of this worthy, and the beautiful chapel lately erected there is to his memory.

About the middle of last century one Mary Morritt, a woman who it is said was gifted with double sight, used to watch the church at midnight of St. Mark's eve, and she professed to foretell the death of any person in the

---

* The temporal side of its ecclesiastical position has maintained itself with great constancy at Barwick. The financial worth of its rectory, reflecting all the wealth and benevolence that may have first created it, has kept it one of the prizes of the northern church. According to the returns of 1525 its position stood thus:

BARWYKE IN ELMETT RECTORY—THOMAS STANLEY, INCUMBENT.

	£	s.	d.
The Rectory, worth in together with the glebe, the tithes of garbs, oblations, and all other profits and emoluments belonging thereto, demised to farm for £30 yearly; the farmer to find a chaplain for the cure and pay him as salary 100s.; in all yearly ..	35	0	0

Reprises in—

Money paid yearly in pension ... to the prebendary in the chapel of the Castle of Pontefract, 25s.; and similarly to the Archbishop "singuli" (for himself individually), 2s. 6d. — .

	£	s.	d.
The clear yearly worth	33	12	6
The tenth part thereof	3	7	3

Like Bolton Percy, a fat rectory had an absentee rector. The bitter scorn with which Chaucer had assailed these absentee shepherds a century and a half before, was equally merited in the days when the nation was demanding drastic reform, and, moreover, in a temper to enforce it. It made a great effort, but do the annals of the New-Style Church say that it accomplished its aim?

There was also a well-endowed chantry in the church:

CHANTRY OF BARWICK IN ELMET—RICHARD ELYS, Incumbent.

	£	s.	d.
The chantry is worth, intents and forms of divers closes, viz. One close in the tenure of William Barden, 29s.; of one close called Brounclose, 40s.; of one close in the tenure of William Briggs, 20s.; one close in the tenure of John Jakson, 13s. 4d.; and one close in the tenure of William Diconson, 8s. yearly; in all ...	5	10	4
In old rent, repaid to our lord the king, issuing from the aforesaid	1	2	6
Clear yearly value	4	7	10
Tenth part thereof	0	8	9½

parish during the following year, by the flitting of their figures passing into the church during her annual midnight vigil. It is said that the death of her own husband was the last she foretold.

North-east of the church are the sites of former extensive lime quarries; Barwick lime being acknowledged of the best, and it was used by Smeaton in the construction of Eddystone lighthouse. Here the road winds down the steep bank to Potterton Bridge, and the trench connecting Barwick to the earthworks can be traced running along the face of the high bank from Wendel Hill to some hundred paces beyond the road, from hence it falls into the valley, climbs the opposite bank, and in its zigzag course runs along the edge of the hill known as Becca Banks to Aberford.

Here, where the road crosses the beck by bridge in the deep hollow to Potterton, was, in bygone times, the scene of many a flood and washing away of bridges. The present structure was erected about a century ago, and the workmen, in digging for the foundation, came upon another complete structure, probably buried with debris in some great spate, and which succeeding floods and their accumulation had completely hidden. From hence the road winds through a deep hollow to Potterton.

VIEW OF BARWICK FROM THE EAST.

The old way to Kiddle (or Kiddhall) Hall—another case of duplicated terms—from Barwick, the way by which the Ellises wended to and from church, is by the street called Bow Hill, running between the two entrenched positions over the Rakes, by a wooden bridge, thence into a lane locally known as Dark Lane, a deep old hollow road where the pack-horse route crossed before the present Leeds and York turnpike was made. Nowadays we only find vestiges of it here and there. Opposite Potterton it crosses Dark Lane at Copple Syke Spring. Half a century ago five skeletons were unearthed near this spring. As no information could be obtained respecting any burial here, it was supposed by the late Canon Hope that they were the bodies of those who had committed suicide, since such were formerly buried near to cross roads, and not in consecrated ground.

Beyond Potterton the old hollow road can be traced for some distance towards Tadcaster. A little distance beyond Potterton, on the open moor, stood the house of one Johnny Monks or Manks (his son and grandson were

KIDDALL HALL.

both called Johnny). It was here the pack-horses were changed and left in charge of Manks, while the relay went forward over the moor to the accompaniment of jingling bells fixed on the head of the leader. This 'belling' was a gay custom of old, and not without purport. Was it to warn of approach, or hearten the beasts to put 'best foot foremost'; or to keep the attendants' courage up after the fashion of the whistling schoolboy of the poet, by dark ways in dark times?

Kiddle Hall is situated by the side of the Leeds and York highway, a little over a mile from Barwick. It is a semi-domestic structure dating from the early fifteenth century, some portions belonging to even an earlier date. From the thirteenth to the eighteenth century the important family of the Ellises flourished here, the last member to reside at the hall being William Ellis, who died in 1725. Before the making of the high road, the house was surrounded by a beautiful park, and wild moor encircled it on three sides, conjoining with the 'white car'—white because of its sheets of silky cotton-grass—and the 'black fen' portions of the Bramham demesne. The map-names alone remain to tell us how the features of this district have unrecognisably changed in a hundred years!

During the Civil War a skirmish took place on Whinmoor between the Cavaliers and the Roundheads, which ended in the complete rout of the latter. Fairfax was gradually retreating across Bramham Moor, before a much superior force of Royalists. After crossing Potterton Beck and reaching the next high land, they were suddenly confronted by another body of Royalists who had reached the moor from the north side of Bramham. The enemy attacking both in front and rear, the soldiers of the Parliament fled; many were slain or taken prisoners, whilst Fairfax and the cavalry escaped with difficulty into Leeds.

During alterations at Kiddle a secret room was discovered, in which were found a coat-of-arms and other relics, supposed to have been hidden during the Civil War. Tradition says the place is haunted by one John Ellis, killed by the Parliamentarians previous to the skirmish on the moor, March, 1643; the Roundheads, ransacking all the houses in the vicinity for food and drink, possibly met with opposition from the Ellises, who were staunch Royalists. To this day people tell one the troubled spirit of the slain Ellis cannot rest, and still flits mysteriously around the precincts of its former home. The house, if not imposing, is very picturesque; the peculiarly shaped bay window, added in the first year of the fifteenth century is full of interest, and on it is the following inscription:

"Orate pro ai-bas Thom Elys et Anna uxoris sue qui istam fenestram fecerunt Anno Dni M.C.C.C.C.C."

Above is a battlemented parapet, with pinnacles adorned with a trailing pattern of vine leaves and grapes, under which are many symbolic ornaments and devices.*

Land between Kiddal and Hazelwood, seventy or eighty years ago, was unenclosed, and it is still known as Bramham Moor, although now enclosed and cultivated. It was formerly the scene of many highway robberies, and also the abode of numerous ghosts, warlocks, and barguests (or bar-ghaist, literally, bier ghost), who nightly peregrinated, to the terror of women and children. One strange, weird, wild, superstitious belief tells how, at death, the soul in a kind of probational journey must pass over the wild waste of "Whinney Moor." Over the dead body the death-song, a dirge-like lament, was sung. It told that if the person had bestowed alms, and performed other good works in his pilgrimage on earth, there need be no dread of crossing the wild waste of Whinney Moor, but, on the contrary—

> "If hosen or shoon thou never gave none,
> Every neght and awle,
> The whinns shall prick thee to the bare bone,
> And Christ receive thy sawle."

Then the soul passes over the "Brig o' Dread" to "Purgatory Fire," and here—

> "If ever thou gave either milk or drink,
> Every neght and awle,
> The fire shall never make thee shrink,
> And Christ receive thy sawle."

Around the district also linger many old-world legends and superstitious customs, such as putting the bees into mourning. On the death of a member of the household, the event is announced to the hive, which is draped with crape, and the bees served with biscuits soaked in wine; the ritual is known as 'telling the bees,' and should the practice be neglected, it is firmly believed the bees will die. Striking the door key on the fire shovel is a sure expedient to bring back to the hive a swarm of bees. Death warnings, mysterious signs and omens, etc. :—a swarm of bees alighting on a dead branch is an unlucky omen, and sure sign of death

* In Torre's *Testamentary Burials* several notices occur of this family.—"William Ellis, of Kiddal, Esq., made his Will, proved April, 1515, giving his soul to God Almighty, St. Mary, and All Saints, and his body to be buried within 'Our Lady's quire' of the Church of All Hallows', in Berwick. Wm. Ellis, of Kiddal, Esq., under his Will, proved November, 1573, giving his soul (as above), and his body to be buried on the south side of the chantry 'quire,' of the Parish Church of Berwick-in-Elmet. Mary Ellis, of Berwick-in-Elmet, gentlewoman, made her Will, proved February, 1630, giving her soul (as above), and her body to be buried in the Parish Church of Berwick-in-Elmet, near unto her late husband."

154   THE OLD KINGDOM OF ELMET.

in the family; children born at midnight are supposed to see 'doubly,' that is, have vision in darkness as well as in light, and are known as double or second sighted.*

We now return into the main valley by way of Potterton, the residence of the Wilkinsons. Here, where the three lanes meet, is locally known as Morgan's Cross, and the name of the adjoining croft is Manor Garth. In the hedgerow yew trees flourish, and formerly the valley sloping down towards Barwick had the appearance of a dark, solemn, and mysterious grove, so dense were the large spreading yews.† The yew-tree is a native of the magnesian limestone tract of Yorkshire, but the finest trees were sadly lopped in the days of archery; some large very old ones still exist, however, on the dry wold beyond Bramham, about Oglethorpe.

CUCKOO HATCHED IN TITLARK'S NEST, NEAR SCHOLES.

To the west of Manor Garth is a wood enclosing a double trench and rampart. This, oral tradition supposes to be the site of King Morgan's castle. Who this King Morgan was we cannot determine for certain, yet

* Connected with this district, by a happy chance I am able to give a unique photographic reproduction of a foster-mothered cuckoo, hatched in a titlark's nest (on the railway bank, near Scholes station), having shouldered out (as is the habit of this ungrateful chick) the last rightful nestling. This was in early July of 1901. The foster mother and father did their duty in feeding their wonderling, and, so far as local watchers could make sure, they successfully reared an alien to wing its maiden way over wide leagues of foam to its first spring or second summer in a far-away foreign land.

† A small field at this place is named, to this day, the King's Paddock.

the place is strangely significant of both a church and stronghold,* and here, says one, any native born can inform the stranger that on this site, in olden time, stood a church which was demolished and burnt by the Scots in one of their raids.

The supposed monastery of the most reverend abbot and priest, Thridwulf, Bede states, stood in the wood of Elmet. In support of this story, there were found in Manor Garth during alterations, about the middle of the last century, three stone coffins, one of which may still be seen in the dog kennels adjoining Potterton Hall; and in the gardens, etc., at the latter place, are various bits of church relics in stone, which tradition reports are from Manor Garth.†

Passing from the latter place we wander down the pleasant vale to where the becks meet. A little nearer Barwick the Ass Bridge spans the Cock, and a few paces to the south in the wood and on the edge of the high cliff, is a fine view of Barwick *(see reproduction)*

This spot is also the scene of the apparition of the cliff lady, a crepuscular spirit, often seen in years gone by. 'Twas said to be the restless ghost of a lady believed to have been murdered at Parlington. A belated traveller relates that, in passing this spot, a carriage emerged from the wood and crossed the road in front of him, and he distinctly saw the white face of a lady, but he heard no sound of horses' feet or crunching of wheels, as the carriage mysteriously glided away. At other times, she has been revealed by the moonlight washing her dress by the beck side. Apart from this apparition, in olden time the Padfoot, with huge saucer eyes and clanking chains, nightly held the bridge, to the terror of the village lads and the continual dread of the superstitious; and the people feared to pass the spot at midnight.

The road from Barwick to Aberford, fringing the beautiful domain of Parlington, is most pleasant; avenues and groves of fine trees, whose umbrageous branches cast lovely shadows, alternating with pretty little dells of sunlight.

* Pelagius, who denied original sin and asserted the doctrine of free-will and the merit of good works (fourth century), and who was the founder of Pelagianism, one of the heresies that crept into the early British Church, was a Briton by birth, and his name, in Celtic, was Morgan; thus it is quite within the bounds of possibility that he may have been connected with a religious house here, and the place, Morgan's Cross, named after him.

† Potterton was formerly noted for the manufacture of a coarse kind of pottery, such as milk bowls, stewpots, etc.

The path by the River Cock is even more charming to those interested in all the wonders of creative nature, luxuriant and beautiful in wildest loveliness, where bee and butterfly love to flit and roam from flower to flower. The bloom of the wild rose, the creamy tint of the elder blossom,

A VIEW OF BARWICK FROM COCK BECK.

and the graceful meadow-sweet, the spikes of the Canterbury bells gleaming in the hedgerows, the chequered flickering of light, imaging the sun's form; while the air is perfumed with the fragrance of flowers and scented with the odour of meadow grass and pine wood.

Wandering through such pastoral scenes we are apt to forget the toil and sorrow of life, yet above us in the woods of Beckhey, twisting and curving with the beck, are the Celtic earthworks carrying the mind back to the stern strife of bygone days!

Crossing the water at Becca Mills, now partly in ruins, we follow the rampart to Aberford. The word Becca, or Becka, has a very much older form in Beckhaugh or hey, making it Norse and probably meaning the hillock at the beck, as the little river is always designated the "Beck." Becca Hall stands on the north bank of the Cock, in a small, yet beautiful park, the residence of A. T. Schreibner, Esq. It was anciently in the possession of the Grammarys. In the seventeenth century it was in the hands of the well-known Carvill family, and from thence passed to the Markhams. Sir Clement Markham, K.C.B., the worthy historian of the Fairfaxes, is a grandson of the Hon. William Markham, of Becca Hall.

THE AVENUE, ON THE ROAD TO ABERFORD.

Aberford—Aber (Celtic), a confluence, with a ford, a passage over a stream or river—hence Aberford. The name has, however, been written variously—Aberforth, Abbeyforth, and Edburforth, the two latter names throwing some suspicion on the derivation of its name from a confluence at the ford. It was undoubtedly an adjunct to the great station at Barwick, both in Celtic and Angle times, its boundaries reaching to the Norse settlement of Grimston and Kirkby.

Aberford church is dedicated to St. Ricarius or Ricquier, not the English saint of that name living during the thirteenth century, but the St. Ricarius of the seventh century. Although existing in ages so far apart, strange to say, the lives of the two men have much in similarity, both in character and incident. The dedication to St. Ricarius is most interesting. This saint appears to have visited England about the middle of the seventh century, the period when the little Christian kingdom of Elmet was falling from the grasp of the Celt into the hands of the Engle-folk. Why then should we not attribute this church to the memory of the man who may have visited the Celts in Elmet, and preached to them in the great station at Barwick?

The church, with its former traces of vast antiquity, is a fine building, enlarged, and in some degree repaired, in 1821, when the early Norman chancel arch was barbarously used; it was rebuilt in 1861, except the tower and chancel, the former being restored in 1891. The Registers date from 1540. The patronage of the church passed from the Grammarys, who presented it to the knightly family of Walkyngham in 1230. The latter held it until 1331, when it was appropriated to the provost and scholars of the house of St. Mary at Oxford, collegiated in that university, and now Oriel College, to which it still belongs.

The churchyard contains several fragments of antiquity, in shape of stone coffins, etc., and its situation, high above the street, is very beautiful.

Near the south wall rest the remains of "Sammy Hick," the famous blacksmith preacher of Micklefield. The church contains a stained glass window to his memory. The old people still relate a miracle performed by Sammy Hick. Between Hook Moor and the south end of Aberford is a disused old windmill, where the miracle is said to have been performed. There had been a long spell of calm, dry weather, and there was no flour for the seed-bread wanted at the love-feast on the coming Sunday. Sammy had great faith in prayer, feeling certain that the meal would be forthcoming; so he went forth with the wheat to the mill, and began earnestly to pray. Strange to say, his prayers were answered. The sails and millstones began slowly to revolve, until grain sufficient for the purpose was ground. News of the mill in motion soon spread, and other persons with corn to be ground appeared, but

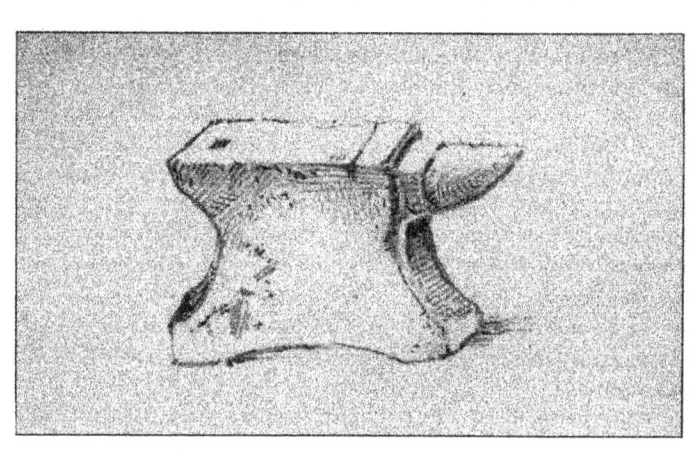

SAMMY HICK'S ANVIL.

for them there was no favouring breeze, for, like St. Thomas, their faith was not even as large as a grain of mustard seed.

One John Walton, vicar of Aberford, who died in 1640, attained the remarkable age of one hundred and fifteen years. The parish is healthily situated, which its record of longevity proves. The Register shows that nearly thirty persons have reached upwards of ninety years since 1780, and two persons have died over a hundred years, one reaching one hundred and seven. Amongst the long age records are the names of Helen Hick, who died in 1795, aged ninety, and one Robert Hick, mason, who died in 1845, aged ninety-two.

John Hick (doubtless ancestor of Sammy Hick, the well-known preacher) was a celebrated manufacturer of pins, locally known as a 'pinner.' This John Hick left "£50 to ye poor of ye p'ish of Abbaford, the interest or clear rent whereof (after a purchase made) is to be divided amongst them three times every year for ever."

The following tragic event, in connection with this church, is on record, June 26th, 1347:—"A general sentence against those who entered Aberford Church, and killed John de Byngham, clerk, whilst kneeling before the high altar in prayer."

Strange to say, Aberford is not mentioned in the Domesday Book, although the adjoining manors of Parlington and Hazelwood are recorded.

Aberford has always been favoured for residential purposes. When the Edwards, in succession, for more than a century occupied the throne, and came north on their rounds of war or pleasure, the quiet little town was one of their hunting stations. State documents still exist in connection with this place, enacted by each of these monarchs. From Edward I., in 1302, one of the barons Despencer, then owner, obtained a charter* for a weekly market there on Wednesday, and also a yearly fair on the eve, day, and morrow of the feast of St. Dionis (Denys). The worthy Longshanks knew the place and patronised it on more than one occasion during his war journeys north.

Just on the south of the village are the almshouses, an institution for the aged poor. They were erected in 1844 by Maria Isabella and Elizabeth Gascoigne to the memory of their dearest father, Richard Oliver Gascoigne, and their beloved brothers, Thomas Oliver and Richard Oliver Gascoigne, all of whom were carried off by death within the short space of twelve months. The institution is for eight pensioners, four of each sex, who have been tenants on the Parlington or Lotherton estates, and who are upwards of sixty years old. The hospital is a stately pile of architecture, with a central tower and beautiful Gothic chapel, and, with the woods of Parlington in the background, forms a noble picture.

The Roman Catholic Church, dedicated to St. Wilfrid, contains exquisite old coloured glass windows.

Camden, in his Britannia, says: "We travelled along the bold ridge of the Roman military way to Aberford, a little village by the side of the way, famous for making pins, which are in great request among the ladies. Below this runs the River Coc, called in books Cocker, and in the descent to the river are to be seen the foundations of an old castle called 'Castle

* The first charter for a weekly market and an annual fair was obtained by Henry-le-Grammary about the year 1250.

Carey.'" This castle, probably built by the Normans on an earlier foundation, is also mentioned by other historians. Its site is in the grounds belonging to the residence of Miss Wharton, known locally as Abbey House.

Traditions of a monastery erected in 655 by the Scottish bishops, trained by Columba in Iona, linger around this spot. There is no positive evidence,* yet there are certain vestiges indicative of such a house, which may have been despoiled and burnt by the Danes two centuries later. But what is

[*W. G. Foster.*]

PARLINGTON PARK.

absolutely more certain, the spot is the site of a Roman fortification, built to guard the passage of the Cock. It is situated on the tongue of land between the latter beck and the deep ravine, down which filters the little stream rising on the confines of Hook Moor, known as the Crow, or Craw.

* Burton says that the second of the religious houses built by the Scottish monks in 655 was at Abberford, Newton Kyne, or Tadcaster. All places are on the line of the old road, but which place has this honour of sanctity seems uncertain.

M

That the Normans had a fortification on this site we have undoubted proof, apart from the testimony of Camden and other old historians. As we have observed, in bygone years a good market and fairs were held, but grew less each succeeding year and are now things of the past.

[*Frank Dean.*

ABERFORD FROM THE NORTH-EAST.

The place is unique in appearance and character, and entirely different from other villages in the basin of the Wharfe, and consists chiefly of one long well-built street, rising from the beck to the opposing ridges on each side.

From different points of vantage, interesting landscapes are to be viewed. The church, with its tapering spire, surrounded by umbrageous trees, rising above the house-roofs of the town, forms a very pleasing scene; the old corn mill, its waterwheel and ivied cottage, and hard by, the slender aspiring poplars; the valley spreading west through lush meadows, with the twisting stream, and the bold wooded escarpment partly hiding the trenches

THE OLD KINGDOM OF ELMET. 163

of Becca, which bring to mind far-reaching memories—historic scenes which pierce the mists of a remote age.

From the bridge, the view north or south, along the course of the old Roman street, which has oft resounded with the tramp of armies and the rumble of mail-coaches, has features interesting to the antiquary and historian. The old ruined windmill, minus the sails, perched on the hill slope east of the town, silhouetted against a pale blue sky, over which huge pack clouds are sailing westwards, casting deep shadows on the landscape, and two quaint white-walled cottages abutting on the circular structure of the mill, make a striking picture in this hill and dale belvedere; one which probably commands the attention of the tourist more than others, although only a thing of yesterday compared with the antiquity of objects around: notably the great Roman way—the Ermyne Street—running, as we have already observed, from Castleford over Hook Moor, where the high causeway is still in good preservation.

Thence the present road passes along the side of the old road until reaching Aberford. A little distance north of the town, beyond Black Horse Farm, the Roman street bears away to the right of the present road, and here it is a very conspicuous landmark, running over the fields, a high, compact ridge.

164   THE OLD KINGDOM OF ELMET.

Practically cultivation seems to have had little effect in lowering the ridge of this original Roman road. At Nip Scaup, or Nut Hill, by the side of the ridge, is an old farm, where the family of the Noverleys have dwelt for hundreds of years. Report says they came in the train of the first Vavasour, and were huntsmen for that House when most of the land hereabouts was wild moor, fen and forest. A little distance south, where the old and new roads part, formerly stood a cross; Highcross Cottage keeps its memory green. Immediately to the north of this place there is a length of the Roman road remaining. It diverges from the present turnpike and passes over the cultivated fields in the vicinity of Headley Bar; the present road is

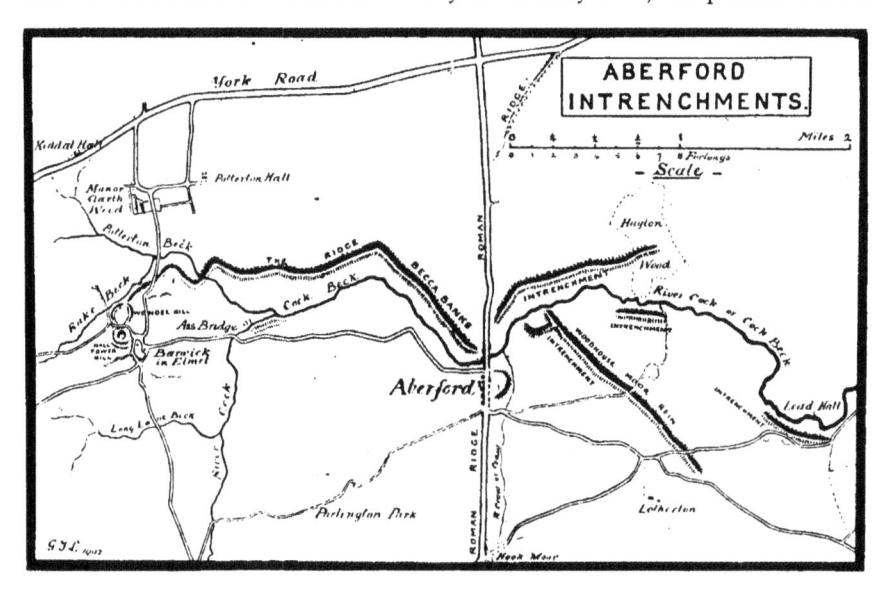

on the track of the Roman way. Apart from the high ridge, other proofs of this old road are strongly in evidence. Here in the fields, after the cultivation year by year, a long line, almost of snowy whiteness, is brought to the surface. This annual earth-ghost is due to the upturning of the Romanway subsoil, chiefly by the plough, but in part by worms, and its subsequent disintegration and bleaching by the weather. Down in the little valley immediately to the west, there is a fine well of water, known as the "Duke of Buckingham's Well." From evidences here there has formerly been a substantial house hereabouts. There is a local tradition which needs no comment: it says that the Duke of Buckingham, riding from the battle of Towton, fell sick of flux; being advised of the astringent properties of the well, he drank and was cured.

From Windmill Hill we may behold, mentally, the legions of Honorius passing southwards never to return; and picture the natives watching the departure of their imperial masters, to some a source of pleasure, to others of sorrow; emblazoned banners wave, yet the cordon is tightly drawn: Rome calls afar to her sons for help. Thus our thoughts mingle with scenes of far-off days and present times.

A PEEP FROM THE LOTHERTON ROAD.

In coaching days Aberford was a place of some fame. The "Swan" and the "Arabian Horse," with their quaint settles and picturesque interiors are evidences of bygone bustle and far greater prosperity. Sixty or seventy years ago, Bramham Moor, "the home of howling winds," was quite enlivened by the passing to and fro of mail-coaches. Now and again, when the hounds meet at the crossing of roads, the scene partakes of the character and picturesqueness of the past. From one coach named the "True Blue," a native of the moor, now fast approaching fourscore, told the writer that as a boy it was his duty to obtain a copy of the " Leeds Mercury," the price of which was sevenpence-halfpenny.

Bramham Moor is said to have been a rendezvous of Nevison, the celebrated highwayman, and the "Black Horse," now a farm, is the place where, report says, he baited his famous mare during his fabled ride on her from London to York.

In our journey down the vale we follow the south bank and note the entrenchments known as the Woodhouse Moor Rein,—rein or rine, a strip or stripe—which extend from Aberford, south east, to Lotherton. Professor Phillips regards them as part of a system of earthworks of an ancient population having its centre at Barwick, but whether raised by Briton or Saxon, he could not be certain. Doubtless this great system of earthworks, so complete in their design and carrying out, are pre-Roman, or were constructed as a barrier against the invasion of the latter people. They are so linked together from Wendel Hill at Barwick to the swampy lands of lowlying Lead, and in some places running on both sides of the river, east and west, and show by their contour a preconceived design. To this day they remain a great monument of that very eventful period to the Briton—the coming of the Romans. Here by the roadside is Mr. Young's small museum of curios and antiquities, many of which have been found in the district: flint implements, Roman coins of Constantinus and Faustina, the famous (and infamous) Empress of Rome.

Hidden in a recess across the road is the old market cross brought hither from Aberford, which formerly stood by the churchyard near the old vicarage. It was removed from there during the time of plague, and the fairs removed hither also, and such was the fear of the plague that the purchase money was placed in a trough containing water, and taken out by the sellers, and here in the hedgerow the old cross still rests. A strange and pathetic interest invests this silent testimony to the fearful plague-time of long past. 'Tis a pity the old stone cannot be removed to its former site, it being a relic around which, to some extent, the history of Aberford centres. The registers of the church tell a fearful and pathetic story of that terrible visitation, when the families of those infected were compelled by force to live with those smitten fatally, and receive, as it were, their certain doom.

Half a mile beyond we turn aside to the right, and a few hundred yards brings us to Lotherton (Lutterington of old). The surroundings of the place are wonderfully picturesque. The antique ivy-clad and gabled house by the road side, with the large overhanging trees, are typical of the past. But apart from this picture the tiny hamlet contains a little private chapel, belonging to an old manor-house, and not much bigger than the squire's pew in some chapels. Like a jewel in a casket, it is hidden by dense foliage and interwoven with ivy. In the summer time, with the exception of the bell gable, it is completely hidden to the passer-by, and to the casual observer its claims to beauty and antiquity are lost. Yet the little chapel is capable of teaching a most instructive lesson, which the thinking pedestrian cannot afford to neglect. As a relic of an age we are apt to despise as barbarous, it is a striking reproof to modern times and builders. Only when one has passed through the intricate maze of foliage and reached the entrance doorway do we grasp the evidence of its antiquity. The north doorway, now walled up, is decidedly Norman— twelfth century. There is an ancient holy-water stoup of the same age as the arch of the north door. The east window is a small narrow slit. The deeply recessed windows, hidden on the outside by dense foliage, give the interior an air of gloom. The fittings are of the rudest description. Through the cracks in the roof tendrils of ivy have crept and now hang from the roof to the floor of the chapel in clusters! The interior of the building is 54 feet by 21. Needless to say, service is not held in the chapel now. The venerable relic is in a most dilapidated condition now evidently used as a pigeon cote, and a place for fowls to roost in.

OLD BELFRY LOTHERTON

The estate was a part of the Archbishop's barony of Sherburn: hence Sherburn is the mother church—nearly four miles away, while Aberford is little more than a mile. Richard de Lutterington held a knight's fee there, in 1202. In 1251 the manor went to Robert Haget, treasurer of York, and

Gilbert Bernevale, his assign, who died in 1276, leaving daughters, Albreda and Cecily. Albreda had a son, Gilbert Conday; Cecily was married to Gilbert Neville, but it was found that Gilbert Bernevale, before his death, had granted the Lotherton lands to Joan, daughter of Alan Sampson, of York, and had placed her in full seisin of them. Afterwards, however, the Nevilles and Sir Robert Fourneaux seem to have divided the estate. John Neville, of Lotherton, took a prominent part in the disastrous Scottish Wars of Edward II., commanding a portion of the West Riding men who were at Bannockburn.

After them the Grammarys occupied, and, in 1495, Sir Guy Fairfax confirmed Lutterington and other lands to his son Guy: "Rendering thereof to Sir Guy one red rose yearly, at the Feast of the Nativity of St. John Baptist;" and so it was that the little chapel of Lotherton, where the knight has kept his vigils before starting on his journey to the Holy Wars, told the tale of England's glory from the Crusades to Marston Moor; and from thence Major (now Colonel) Gascoigne rode forth to take part in our late war against the Boers.

INTERIOR (LOOKING WEST) LOTHERTON CHAPEL

A mile further down in the vale is the little Church of Lead, or Lede (another proof of Celtic occupation), erected in the thirteenth century as a private chapel to Lead Hall: in bygone days a place of some importance, now deserted and falling to ruins. In the early centuries it was the home of the Teyes family, afterwards the Scargills.

About this very ancient domain Leland tells us not a little of what we want to know. He saw it about 1540, and thus reporteth :—" Aberford is a poor thoroughfare on Watling Street. Cock Beck springeth west of it and so runneth through it, and thence, by much turning to Lead, a hamlet where Skargill had a fair manor place of timber. Scargill, late knight, left two daughters to his heirs, whereof Tunstall wedded one, and Gascoyne of Bedfordshire, the other. Cock Beck after crosseth by Saxton and Towton village and fields and forth into Wharfe River, beneath Tadcaster."

In its palmy days this fair domain, with its then timber manor-house and outbuildings, as described by Leland, must, indeed, have been a charming spot. In the midst of fertile meadow land stands the church; the ground on either side rising more boldly, encloses the picturesque vale. The eye that loves to rest on quiet scenes, and see the inexhaustible beauties of natural detail, finds much to admire here.

NORTH DOORWAY, LOTHERTON CHAPEL.

The interior of the chapel is very roughly furnished with a few rude benches, a plain deal communion table, font, and an ancient chest. On the floor are four tombstones, from which the brasses have been removed. The arms on the tombs are a fesse with three mallets; also the names of Margeria, Baldwinius, and Franconis, members of the ancient Teyes family.

Margaret was the daughter of Roger le Teyes and niece and heiress to Walter le Teyes, Baron of Steingrieve, who also owned lands in Yorkshire,

Bedfordshire, Essex, and Buckinghamshire. He was summoned as baron, February 6th, 1298, and fought in the Scotch campaign. He and Henry le Teyes were the two barons who affixed their seals to the letter addressed to the Pope from the Parliament held at Lincoln in 1301, protesting against the Pope's interference with the claims of Edward I. to the crown of Scotland.

LEAD CHURCH (TREE IN FOREGROUND NOW GONE).

A Franco Tyays, of the county of York, was summoned to come, with horse and arms, to Parliament at Berwick. Walter le Teyes died in the eighteenth year of Edward II.; Margaret, his niece and heiress, being about twenty-six years of age. A representative of this old and important family remains in the person of the Rev. James Tyas, the present Vicar of Padiham.*

    * The Tyases held Lede Hall for some generations. In 1278 Franco le Tyays having to answer for free warren and his lands quit of service at Lede and elsewhere, claimed by charter of Henry III., granting to him, Franco, and his heirs free warren in all his domain lands of Lede, Wodçhuse, and Farnley. This was to be inquired into with reference to usurped privileges. He did service in person at the county service nearest after Michaelmas, and at the 'trithing' after that feast. The word 'trithing,' or 'tryering,' is obsolete; it meant the sessions whereat the specious 'special pleader' (whence our phrase of to-day) had liberty to say what was—not the truth. The word occurs in one of Alex. Brome's songs, who himself was an attorney, and he makes the versed assertion:—

Chiefly by the efforts of the Vicar of Ryther, Lede Chapel* has lately been put into a state of repair.

For the present, instead of continuing down the vale, let us go by field, path, and hedgerow, up the rising ground, north-west to the fine elevation on which presides the historic hall of the famed Vavasours, Vavasor, or Valvasor. The King's Valvasor was an office of great honour in olden time—a sort of land-valet or steward of the vassals. The massive hall, with embattled frontage and two projecting wings and fine flight of steps built of grey limestone, stands forth in bold relief against a dark background of wood.

This ancestral seat of the Vavasours represents an unbroken tenure, extending even beyond the Conquest, but how long we cannot say. Such evidence as can be obtained on the subject goes to show that this family sprang from one of the Celtic chieftains, who, though subjected to Teutonic rule, have never been dispossessed of all their lands, and in that position were the hereditary rulers of Tadcaster.

INTERIOR, LEAD CHURCH.

"And shew'd then selves as erraut lyars,
As they were 'prentice to the tryers."

At the wapentake of Barkeston and Aggebrigg after that feast, he gave 6s. 4d., wapentake fine, to be quit of all other services, county, trithing, and wapentake. These Tavases were tenants of the De Laci, of whom they had been retainers for more than a century.

* Two services are held in the church yearly. The reason for this singular custom seems to be lost in mists of antiquity. The following is an extract from a Ryther terrier dated July 28, 1853:—"Annexed to the mother church and in the parish is a small chapel called Lead or Lede Hall Chapel where Divine Service is performed by custom on the first Sunday after the Feasts of St. Mark and St. Luke respectively." The Rector of Ryther receives from this chapel, in lieu of tithe, an annual income of £1 18s. 8d., irrespective of any obligation or service held in the chapel.

The prominence of the Vavasours in the early grants of the Percys is a circumstance pointing strongly to that fact. The early machinery of the government of the district with Nigel, the provost at Huddlestone in the first decade of the twelfth century, and with the authority and ownership of the Vavasour, extending west to Addingham, is all in accordance with the permitted rule of a Tributary chief. Their name, Valvasor, was derived from the office and not from the territory.

The inheritor of Haselwood was a Valvasor, not by blood but by position; doubtless the office was hereditary, but all the same the title continued to be that of an officer and not of an inheritor. It was exactly in that position which the Vavasours of Haselwood were when Percy and De Laci had to settle the bounds of their respective fees, for record in the Domesday Survey.

A DISTANT VIEW OF HAZELWOOD.

The difficulty which presented itself to them arose from the long-permitted rule of the Vavasours. Eventually the territory in the Iselwood and the Saxton (the latter name bespeaking its Saxon and stone-quarry origin) went to the Percy. The lands adjoining, at Towton, went to the De Laci, in the swamps of which extending on both sides of the River Cock the native "Leedes," or Leods, the Celtic people of Elmet—the men bound to the soil—were left to settle.

At Lead there is still this further peculiarity—that Lead is a chapelry in the parish of Ryther, miles away, while Lotherton, although close to Aberford, is in the Parish of Sherburn, whose Parish Church is also four miles off. The only possible explanation of these peculiarities lies in the old Celtic entrenchments, called, on the east of Aberford, Woodhouse Moor Rein, the Wodchuse of the Charter. West of that are Becca Banks and the Ridge, the whole having been one of the defences of the British Kingdom of Elmet, beyond which Edwin's conquest did not reach.

At Hazelwood, Ryther, and the swampy ground of the Fen district, the local Celtic chieftains have been firmly established. At both places the families evidently there at the time of the first records demonstrate well-settled possession, and many Celtic names and customs.

The old name of Haselwood (Iselwood) establishes the "hall" or "hael" that always implies local government. At least since the days of the Conquest this ancient and noble family have held the lands of Hazelwood, except for a short time in the reign of Henry III., when it was in pawn to Aaron, a Jew at York, for the sum of £350. He made a conveyance of his security to Queen Eleanor, in discharge of a debt due to her, from whom John le Vavasor received it again on payment of the money.

In its feudal aspect, Hazelwood presents the earliest features of a Seat in rank just below the dignity of a baronial Castle. As a stone edifice capable of supporting the operations of war as then known, it had an early beginning. In 1286, King Edward I. gave leave to castellate the mansion, which really means that, by that time, what Mauger had left of the old timber hall of his ancestors had become decrepit by wear and time, and, action being necessary, stone might be used in the erection of a strong and warlike edifice.

The venerable Gothic chapel, founded in that year, gives an evidence of the castellated structure, not externally altered by the present hall, the front of which has been remodelled with some incongruity of taste. The fatal influence of the times, exhibited in the Jacobean architectural alterations inside the chapel, gives some clue to the execution of the present front of the hall.

Sir Thomas Vavasour, the first who dropped the ancestral "le," was knight-marshal of the King's household, and created a baronet in 1628; had he remained a simple knight, the Gothic features of the castellated mansion of Sir Robert le Vavasour would have existed to this present day. The exterior consists of a centre and two wings; unfortunately the effect is marred by the Jacobean work in the approach to the entrance hall—a magnificent room, around which are the shields emblazoned with the family arms. From the battlements an expanse of country spreads before the eye, the battlefield of Towton appearing in the foreground.

The hall stands about midway between Stutton and Aberford, on the high ground, facing a most beautiful park. From the castle is a fine panoramic view of hill and dale, east and north-east the eye roams with pleasure across the rich vales of Mowbray and York, through which can be seen glimpses of the shining Ouse, passing village, church, hamlet, and the stately towers of York. Far away over this fertile vale eastward stretch the outlines of the Wold hills; northward the heather-clad moors blend their contours sweetly with the clouds. Standing in front of the castellated mansion, the spectator cannot but be impressed by this imposing palace of ancient England. The whole place breathes of mediæval times, and yet not in the same way as the hoary ruin or the dismantled fortress, for it is as perfect as when the Vavasour knights led forth their retainers to the battle-field, or when the loud blast of the horn peopled the park with a grand

HAZELWOOD CASTLE.

array of barons and their ladies going forth, hawk on wrist (for falconry was the sport of the time), to hunt over the wild moor, or to chase the fleet deer through the wide forest. In imagination we hear the trampling of horse and jingle of armour; round the bend in the park appears the best of English chivalry, accoutred in their vestments of war or the chase; above them floats the symbol of the Crusade, under which they fought and won the Holy City from the Infidel. Such are the visions which rise up before our eyes as we look on this stately structure.

The scene changes! It is night: unbounded hospitality prevails. Through the latticed windows we see a numerous throng; the banquet hall is brilliant with the glare of lights in sconces against the walls, resonant with the greetings of friends and expressions of merriment; servitors and retainers carry savoury dishes; on the walls are a vast number of banners and other trophies of war; goblets of wine are quaffed to the health of the noble host and hostess. The scene grows brighter as some hero recites his adventures in the deathful storm of battle, while the harper sings those inspiring and romantic ballads of love and war, handed down through unbroken generations of a long and distinguished ancestry!

Hazelwood seems deserted now; the mansion is still there, the park, as of old, beautiful; the spacious courtyard and surrounding buildings are perfect, yet how lonely and empty the place seems, the body remaining, but the spirit departed hence. The life to which it was born and dedicated is no longer possible. Hazelwood is a reminiscence!

Standing against the walls of the mansion, and under its protective shade, is the Gothic Chapel, dedicated to St. Leonard, and built by Sir William le Vavasour in the thirteenth century.* For six hundred years, services have been held without intermission in this sanctuary, the only place of Roman Catholic faith not closed during the reign of Elizabeth; so great, it is said, was her esteem for that renowned family. This venerable chapel contains many other memorials of its patrons. Along its north wall a group of statues represent a Vavasour family of the sixteenth century, all in a good state of preservation. On the same wall are two mural recesses containing

* One very noteworthy feature of the Haselwood Chantry seems to have been missed as to its true import. For all local purposes the chapel has served as a parish church. Yet while its independence in Purpose has been maintained, its subordination to Tadcaster has never been disputed. It is further remarkable that the Vavasours made their private chapel at Weston into a parish church also. These facts go far to support the explanation of their name in the authority of a Celtic chieftain, with which other facts quite agree.

The chantry of St. Leonard's, at Haselwood, being a parish church as they say, and within the precincts of the parish of Tadcaster.

JOHN BEVERLEY, Incumbent.

Founded by the ancestors of Sir William Vavasor, Kt., sans date, to th' extent the said incumbent shall minister all sacraments and sacramentals to all the inhabitants within the Mansion Place of Haselwood aforesaid, and to bury, wedd, and christen within the same chappel, according to the said graunte; which mansion is distant from Tadcaster, which they call the mother church, 2 myles and above; and the said incumbent haith yerely out of the terme of the mylles of Stourton, 8s. for all gross tythes as the incumbent allodgeth; and further, the Incumbent haith over and beside the 8s., all offerings and other petty tythes, with renewe within 11s. 6d. for the said Mansion Place, whereby it should seme the same rather to be a parsonage than a free chappel or chauntry, and payeth tenthes after the rate of £4 16s. 4d. for the said annuitie, tythes, and valet, tenthes deducted   £3 8s. 3½d.

recumbent effigies, one of them probably representing Sir William, the founder of the chapel. Both have the appearance of thirteenth-century work; their martial figures repose in complete armour, and tell of siege and war, and the reward of 'the good fight'—the peace which passeth understanding. The north end contains a very undesirable mixture of Gothic and Jacobean architecture. Besides other tombs there are two painted windows, and a beautiful painted altar-piece.

ROMAN CATHOLIC CHAPEL, HAZELWOOD.

The religious splendour contained in the chapel may be seen from the will of the founder, Sir William Vavasour, who died in 1311. "To the six chaplains celebrating in the 'new chapel' of Haselwood during the first year of his decease he leaves thirty marks. To his wife, Nichola Waleys, he leaves all his ploughs and their oxen. He also leaves money to celebrate masses for the souls of his dead father, John, and mother, Alice. He designates the chapel as the new chapel of St. Leonard of Heselwood." His daughter Alice was a nun at Sinyngthwayte. Peter le Vavasour, rector of Staynton, was a kinsman, perhaps brother.

The fine array of blue marble tombs of the Vavasours, who have been buried here since the foundation of the chapel, is the evidence of their succession. The simplest of them, that of the founder, is described by Dodsworth. On the floor lies a flat stone with his coat, Vavasour, impaling a pegasus rampant within a bordure componed argent and vert, and this epitaph: "Orate pro animabus Gulielmi Vavasour, Militis, et Elizabathe consortis ejus,"—the pious invocation of so many generations of our forefathers.*

One and not by any means the only effort of Vavasour chivalry will always be remembered by Yorkshiremen. Sir Thomas le Vavasour, the lineal descendant of Sir William le Vavasour (who so distinguished himself in the Scottish wars as to win the praise and high favour of Edward I.), made himself honourably conspicuous by raising forces and equipping vessels for service against the Spanish Armada, 1588. Queen Elizabeth, in reward for his great zeal and energy, and also out of particular regard for one of her maids of honour—a Vavasour, and acknowledged by the Queen as her kinswoman, would never suffer the chapel or service therein to be molested. And so it came to pass that amid all the persecutions directed against the Roman Catholics throughout England, the rites of the ancient faith were allowed to continue at Hazelwood, and so onward to the present time. A striking example which shows there is more true religion in toleration than in the dogmas of all the churches.

* In connection with donation of stone to York Minster by the Vavasours from their quarry in Thevedale, the following is from Drake's History of York. The Robert le Vavasour possessed of Hazelwood in the reign of Henry III., extending from 1216 to 1272, during which interval the south transept was added to the noble structure. "It appears," says the historian, "by a deed that Robert le Vavasour granted to God, St. Peter, and the Church of York, for the health of his own soul, and the souls of his wife Julian and his ancestors, full and free use of his quarry at Tadcaster, in Thevedale; with liberty to take and carry thence a sufficient quantity of stone for the fabric of this church so oft as they had need to repair, re-edify, or enlarge the same. Robert de Percy, lord of Boulton, made a similar grant of his wood at Boulton for roofing the new building. In memory of these two extraordinary benefices, the church thought fit to erect two statues; one represented with a piece of rough unhewn stone in his hands; the other with a similitude of a piece of wrought timber." Camden says, "That near Hesselwood, within twelve miles of York, lyeth a most famous quarry of stone, called Peter's Post, for that with the stones hewed out of it, by the liberal grant of the Vavasours, that stately and sumptuous Church of St. Peter's, at York, was re-edify'd; and some tell us that the property of that stone is such as to be very soft, and consequently more easy for the carvers, when newly taken away, which after hardens the more the longer it is exposed to the air. A stone as if Nature herself had contrived to further on the workmanship."

The present Sir William, although a Catholic, we understand, holds very tolerant views on religious matters. How quiet the pretty little church yard seems, with its tombstones crumbling from time and exposure, still beseeching all out of their charity to pray for the souls of those who sleep beneath!

Many incidents in song and story are related of this ancient family,* all redounding to the esteem and honour in which they were held in bygone days. The homeless wayfarer and aged labourer, bowed with years of toil, tells with pride, how this hospitable family gave refreshment to the poor, as to the rich.

* There was a Justice, but late in the realme of England, callyd Master Vavesour, a very honely man and rude of condycions, and lovyd, never to spend mych, mych noney. This Master Vavesour rode on a tyme in hys cyrceutyee (circuit) in the northe countrey, where he had agreed wyth the sheryf for a certain sone of noney for hys charges thorowe the shyre, so that at every inne and lodgynge this Master Vavasour payed for his own costys. It fortuned so, that when he cam to a certayn lodgyng he connanded one Turpyn, hys servant to see that he used good husbondry, and to save suche thynges as were left, and to carry it wyth hym to serve hym baytynge. Thys Turpyn, doying his nayster's connandnent, take the broken bred, broken nete, and all such tying that was left, and put it in his mayster's cloth sak. The wyf of the hous, perceywing that he toke all such fragmentys and vytayle wyth hym that was left, and put it in the clothe sak, she brought up the podage that was left in the pot; and when Turpyn had turned hys bake a lytyl asyde, she pouryd the podage into the clothe sak whych ran upon hys robe of skarlet and other of hys garmentys, and rayed then very evyll, that they were nuch hurt therewyth. Thys Turpyn, sodegnly turnying hym, and seeing it, revyled the wyfe, therfore, and ran to hys nayster, and told hym what she had don; wherfore Master Vavesour incontinest, callyd the wyfe, and said to her thus: "Thou drab," quoth he, "what has thou don? Why hast thou pourd the podage in my clothe sak, and marrd my rayment and gere?" "O, sir," quoth the wyfe, "I know wel ye are a judge of the realme, and I perceyve by your nind is to do ryght as to have that is your owen; and your nyud is to have all thyng wyth you that ye have payd for, both broken nete and other thynges that is left, and so it is reson that ye have: and, therefore, because your servant hath taken the broken nete and put it in your cloth sake, I have therin put the podage that be left, because ye have wel and truly payed for then. Yf I shoulde kepe any thynge fron you that he hath payed for, per-adventure, ye wold trouble me in the law another tyme." Here ye may se, that he that playeth the niygards so mych, son tyme it torneth hym to hys owne losse.—Fron "The Hundred Mery Talys."

CHAPTER VIII.

TOWTON AND SAXTON.

THE STORY OF A FAMOUS FIGHT.

RETURNING to Lede by way of Newstead (situated half a mile west of the beck, where also is the old stead and signs of early occupation, a unique moated site very indicative of a long history) we now follow the beck to the old mill, known as Lead Mill, although standing in the parish of Saxton.

A twelfth-century deed of Robert Patefin, lord of Towton, to Roger Berkin and Alice his wife (whose first husband was Roger Paytefin), grants them all the town of Towton, yet so that the men of Towton, as they were wont to do, should grind at Paytefin's Mill of Saxton, saving to Roger and Alice, his wife, the "multure of their house quit," for all the life of the same Alice.

In the reign of Edward I. Alice de Laci gave to Margaret Kirkton (daughter of Alexander de Kirkton, sheriff of Yorkshire), her damsel and a great favourite, the bodies and lands (holden in villeinage) of Ralph Brown and George Saxton, both of Lede. The grant says: "I, Alice Laci, have given to Margaret Kirkton, my mayd servant, my manor of Saxton and five score and two acres of arable land in Saxton, wherof twenty acres lie in a place called Towton-dale, and two 'placeas' of pasture lying at Maydencastell, and the mill of Lede. Witnesses: Sir William Vavasour, Richard Tvas, John Reygate, Gilbert Singleton."

The mill formerly stood further down the beck near to where the bridge crosses the stream, and close by the south shoulder of Mayden Castle Wood.

A breath of antiquity surrounds this old mill. The interior, musty and cobwebbed, seems to groan and creak with the labours and cares of numberless years. It still retains, dented and crumbled with time, the old multure board, although the custom is now obsolete.

We are now merging on the western fringe of the great battlefield of Towton. A mile or so down the beck from Lede, which hitherto, in many sweeping curves, has run in an easterly direction, here bends more to the north under the dark shadow of Castle Hill and Renshaw Wood, winding through a deep, silent vale, sombre and melancholy as if reflecting on the tragedy of the past. Here can be seen the solitary heron and other wild fowl, a thousand sights in animal and vegetable life arrest our attention, the cry and splash of startled water-hens amongst the rushes. In the hedgerow bloom the bramble and sweet wild-rose from which now and again flits the sportive butterfly. All is strangely quiet in this isolated spot except the hum of insects passing to and fro, the gentle flow of the rivulet, murmuring over slight obstruction, the song of the lark rising higher and higher, and the soft cooing of the ringdove. What a contrast is this quiet spot to the noisy hum of our large towns! Here, a deep and silent vale, through which the ever-restless streamlet laves its course, the scene enclosed by woods and hills; above, the glorious sky and fleecy clouds, and the bright sun smiling down on the peaceful vale. Yet on this spot a tragedy fateful to England was enacted. The dale resounding with the awful clang of arms, the shriek and tumult of men in deadly combat. On the plateau above, a most fearful battle was fought between Englishmen, which, for the dire struggle, carnage, and numbers slain, mark it as one, if not the greatest fight ever witnessed on English soil.

THE DAY BEFORE THE BATTLE.

On the Saturday morning, 28th of March, preceding the battle, the Lancastrian army was moving southwards towards Towton. The Yorkists, under the personal command of Edward and Warwick, were encamped at Pontefract, from whence Lord Fitz-Walter, with a body of picked troops, had been despatched to guard the ford at Ferrybridge, the only available crossing place in the district.

News of this detachment coming to the knowledge of Lord Clifford (the bloody Clifford), he, in the early hours of the following morning (Saturday), in charge of the men of Craven, fell like a thunderbolt on the advanced guard holding the ford. Fitz-Walter, hearing the tumult, leaped from his bed, seizing the first available weapon, rushed into the conflict, only to be slain with nearly all his men. It was at this juncture of affairs when the news of this defeat and capture of the ford by Clifford reached

Edward and Warwick. The latter is said to have leaped from his saddle, and, stabbing his charger with his sword, said, "Let him flee that will, for surely I will tarry with him that will tarry with me;" then, holding up the reeking sword by the blade, he kissed the cross formed by the handle.

An attempt to dislodge Clifford at the ford being of no avail, a detachment crossed three miles higher up the Aire, at Castleford, to cut off Clifford from the main body of Lancastrians. Perceiving the ruse, he, however, fell back towards Towton, but not sharp enough to elude the advanced guard of the Yorkists who probably pushed forward by the old Roman way, and

THE BATTLEFIELD OF TOWTON (LOOKING SOUTH).

over Hook Moor, reaching Dintingdale, a small valley running between Saxton and the Ferrybridge and York Road, the way by which Clifford and his staunch men of Craven were retreating. There, in the little valley, a smart skirmish took place; Clifford and the yeomen of the west fought bravely against overpowering numbers; their fate, however, was sealed: few escaped to tell the story of disaster. Clifford, we are told, had taken off his gorget to relieve pressure, and so was slain, pierced in the throat by a headless arrow.

Late on that Saturday, the whole human machinery of war and destruction was in motion, and, in the cold dusk of a March evening, settled down almost within sight and hearing of each other, the lurid flame of watch fires gleaming in the evening sky. The Yorkists occupied the high ridge of land immediately south of Saxton, stretching from Scarthingwell towards the Cock at the 'Crooked Billet.' The Lancastrian divisions occupied the high land immediately around Towton, having about two miles of front, the left wing spreading south-east of Towton, the right reaching from Towton half a mile or more west, to where the land falls sharply down into the swamp of the Cock at Renshaw Wood, with an outpost to guard the right flank at Castle Hill (the site of Mayden Castle) a few hundred yards nearer Lead Mill. Thus was the disposition of the two armies within sight and hearing of each other, on that fatal eve, the prelude to the carnage and death of the morrow's fight.

LOOKING NORTH OVER SAXTON ON TO THE BATTLEFIELD, RENSHAW WOOD IN THE BACKGROUND.

BATTLE OF TOWTON FIELD.

This battle took place on the morning of Palm Sunday, 1461. The Sabbath had only just broken into day, which found the two armies, composed of the best and bravest of England's sons, ready for the coming fight. As they came in full sight of each other they "rent the air with a mighty shout," the challenge and defiance to mortal combat.

The morning was wild and stormy, the heavens overcast, the fierce March wind driving a blinding snowstorm full into the faces of the Lancastrians. The Yorkists, quickly taking advantage of the storm, advanced and sent many furious showers of arrows from their strong bows full into the ranks of the enemy, causing fearful havoc at the first onset. The arrows were shot from the rising ground, after which the archers retired a few paces into the hollow until the enemy had emptied their quivers. The snowstorm blowing into the faces of the Lancastrians, prevented them from seeing this manœuvre; in turn, their arrows, flying fast and thick against a foe they could not see, fell short of the mark. Several times Edward's archers advanced, each time speeding their arrows full into the faces of their foemen, causing great confusion.*

[F. Dean.
TOWTON BRIDGE, NORTH-WEST CORNER OF RENSHAW WOOD.

Nearer and nearer gradually crept the hosts of death. The Lancastrians, perceiving their disadvantage, rushed through the blinding hail and storm of arrows and smote their foes with sword, pike, battleaxe, and bill; and so, nearly the whole of that Sabbath day the battle raged. The huge mass of

* During the Middle Ages, the long bow wielded by sturdy English yeomen proved a terrible weapon of war. On the battlefield of Crécy and Poitiers the English archers won in perishable fane and renown, speeding their cloth yard shaft with a swiftness and force hitherto unknown.

struggling humanity fought like demons; many times during this fatal day did the fortune of war hang in the balance, sometimes the white rose trembling, then the red; "men fought as if the battle was the Gate of Paradise." "For ten hours," says one historian, "the conflict raged with uncertain result;" compared by Shakespeare to the tide of a mighty sea, contending with a strong opposing wind.

The tide of battle at last set against the House of Lancaster by the arrival of five thousand fresh Yorkist troops. No quarter had been given at the battle of Wakefield, where the black-faced Clifford, in cold blood, slew the innocent Rutland; now at Towton Edward commanded that no quarter should be given, and only too well were his orders carried out, for at eventide, upwards of thirty-six thousand of the bravest and noblest of England's sons lay dead or dying on the ghastly field.

The wreck of the vanquished army fled north-west; across their path ran the little River Cock, into whose waters many fell, never to rise again. Dire was the confusion at the bridge, which was choked by a mass of struggling humanity, and which at length gave way beneath the pressure. Over a bridge of bodies fled the remnant of the Lancastrians. Not only at this spot, but for the space of two miles or more, the valley of the Cock became a veritable death-trap to the vanquished. Down the valley ran the blood of the slain, changing the waters of the rivulet and the Wharfe to crimson; even the brown waters of the Ouse, it is said, became tinged with human blood.

A stranger passing over this ground would see nothing to indicate that on this spot was fought the most fierce and deadly battle of ancient or modern times. A few mounds and depressions mark the place where many of the bravest of our land lie in their last sleep. It is said the titled slain are interred in the churchyards of the surrounding district, but with, I believe, a few exceptions, history is silent. No monument marks the site of battle, yet there is one beautiful memorial on the field which the villagers tell us cannot be effaced—above where the warrior sleeps, white and red roses bloom, emblems of the fatal feud. How they came thus is not known, but they do not grow well on other soil than that on which was poured out old England's noblest blood.

"Oh, the red and white rose, upon Towton Moor it grows,
And red and white it blows upon that swarthe for evermore,
In memorial of the slaughter, when the red blood ran like water
And the victors gave no quarter in the flight from Towton Moor.

" When the banners gay were beaming, and the steel cuirasses gleaning,
And the martial music streaming o'er the wide and lonely heath ;
And many a heart was beating that dreamed not of retreating,
Which, ere the sun was setting, lay still and cold in death.

" When the snow that fell at morning lay as a type and warning,
All stained and streaked with crimson, like the roses white and red
And filled each thirsty furrow with its token of the sorrow
That wailed for many a morrow through the mansions of the dead.

Now for twice two hundred years, when the month of March appears,
All unchecked by plough or shears spring the roses red and white ·
Nor can the hand of mortal close the subterranean portal
That gives to life in mortal these emblems of the fight.

" And as if they were enchanted, not a flower may be transplanted
From those fatal precincts, haunted by the spirits of the slain ;
For howe'er the root you cherish, it shall fade away and perish,
When removed beyond the marish of Towton's gory plain."

I have somewhere heard it remarked that on one occasion the Iron Duke was asked, by an expert in war, what calculation he made at Waterloo for a retreat, in case of defeat; his answer was, "None!" Be that as it may, it was thus with the leaders of the Lancastrians at Towton heath, otherwise the carnage of that day would not have been nearly so appalling. Their position for fighting, on the high plateau, was even more advantageous than that of the Yorkists; but for the retreat of a large army in confusion, nothing could be more dangerous and deadly: it proved a veritable death-trap.

Immediately to the rear of their position and extending from the site of Mayden Castle, hard by Lead corn mill, to the outlying lands of Grimston (a distance of two miles or more), the ground drops abruptly down to the treacherous, oozy fen-banks of the River Cock, which, if insignificant, were not the less deadly, the latter not more than from seven to twelve feet across, easy enough for an agile man to jump, yet too wide for the vanquished to leap, laden with their armour and wearied with the exertion and turmoil of the day's fight. And even to this day the ground on either bank (in most places), for a hundred yards or more, is a dangerous morass, yet tenfold worse four hundred and fifty years ago, as at that period the length of the valley from Lead Mill to Stutton, or even lower, to where the beck joins the Wharfe, was one continuous mire and swamp, impossible to cross without becoming engulfed. The old Norman bridge which stood at the north-west corner of Renshaw Wood was, at that period, the only available crossing-place.

We make this statement so that the reader can understand the death trap awaiting the Lancastrians if the battle proved disastrous to their cause. The reader must also remember that the present good road from Towton to Tadcaster was not in existence until three centuries later. The old Norman track turned sharply to the left at Towton town end, passed down the precipitous slope on the north side of Renshaw Wood to Cock Bridge, climbed the opposite ridge, and thence along the west side of Stutton into Tadcaster; such was the ground the beaten army had to retreat by, exhausted. When broken all along the line, they turned and fled down the slippery bank into that sullen water-way of ignoble death: as we have already observed, it was a day of storm *

RENSHAW WOODSIDE.

With deep pathos, one old writer tells that "All the while it snew," presenting a conflicting element to fierce passions, burning in the hearts of the victors, to kill, without mercy or distinction, every fugitive in their path. The awful carnage which took place in the valley on this day will never be forgotten. The numbers who fell here, on the side of the Lancastrians, were, perhaps, equal to those who fell on the field of battle, with their faces to the foe.

* "So many of them fell into the Cock, as quite filled it up, and the Yorkists went over their backs in pursuit of their brethren . . . over thirty-six thousand English men here fell a sacrifice for their fathers' transgressions; and the wounds of which they died, being made by arrows, battleaxes, pike, and sword, would bleed profusely."

"Men alyve pass'd the ryuer uppn deade carcasses, and that the greate ryuer of Wharfe, the greate sewer of all the water coming from Towton, was coloured with blood."

We need feel no surprise concerning the scarcity of relics connected with this battle (found in late years), considering the lapse of time and the nature of the ground on which the main issue of the battle was contested. It was March, the vegetation of the past year on the moor had assimilated with the earth, to make way for the return of spring. Thus the land would be nearly bare of undergrowth, and, doubtless, the greater part of the weapons would be easily found and removed by the victors, and the inhabitants of the villages around, following in their wake, gleaned up most of the remainder, which, during the course of centuries, if not even used again, would be dispersed hither and thither to different parts of the empire; apart from which, antiquaries have been continually calling on the farm men and cotters, and purchasing for a trifle any relic of the battle worth removing. To-day, few weapons, we should say, remain hidden in the soil of the actual battlefield. Middle-aged and elderly men will speak of finding the barbed end of a rusty arrow, the head of axe and pike, or handle of a broken sword, etc.; and one John Hargreaves relates that he has, on different occasions, found barbed arrows in a field known locally as "Nor Acres" (now historic), but the farm men always hark back to the days of their fathers, or even grandfathers, when reporting to us the more important finds.

It may seem strange, yet there is not a single stone or monument (with the exception of Lord Dacre's, in Saxton churchyard), to mark the places where the vast army of dead warriors (thirty-eight thousand) lay in their last long sleep.*

Leland records that "Five pittes yet appearing half a mile by north Saxton fields." The same antiquary also records that a Mr. Hungate, of Saxton, collected a great number of bones, and caused them to be buried in Saxton churchyard; and here the late sexton related to the writer that all along the north side of the church, from Lord Dacre's tomb to the tower, was a vast receptacle of bones of the slain, brought hither from the field of battle.

* In the hedgerow, about four paces from the highway leading from Saxton to Towton, and a little east of the quarries, there is to be seen a stone cross, which may have been placed to mark the site of a grave, or the spot where a noble fell. It is known as Lord Dacre's Cross, and possibly it is a relic of the Chapel at Towton, which Richard III. began to build, but which was never finished, and has now totally disappeared.

In the ings, between the site of May-den (May-dene) Castle and Lead Mill, are three mounds, having the appearance of tumuli, two of which have evidently been disturbed, and we were told a broken sword was found just below the surface of one. On the opposite side of the vale from the north-west corner of Renshaw Wood, is a long mound, bearing the impression of a huge grave. In the field where tradition avers still grow the red and white roses, several graves were formerly to be distinctly traced; now, faintly. Another huge tumulus, thirty-two yards in length by nineteen in width, was formerly to be seen in the field still known as the "graves."

The peculiar variety of wild white rose, tinged (not streaked) with red, formerly plentiful on the battlefield, has been cut and uprooted until now it is very scarce. There was formerly a large bed in the field known as Towtondale, or bloody vale; here a farmer told the

[E. Bogg,
LORD DACRE'S TOMB, SAXTON CHURCHYARD.

writer that he netted the bed of some thirty yards square, and made it into a sheepfold, which was the means of destroying the plants. The country people attribute the rich red tinge of the roses to the soil being impregnated with blood at that fatal fight. Botanically speaking, Dr. Arnold Lees informs me this cannot be the case. The 'field,' being glacial drift over limestone, is rich in species of wild flowers, four different kinds of roses growing there. The white York rose, a spiny neat-leaved plant, is always creamy-hned. The common dog-rose, the Lancastrian, is a blush pink, more or less deep. The field rose is also white, not very prickly, and easily destroyed; it has been found with the petals streaked with pink—probably from hybridization—but very rarely. Blood in soil could not cause it until the iron in it had been oxidized. The primrose, however, has been changed into the mauve and red polyanth of the garden by an ironized and blood manure. Iron in solution is a poison to most plants, but in minute quantity, like "pink pills for pale people," it will deepen the colour of tissues. The soil on Towton is, doubtless, very complex, and wild flowers flourish wonderfully hereabouts.

> "There still wild roses growing,
> Frail tokens of the fray,
> And the hedgerow green bears witness
> Of Towton field that day."

Far and wide, across highland and lowland, in mud-built cabin or baronial hall, in simple chapel or stately minster, lowly village or thriving city, were to be heard the wailing of sorrow, the continual pealing of muffled bells, and the long, weary vigils of the bereaved widow and the fatherless, the mournful sound of the requiem sung for the repose of the souls of the slain.

Litanies for the departed, sobbing sounds in broken accents, filled the sacred fane! Priests were hired with land and treasure for unceasing intercessory prayer; candles on the altars burn, and clouds of incense veil the Holy Pix, as the sobbing prayers rise from hearts torn with anguish, for the brave hearts that late beat in youthful breast and hoary sire. "Out of the depth of our grief we cry unto Thee! from the morning watch even until night! *Miserere nostri Domine*. May they rest in peace."

From the name of the great battle Towton is known the wide world over. The place is not mentioned in the Domesday Book.

On the parcelling out of land by the Norman, Towton fell into the family of the Pictavenses, or Pavtefius, lords of Headingley, who were afterwards great patrons to the monks of Kirkstall. Early in the thirteenth century it came into the possession of Robert Berkin and Alice, his wife; to the latter, as reasonable dower from her former husband, one Robert Paytefin. Late in the thirteenth century the manor passed into the possession of the Stophams, of Weston.

In 1310, Sir William Stopham was ordered to muster his followers at Berwick-on-Tweed for service against the Scots, and in 1316, besides his other possessions, this knight was certified as Lord of the township of

Baildon. His daughter and heiress married Sir John Vavasour, and the name of Stópham ended. A further account of this family will be found in Vol. II. of this work. Towton thence passed to the powerful family of Roos or Ros, and from them to the knightly family of Melton of Aston, representatives of Archbishop Melton. The last of the Meltons who held

THE DACRES TOMB, LANERCOST PRIORY. [*E. Bogg.*

Towton was John, who died in 1544, when George D'Arcy and the Lady Dorothy, his wife, daughter and heiress of John Melton, obtained possession. For his bravery at the siege of Tournay, George received the distinctive mark of knighthood, and after the delinquency of Thomas, Lord D'Arcy, his father, was restored in blood with the dignity of Baron D'Arcy to himself and his heirs male.

Towton is on the eastern fringe of the Elmet district; it stands on the edge of the high ridge of land, from whence the ground shelves rapidly down into the fenland of the Vale of York.

The village consists of one single street, through which runs the London and Edinburgh highway; there is not anything of more than passing interest, the scenery around is finely diversified, and far-reaching views to the east can be obtained. In a field behind the hall is a site known

THE OLD KINGDOM OF ELMET. 191

as Chapel Garth ; nothing remains, but the foundations of a chapel have from time to time been found. On a part of the field "most remote from Saxton," a great chapel was intended to have been built by Richard III., "in token of praier, and for the souls of the men slain at Palme Sunday Field." Stowe says that "Towton, village is a mile from Saxton, where a great chapelle was

LORD DACRE'S CROSS, IN THE HEDGEROW (NEAR TO THE FIELD KNOWN AS 'THE GRAVES'), TOWTON.

begun by Richard III., but not finished, in which chapelle were buried also many of the men slain at Palm Sunday Fielde."

Nearly a mile south-west of the battlefield, in a gentle hollow, through which flows a wimpling stream, rests the village of Saxton, which, like Towton, is part of the honour of Pontefract. Saxton was granted by Alice de Laci to her handmaiden, Margaret de Kirkton. When Henry de Laci, Alice's son and Earl of Lincoln, was lord of the honour, Saxton was in the possession of Sir Roger de Saxton, who founded a chapel there in 1292, dedicated to St. Mary.

The parish church is dedicated to All Saints', and in the reign of Edward III. belonged to the hospital of St. Leonard of York. The chancel arch is late Norman; there are also two ancient windows. On the walls and floor of the chancel are many memorials to the Hungate family, of whom one, William Hungate, founded the grammar school at Sherburn, and did many other benevolent things; the last one reads:

"INTERRED THE BODY OF SIR CHARLES HUNGATE,
OF HUDLESTON HALL, BR.,
THE LAST MALE HEIR
OF THAT ANTIENT FAMILY, NOV. 6TH, 1749,
AGED 63."

At the latter end of the fifteenth century the estates of the ancient family of St. Ley, or generally Sallay, fell into the hands of William Hungate, through his marriage with Olive, daughter of William Sallay, the last male representative of a house which had been settled at Saxton for several centuries.

William Hungate was the son of William Hungate, of Borneby; his marriage is likely to have occurred not long after the battle of Towton, for Leland tells that it was he who gathered together the bodies of the slain and caused them to be buried in Saxton churchyard. William Hungate died about the accession of Henry VIII., in the first year of whose reign, William Hungate, the son, paid relief for his lands and succeeded thereto. This second William married Alice, daughter of Sir Thomas Gower, of Stitenham, illustrious as of the family of the eminent poet, "the morall Gower," to whom Chaucer dedicated his "Troilus and Cressida." From this period the family of the Hungates rose in reputation and wealth, allying itself with its neighbours, the Vavasours of Hazelwood, of the first rank of the feudal nobility. William Hungate seems to have passed an uneventful life. By his will, dated June 26th, 1547, proved April 19th, 1548, he orders his body to be buried in Saxton church. He was succeeded by his son William Hungate, who married Andria, daughter of John Saltmarshe, Esq., of Saltmarshe. The line of the Hungates terminated in 1710 by the death of Sir Francis Hungate, Bart., who is buried at Saxton.

Some twenty-six years ago Saxton Church was restored, when many memorials were destroyed or lost. Under the pulpit are the tombs of the Hammonds and Widdringtons, date 1671—one requests, "Gentill reeders and hearers hereof of ye charatie pray ffor ye soule of Anthony Hamond, Esquier, who departed oute of this missarable worlde ye ii^o of August, in ye yere of our Lorde God, MCCCCCLXIII, and lieth buride under this stone, whose soule it may please God to p'don."

Teresa Sempson, who died about forty years ago, at a great age, was the last female who did penance in this church; with a white sheet thrown over her shoulders, she silently walked the aisle during part of the service, as a punishment for her misdeeds. Near to the porch is a stone with the following quaint inscription :—

HERE LYETH THE BODY OF RICHARD
FLETCHER, WHO DEPARTED THIS LIFE
YE 8TH OF APRIL, 1739, AGED 63 YRS.,
WHO LEFT THE USE OF TEN POU^D TO YE WIDOWS OF SAXTON.

On the north side, in the God's-acre, is the tomb to the memory of Lord Dacre, who fell on the adjoining battlefield.* Along the whole length of the north side, some few feet below the surface, are immense quantities of bones, supposed to be part of the slain from the battlefield. The late sexton told the writer that he had seen them when digging some years ago, several feet in thickness. It is now understood that this part of the burial ground remains undisturbed.

In the meadows east of the church are distinct traces of an encampment, near to which, in the midst of a fine park, stood the mansion of the Sallays, and later of the Hungates, surrounded by many large trees. Their crest is

A PEEP OF SAXTON, FROM DINTINGDALE.

still to be seen over the front of the manor-house. In the adjoining field, west of this house, and near to the village street, is an eminence, enclosed by a double trench; whether raised by Saxon, Dane, or Norman we know not; but we should imagine, from the many signs left on the surface of the earth, that a great struggle took place on this spot centuries before the fatal fight

* Local tradition says that Lord Dacre and his charger were interred in one grave, which may account for the skull of a horse being found when the tomb was restored, a few years ago. Lord Dacre's skeleton was found in an upright position.

on Towton heath. Saxton, apart from its association with the great battlefield, around which memory mournfully lingers, is a pleasant and rural village, where many signs of the 'Merrie England' of old remain.

During the sixteenth and seventeenth centuries the Hungates were nearly always involved in continual trouble and in lawsuits with their neighbours. The line of this ancient family ended in the death of Sir Charles Hungate, 1749, and by the marriage of Mary, daughter of Sir Francis Hungate, to Sir Edward Gascoigne, the estates of the Hungates came into the hands of the Gascoignes. There appears to have been another branch of the Hungates, between whom and the Gascoignes a trial took place in 1833. The Register Book at Saxton says:—

"In chancery, 19th April, 1833, between William Hungate, otherwise Wm. Anning Hungate, complainant, and Richard Oliver Gascoigne, Thomas Oliver Gascoigne, and Richard Oliver Gascoigne the younger, defendants. At the execution of a commission for the examination of witnesses in the cause, this book was produced and shewn to the Rev. John Carter, a witness sworn and examined, and by him deposed unto at the time of his examination on behalf of the defendants. Signed, Thomas W. Totty, G. S. Rowles, Robert Spencer, R. Bailley."

This William Anning Hungate was a lieutenant in the Royal Navy, and in great favour with William IV.; for him, however, the trial was of little avail: the Gascoignes still possess the estate. Many years ago the late sexton (with almost melancholy sadness) told the writer of the visits made by this branch of the Hungates to Saxton, telling how, in his younger days, both he and his father visited the church in the company of this Hungate claimant, and how reverently the latter examined the tombs and registers of his family, and also inquired about certain relics that were then missing, etc., requesting them, if possible, to restore the same, as the Hungates would be returning to claim their lost heritage. A dream of his never to be realized! possession is nine points of the law.

The Hungates were staunch Roman Catholics, and many of their kin appear in the list of Recusants compiled in 1604. Among the latter is the following account of a secret marriage

"Richard Chomley, Esquier, maryed with Mary Hungate (a daughter of William Hungate, of Saxton), in the presence of John Wilson, William Martin, Huge Hope, and Christopher Danyell, in a 'fell' with a Popish priest."

A 'fell' is not only a mountain side, but, in archaic early English language, meant any uninclosed place in the open air, secluded, but without many trees.

The record of this marriage is most interesting. The lovers dare not marry in the hall of the Hungates at Saxton, for fear of spies, so an arrangement with a priest and witnesses is made to meet at some solitary and secluded spot, where the marriage ceremony is performed and the wedding party scatter and return home without discovery. Such scenes would be common during the period of Roman Catholic persecution in England, showing the oppression and bigotry the Catholics of this age were the subjects of.

Anent the adjoining battlefield, there are many side-lights and touches of oral tradition, handed down from sire to son. It is told how

[F. Dean.

SHERBURN, FROM THE NORTH.

Lord Clifford, nicknamed "the butcher," was slain by a headless arrow in Dintingdale, some few hundred yards east of Saxton Church, and the spot where the "bur-tree-bush" stood in "Nor acres," from whence the lad shot Lord Dacre, can still be pointed out. This is about the centre of the battle-field, where the brunt of the fighting took place: how the boy could hide in the midst of sixty thousand men in the fierce struggle of war is more than we can understand. One hears, too, of a vast white sheet of snow that fell unceasingly all through that fatal day, and how both morn and evensong were over at Saxton Church before the worshippers were aware that the fight had taken place—

> "Palm Sunday chines were chining
> All gladsome through the air,
> And village churls and maidens
> Knelt in the church at prayer."

An utter impossibility—the noisy fiend of war would only be too palpable to the terror-stricken villagers, all through Saturday night and Sunday, to even admit of any service being held.

Dintingdale, east of Saxton, down which a little brook meanders towards Scarthingdale, is interesting from the skirmish which took place in it on the eve of the battle. From hence, by fieldpath and hedgerow, pranked with wild flowers, we pass to Sherburn,—its church showing out prominently in the landscape before us. In our way there is much to interest. From the moor, now enclosed, we drop into a deep valley, which in olden time cut off access to Saxton from Sherburn, and thence following the footpath over the green pastures, we climb up the steep ascent to the church.

CHAPTER IX.

ROUND ABOUT SHERBURN-IN-ELMET,

NAMED from the shire-burn, was the capital of the eastern frontier of the kingdom of Elmet: a division, the edge or boundary of a kingdom, the eastern limit of Elmet Setna, the last fringe of inhabitable land on this side. The region beyond, to the north and east, was interminable marsh, forest, and 'fell'—a wilderness, wild and desolate, the silence broken only by the howl of wild beasts, and the cry and flight of innumerable birds, among which were the long-lost bustard and thick-knee plover, on the drier land, and the 'hollow-sounding butter bump,' or bittern, among the reed beds.

Sherburn, doubtless, registers a Christianity dating back to Celtic time. Here was a church previous to Athelstan's reign, and a list of the "Utensilia," date about 900, still extant, mentions a peal of six bells and four hanging bells. Nearly every vestige of this church has disappeared, and so has King Athelstan's palace, later the Archbishop's. The site, however, is to be seen on the north slope of the hill, with part of the moat which enclosed it on the west and north.

In celebration of the victory at Brunanburgh, Athelstan presented the house to the see of York, as a thank-offering to the Almighty for his great victory; and as a palace of the Archbishop's it remained for over three hundred years. The Archbishop held his court at Sherburn, and the knights of the barony did their service until about the middle of the fourteenth century, when Cawood, having become more suitable for a residence of the Archbishop, the palace at Sherburn was dismantled and the material dispersed.

After the disaster to the English, at Myton, the Scots raided Wharfe dale, causing fearful havoc and loss to the inhabitants. Amongst other places they destroyed were the manors of Ripon, Otley, and Sherburn. During this shameful state of things, when the government of the kingdom suddenly fell into a strange state of impotency, a few daring spirits relieved this monotony of wretchedness: Robert de Ryther and John de Vavasour were distinguished for their great zeal and activity. It was one of the Vavasours, with the assistance of Henry de Scargill and others, in 1322, harried Parlington—"turned out the king's favourite, Hugh le Despencer, le pere, and pulled his house down about his ears." Soon after the disaster at Myton, the Archbishop, in a letter dated at Cawood, writes to the rural Dean of Sherburn that, whereas many of his tenants had been slain in the battle, the Dean was to take care and have their effects properly administered to.

Since those stirring scenes enacted during the Civil Wars, Sherburn has settled down into a quiet, regular state of·existence. Once the capital of the surrounding district, it takes a pride in the evidences of its vanished importance, former homes of kings and princes still remaining within its bounds to testify to its passed greatness.

The town is a most interesting study. In the grandeur and massive proportions of the Norman Church, and the emblazoned scroll, telling of knightly fame and glory, decorating its west window, the historian and antiquary can each find inspiration and delight; and the diversity of its landscape views, the sweetness of its orchards, hedgerows, and pasture land, the rusticity of its winding lanes, the charming outlook over the Fenland, stretching from its doors to the Wolds, are so combined as to give those in quest of health and pleasure ample reward for their visit. The towers and spires of minster, abbey, and church appearing in the middle distance, with the smiling cornfields and meadows we now gaze over, is the reward of many centuries of toil by the descendants of the Angle and wild Norseman, who steered their galleys up the tawny waters of the Ouse and its tributaries, and made their settlements on the banks thereof. 'A History of England' in little, the Sherburn domain happily epitomizes.

As a structure, the church of All Saints, in which the works of at least eight bygone centuries survive, is a type of superior dignity and imperishable endurance. Within its now existing walls the voice of Aldred, the last Archbishop of the Saxon race, and also the first Archbishop of the Norman regime, has resounded, and we need not doubt that the men who looked the haughty Norman in the face as the battle raged at

Senlac (when the noble patrimony was wrested by William from the ill-fated Harold) knelt in prayer for the success of their king and the safety of their wives and little ones on the same spot as the wives and little ones kneel in prayer to-day. Here, within the old church at Sherburn, has been witnessed the consummation of the highest ambition of chivalric enterprise, and all the pomp and circumstance attending the great victory of Athelstan at Brunanburgh. Here, during the prosecution of the Papists, lights, we

SHERBURN CHURCH.

are told, were oft seen burning on the high altar, during the silence and solitude of night. Hither came the Hungates and others to worship in secret; how they obtained admission was beyond the knowledge of human ken, yet tradition mysteriously whispered of certain underground passages which led from their halls hither.

Within the precincts of this sacred edifice, in the year 1321, a most memorable incident in English history took place; foregone events demanded the private conclave, the outcome of troublous times and the misgovernment of Edward II. Weak and vacillating, the very antithesis of his father, whose advice and memory he so disregarded by recalling Piers Gaveston and making a prime favourite of him whom the great king had exiled, and who, just previous to his death, had exacted from his son a solemn oath that he should never be allowed to set foot in England again. Neither before nor since that convocation of churchmen and barons on that momentous midsummer Sunday, have the streets of Sherburn resounded to such a tramp as was heard in the old *ville* on that day. The Archbishop, the Bishops of Durham and Carlisle, and the Abbots from near and far, the Earls of Lancaster and Hereford, many Barons, Baronets, and Knights, with their attendants, assembled in the church of Sherburn-in-Elmet. To this assembly Sir John de Bek, a belted knight, read out the Articles Lancaster and his adherents intended to insist upon. The first one struck especially at the evil counsels of the less worthy ministers of the king, the Chancellor, the Justicier (who ought to be constituted by election), the misrule of the king's favourites, the younger and elder Hugh le Despenser, " who are the main causes of the new evils and oppressions by which the people are excessively aggravated."

Thus we see the meeting was one advocating the most radical reform; its bold and trenchant demands, however, took the prelates by surprise, they could not answer instantly and requested a short adjournment. This being agreed to, copies of the Articles were supplied and they retired "to the manse of the rector" (probably the old palace). The result of their deliberations was futile, as after events testified, still the convocation was a starting point in history, its Principle more popular government and Justice to the people, which only came to pass in after generations.

What an impressive scene this great gathering of churchmen (men of peace) and mailed warriors must have been! But there was treason in the camp. The headsman's axe soon became busy. Fearful tragedies, now in Time's dim distance, flit before our mental view. The shadowy figures of Lancaster, Harcla, and other great men, headless, are seen passing from the block. Never since the Conquest had the scaffold been deluged with such torrents of noble English blood. Ever so in working out the charter and freedom of a great nation such things must be witnessed.

The church at Sherburn is capable of teaching this most powerful lesson; while time after time the old order has given place to the new, this church has remained true to its purpose, and is capable of remaining so for centuries to come. It has undergone many alterations and repairs, and was restored in 1857, but not with that judicious reverence and care for the work of past

NORMAN NAVE, SHERBURN CHURCH.
[G. F. Jones.

masters the architect ought to have taken, which is much to be deplored, especially in the restoration of the chancel. Previous to the Reformation this church must have been architecturally a priceless work of art. An undying care for the fabric of their churches was ever the virtue of the great body of the Romish priesthood. Would that we could say the same of their successors when the grand old parish churches came under their control.

The church consisted of nave, notable for massiveness and grand simplicity, two aisles, formerly with chapels at the end of each, chancel, tower, porch, and a mortuary chapel. Whittaker attributes part of the structure to Saxon work. The tower, arches, and inner walling may be of that era, the arcading of the nave, from the height of the pillars and narrow arches, gives it somewhat this character, and seems to warrant this conclusion. The carved capitals and enriched arch mouldings are fine examples of early Norman work. The clerestory windows, of three lights, are late perpendicular, as well as the outer casing of the tower, with the large buttresses required for its support. The arch of the porch was originally transitional, with chevron moulding and shafts, now much altered by rebuilding. The west or tower window, with many fragments of rare old glass, is specially interesting to one versed in heraldry. The south aisle contains a rare Janus cross, which has rather a curious history. It was found in the ruins of a small chapel, at the south-east corner of the churchyard. This chapel was dedicated to the "Honour of St. Mary and the Holy Angels," and is said by Wheater to have been a sumptuously furnished shrine.

Less than a century ago, one of the churchwardens, a boor, with little veneration for the past, thought it would adorn the walls of his residence, but this robber of relics was not allowed by the parishioners to remove it without a protest beyond words. The feud was finally compromised by some wise Solomon of the rival parties. The cross was sawn vertically into two parts and one side awarded to each. After this wanton act of vandalism half the cross was removed to Steeton Hall, where it long adorned a niche over a doorway there. The writer has in his possession a photograph taken by G. Fowler Jones, showing half of the trophy in that position. Happily the cross has been restored to its original state, and is to be seen in the south aisle of the church and is possibly now the only relic left of the Chapel of St. Mary and the Holy Angels. The date of the cross is late fourteenth century or early fifteenth.

THE OLD KINGDOM OF ELMET. 203

The town of Sherburn contains many antique and interesting features of bygone times. In the main street is the old courthouse, and the Grammar School, built by Robert Hungate, 1656. From nearly any point the massive church tower, uprearing high above the roofs, from its prominent position, with the red and white roofed houses and varied patches of colour intervening, forms a picture of more than ordinary interest.*

The villages and hamlets surrounding Sherburn are nearly all of importance in local history of old. The heads of these families played conspicuous parts in the Court world of their time as the ruins and relics of their manor-houses still testify, and striking and very varied phases of life and vicissitudes of fortune do these manor-houses expose. Many a story, more startling than romance, might be told anent the old houses, once the resting place of kings, and the former home of minstrelsy and chivalry; their names and deeds are emblazoned on the scroll of history.

JANUS CROSS AT SHERBURN.

[G. F. Jones.

* There were several skirmishes hereabouts, during the Civil War, and history says Lord Digby was surprised and defeated in the war between the King and Parliament, at Sherburn; but the place where his coach was captured, and where the slain in the action were interred, is pointed out by tradition at Milford, about a mile distant from the Parish Church.

We will commence with the manor of Huddleston—old-time Hudereston, or Huderston. It is in the parish of Sherburn, and about one and a half miles south-west from that place, and stands in a most secluded valley. Here at the Domesday survey, dwelt one Hunchel or Huddor, a Saxon, from whence it has been said the place received its name; but 'hudr' or 'huddel' in old English meant a heap—an abundant accumulation of anything; and it is quite as likely that the place-name (like that of others about), and the Domesday dweller there, alike derived their cognomens from the fact of stone being so plentiful, and in early days so easily got at, and of such quality, that the quarries once opened have been delved into fame, as the source of many an imposing tower and pile throughout the county of broadacres, and farther afield as well. In the wood adjoining, called Huddleston Old Wood, are the remains of a double trench, and on the moor, in the direction of Newthorpe, are traces of similar entrenchments, evidently salient points in the vast system of entrenchments beginning at Barwick, and stretching hither, more or less, a distance of eight miles, guarding, in pre-Norman times, the only approach north between the Ouse and the Aire valleys.

HUDDLESTON FROM THE MOAT.

The Hunchils are supposed to have been settled here generations previous to the Conquest, but they fled before the scourge and devastation of the Conqueror, returning to their old home some time after and becoming tenants of the De Laci. This family evidently soon rose into position and dignity. About the year 1110, one Nigel de Huddleston presented lands to the monastery of Selby, and, being weary of the sinful ways of the wicked world, entered that establishment as a monk. Again, in 1296, one Sir Richard de Huddleston, by license from Dean Sewal de Bovill, had leave to attach a chapel to his manor-house, "To hear divine service, this year in my chapel, kept in my court of Hodelston, yet so that on chief feast days I am to repair to the mother church of Sherburn." Richard, the last of the male line to dwell at the hall, died here early in the fourteenth century; the estate then went by marriage to John de Melsa. A Sir John Huddleston, however, established the old name in Cumberland, where it lasted until 1774, when his estate passed by marriage of Elizabeth, his heiress, to Sir Hedworth Williams, who, in turn, sold it to the Lowthers.

HUDDLESTON QUARRY.

This family appear to have been ever brave soldiers on the battlefield; a Sir Richard Huddleston was made a knight banneret at the hands of Henry V., on the field of Agincourt; Johan de Odelstone was with Edward I. at the siege of Caerlaverock. One Ferdinand was a staunch cavalier, who took to wife Jane (daughter of Sir Ralph Grey of Chillingham), who bore him nine sons, all of whom became officers, and fought in the cause of King Charles. William, the eldest, was made a knight banneret by Charles for his gallant effort in recapturing the royal standard at the battle of Edgehill. His brother Richard, a lieutenant colonel, was slain at York during the sortie and repulse of the Roundheads, Sunday, June 17th, 1644. His body was buried in the Minster the day following.

The old hall has a wonderful chain of unbroken history stretching over a thousand years, before which it is speculative. It is now a farmhouse, and, although much altered, still retains features picturesque and quaint. The shell of the chapel, built in the thirteenth century, is still remaining, but not used for religious purposes

Huddleston is also interesting by reason of its great limestone quarry, famed for building purposes—the best and most durable in Yorkshire—whence the great use of this stone in the construction of cathedrals, castles, and the surrounding churches and manor-houses. Thoresby says: "The quarry at Huddleston is also a delicate stone and has this peculiarity in it, that when the stone is new dug out it is so soft that it may be cut or wrought with a knife, but afterwards hardens by exposure to the air, the colour is also pure white, so that not only chimney pieces, but monuments in churches are made; it is little inferior to marble." The antiquary's description is to the point, Huddleston quarries (Celtic: *ceraig*, rock) can easily be detected by their hardness and silvery whiteness. Tradition reports that Bishop Dyke, reaching from Sherburn to Cawood, was made deeper and wider and its course cut straight by the Archbishops, so that stone from this quarry might be floated down on rafts to Cawood and from thence by boat to York. In 1358 the Dean and Chapter of York took 'Huddleston delph' on a lease for a period of eighty years and afterwards for another period of nineteen years. This quarry is said to have been known and used by the Romans.

One and a half miles south-east of this place, by the path leading over waste (of old a wild forest region), is Newthorpe (Norse—the new settlement). It lies between Milford and Micklefield, about a mile from the latter. Here, whilst removing surface 'bearings' in 1881, trenches running east and west, and north and south, and V-shaped, about six feet deep, were discovered, the outer belt of earthwork having been thrown up round the crest of the hill; these trenches were probably part of the same system as those already mentioned as existing in Huddleston old wood beyond. Near the trench was found the upper half of a hand millstone. Newthorpe, standing on the edge of a small vale, is a most primitive spot. From hence we pass to Steeton, one and a half miles away; the land, as we go, gradually changing from limestone to sandstone, is gently undulating, and though all is now enclosed some part of the surface still bears signs of its primitive wildness.

STEETON HALL.

Steeton stands on a plateau rising from a small valley which runs down to Milford. From evidences still remaining it has been a fair and stately structure in the 'brave days of old.' It is now a farmhouse, and a mere cantle of its former size.

Under a grey massive specimen of a Gothic gateway, early fifteenth century, we pass into the courtyard to the house—a centre and one wing alone remaining, and this only a confused jumble. The interior contains a huge fireplace, and in the wall of what is now used as a dining room is a piscina, suggesting this part of the house to have been the chapel built by the "Wilghbys" early in the thirteenth century. From the above family Steeton came into the hands of the Reygates, and from them by marriage to the Foljambes. The chapel formerly at the end of the south aisle in Sherburn Church, belonging to this family, was known as the Steeton Chapel.

[G. Fowler Jones.
GATEWAY, STEETON HALL.

On the outer wall of the dining room, or supposed chapel, of the 'Hall' farm runs a tabular corbelled course, on which are a number of old shields and sculptured crests. The one most prominent, in the centre, seems to represent the Paschal Lamb, and is known, locally, as the "Steeton Rackett" (or Reckitt), connecting a ghost story to the hall, which has been repeated from father to son for generations.

The story of the Reckett or Reckling—the smallest or weakest of a brood, be it lamb, kitten, or whelp, in the folk-speech of the north —is variously described: one version reports that it was brought hither from the quarry, during the building of the Hall, with the last load of stones; and its effigy, to be seen on the corbelled table, and known as the "Steeton Rackett," is thought to be the outward and visible sign of its having actually existed, now doomed for ever to wander around the Hall for good or evil. This uncanny sprite is of a peaceable nature except when interfered with; then its rage is noisy and fearsome; whence we say, to kick up a 'racket.'

STEETON HALL, SHEWING FORMER POSITION OF HALF OF JANUS CROSS. [*G. Fowler Jones.*]

Black spleenwort—a fern, nowhere else to be found in such quantity within twelve miles of Leeds—is to be found flourishing on the interior walls, and also on the wall of an outbuilding. Originally, there were four gateway towers—one on each side of the walled square surrounding the house. Foundations of these outer walls are in many places to be traced, enclosing a goodly plot of land. In its palmy days, it has, indeed, been a fair and stately structure, with its battlemented walls and towers.

Standing before the old gateway, imagination can easily picture the events and fill in the shadows of other days. The old tower is now the sole survivor of the pomp and pageantry which in mediæval times passed through its portal.

A mile or so over the fields rests, peacefully slumbering, the hamlet of Lumby, picturesque with its old nooks and corners, farm buildings, ivy-clad walls and thatched cots.

To the east, crossing the great North Road, Monk Fryston is soon reached, a village with many picturesque features and touches of old-worldism; it is, however, outside our limit, so we return by way of Milford, a place of Angle origin—" The ford at the mill." It possesses no distinct characteristic feature. The Domesday record says:

"In Mileforde (Milford) Ulfstan had two carucates of land to be taxed, where there may be one plough. Turften now has it of Ilbert. There are there four villanes and five bordars, but they do not plough. Value in King Edward's tine ten shillings, now ten shillings."

Like Sherburn it lay right in the track of the Conqueror when on his work of retribution and revenge, but at neither place do we find the ominous words "it is waste" appended to the record.

Here we obtain a proof of William's clemency to Archbishop Aldred, or "Ealdred," the man from whose hands he had received the crown of England at Westminster, and who at that ceremonial exacted from the king a solemn promise to protect his Saxon subjects, which doubtless in good faith he intended to do had not circumstances altered the tenor of his resolution.

From the south side, looking over the roofs of the village, with its admixture of orchard, garden, and old farmsteads (some of the latter still retaining the quaint thatched outbuildings), the place is very interesting and suggestive of olden time. We take a glance at Bondbridge Farm with its antique kraal-like outbuildings. Just beyond is the little double-arched stone bridge marking the division of the two parishes, South Milford and Sherburn. Here in the pool the ducks and geese disport, and the little glen down which the stream flows is very delightful.

Just over the meadow, on the north side of the brook, is the old water-mill; though much nearer Milford it is in the parish of Sherburn. How poetical the spot appears as one lingers in the sombre twilight, listening to the plash of falling water, and watching the shadows deepen around the ancient mill.

Following a branch of the great North Road from Milford through the long street of Sherburn, past the 'Red Bear' (reminiscent of coaching days), a mile or so from the latter place we reach Barkston. Barkston Ash is the head of a Wapentake of nearly one hundred thousand acres.

"In Barcheston (Barkston) Saxulf had one carucate of land to be taxed. Land to half a plough. Ilbert has now there one soken au with one plough. Value in King Edward's time, ten shillings; the same now."

There is not much of importance architecturally in the place. A stranger might find much to interest and charm around the farm buildings of an earlier age; yet it is a focus of vast antiquity. The ash tree—the trysting spot of olden time—is not of great growth or age, but it forms a visible evidence and link, and is the successor of a patriarch which once flourished on the same

BARKSTON ASH.

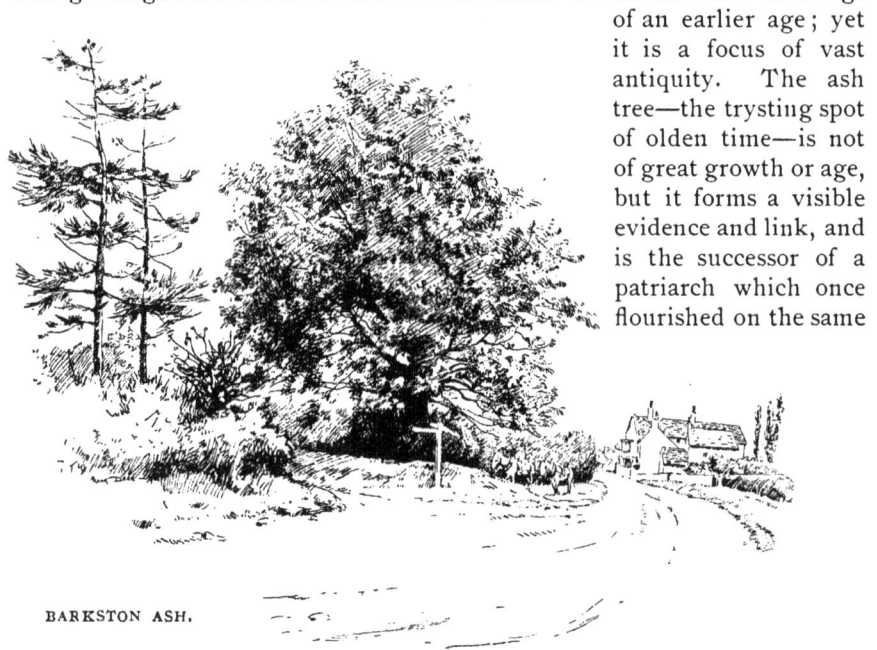

spot, pointing to institutions and customs belonging to the far past. The hamlet gave its name to a knightly family, the De Barkeston, who held lands here for four centuries, but who have been long extinct.

Scarthingwell Hall adjoins Barkeston. The mansion stands in the centre of a beautiful park, well timbered and adorned with stretches of water, grassy dell and woodland glade. It is a natural aviary for birds, amongst which are to be seen a few rare visitants.

From the higher ground beyond, the outlook over the Fen district, when light and shadow play across the wide expanse, is ever changing—now a flickering sunbeam, then shade. A soft, diffused silver-grey hue, like a shimmering veil, at times shrouds the landscape. Through this film a church or abbey tower looms strongly, or a glimmer of sunlight locates the red-tiled roofs of a fen village, and in the middle distance the Minster towers of York reveal the position of the old city.

Not a little of the history of Lower Wharfedale has been moulded by the extent of its flat lands and vast water patches. For instance, if we glance at the great military position of Barwick, we find the chief obstacle which contributed mainly to its strength was the several reaches of river and fen which nearly surrounded it in the past, the retreat and refuge of the vanquished Celt. The forcing of the swampy line of the River Cock at Aberford was a work of no small difficulty to the Roman, and the natural strength of the position defended is still very obvious. The same difficulty occurred later to the Angles and Normans, but not to the Norsemen and Danes for they were 'shipmen'; a life on the water was theirs by nature, to them the surging of the sea was like the sweetest music, and they found a convenient passage for their keels along the River Ouse and its tributaries. Thus they gained a foothold into the fenland and river valleys and turned the flank of the position where preceding invaders had been brought to a halt. Hence it is from the swamps of the Don to York we find Norse names indicating the majority of settlements, and from the mouth of the Wharfe westward and northward we find such names predominating.

Men of fourscore years tell us how greatly the flats have changed since their youth, vast reaches of swamp and uncultivated land existed between Ryther, Ulleskelf, Fenton, and Sherburn, tenanted by flocks of wild fowl. It is now nearly all reclaimed and the farmer seems to be a fairly prosperous individual hereabouts.

A thousand or twelve hundred years ago the state of the fenland, between the course of the lower Aire and Wharfe, was strangely different. There hung a wilderness, wild, lonesome, and desolate, darkened by fog and rolling mist, through which the rivers sullenly crept; even at this time in winter the long stretches of lowland wears an uninteresting and gloomy aspect. The Romans had done something in their day by dyke and drain to improve the state of things, and one Roman relates about a curious and strange people who dwelt in the fens partly swimming and partly wading. Another historian tells how vast flocks of wild fowl nearly darkened the fens; here congregated swans, herons, storks, geese, bitterns, curlews, snipe, ruffs, plovers, godwits, moor buzzards, water crakes and coots, widgeon, teal, sheldrake, pintailed duck, and a host of other birds, many of which have now become extinct or disappeared on the breaking up of the land.

Church, or Kirk, Fenton, about one and a half miles from Barkston, in pre-railway days lay fairly off the beaten track; to-day it is connected with the busy centres by a good train service.

On every hand, in our walk, we note the evidence of a vast amount of labour performed by yeomen in reclaiming the land. The chartulary of the priory of Helaugh, to which a large portion of the lands of Fenton were given, throws some light on the early history of this place. It was late in the thirteenth century before very much reclamation had taken place, and the church then was very incomplete. About that time Nicholas de Percy, of Fenton, when William, the chaplain, was vicar, gave a rent of one penny out of a toft to find a light to burn before the image of the Blessed Virgin; perhaps there seems no great splendour in such a gift, nor can we ascribe a very high development to the Fenton of that day. The place from which the rent was derived is, however, interesting. It is the homestead of William, son of Gamel, at Biggan, a township which in after years the Canons of

FENTON CHURCH FROM THE NORTH. *F. Bogg.*

Helaugh always speak of as "New Biggying." The land about the church was called the "Aldfeld" (Oldfield), and there the parson was located, dwelling about the "head landis." We find such names as a John de Brunne, a Robert de Wextow, Henry de Huk, and a Robert Golyff, etc.

Seen from many points the church makes a striking feature in the Fen landscape. Originally a Norman church, it has been added to and considerably altered from time to time, and its architecture is thus varied from transitional to decorated and perpendicular. It consists of nave, one aisle,

FENTON CHURCH FROM THE SOUTH.

transepts, chancel, and square tower in the centre resting on four massive early English columns. The lancet windows and transitional arches are noticeable features. In the floor of the chapel, south transept, there were found, at the last restoration, two stone coffins, one containing the bones of an adult, and the other the remains of a child. The walls of this transept contain an ogee canopied recess, which formerly held the effigy of a lady, now to be seen on the chancel floor; the costume is that of late fourteenth century, the symbolical device at her feet represents a lion and some foul fiend in deadly combat; and here also are two altar slabs bearing the five crosses, and also an early English piscina. One relic denotes the existence of a Norman church, the bowl of the original font resting on the sill of the window at the west end.

Fenton forms a most interesting study; around it linger curious survivals, and primitive ideas and customs still tenaciously cling to it. The rustic porch covered with woodbine, red brick walls, tiled roofs of the same hue resting amidst green surroundings—the footpaths over meadow and cornfield, over which the lark floods the air with melody, and wild flowers grow, the undisturbed antiquity and beauty around the churchyard. Only a small remnant of what has been the village green, locally the "green hill," on slightly rising ground, remains.

A portion of what appears to have been a market cross is still left standing in the centre of the former market-place*; on the opposite side of the street of old stood a substantial hall (in the Subsidy Roll taken 1379 there is mention of one Isabella, at ye Halle, by this we obtain evidence of the existence of the house at that early date); about half of the moat which enclosed a large plot of land, in which the house stood, still exists, to the south of which the fenland for some distance is still known locally as the 'oad pake' (park). During the demolition of the old house a piscina and other relics were discovered in the walls, the latter were of extraordinary thickness. A few other antique features, a font, etc., are in the garden, and the above, with the remains of the moat, are the only mementoes of the old hall.

Around the aged walls of the farm adjoining the churchyard, lingers all that peculiar charm and old-time peacefulness and rusticity; the duck pond is a survival of the moat which formerly surrounded it. Here the ducks and geese disport, birds sing in the trees and hedgerows, the turkey-cock (whose name—Turk—is no misnomer) gabbles defiantly at our intrusion, a swarm of crows wheel and circle high above the roofs and weather-beaten tower, even the implements, strewn about in random confusion amongst the nettles and other weeds, are all characteristic of old time.

Vine Cottage, situated at the east end of straggling Fenton, is another interesting and picturesque feature: a rough-hewn timbered structure, retaining its thatched roof, overhanging eaves, and leaded-paned windows. The grape, from whence it receives its name, ripens under its eaves; trailing plants, fruiting ivy, woodbine, and old English flowers, cling tenaciously about the crevices of its walls. In springtime, when sunlight gilds and shadows flicker, birds trill their sweetest lays, and flowers shed delicious fragrance, 'tis, indeed, a charming old-world picture. The structure has undergone slight alterations; the original building dates from Tudor

* There appears to be no account of a market held here.

days, evidences of a moat which, in the past, surrounded it can still be traced. The interior, with ingle nook, and primitive posts, beams, and joists, is replete with age and imagery; every object the eye rests upon, in the farmstead and large orchard adjoining, is full of rustic beauty and old-world sleepiness. The weather-beaten gnarled trees, twisting hedgerows, and the obsolete farm domestic utensils, thrown carelessly into such picturesque grouping, are all pregnant with an odour of the past; apart from which is that sweet commingling of vocal sound from bird and fowl, arousing pleasant reminiscences of other homesteads and days gone by.

A mile or so south-east of Church Fenton is Little Fenton, a small hamlet; Hall Garth, a moated site, is, perhaps, the only remaining vestige here of other days. The village folk say there are ghosts still existing hereabouts: at the house yonder in the fields some unearthly visitant, whose spirit cannot rest, wanders in the lonely hours between night and morning; uncanny noises are heard, pots are at times banged about, doors flung open, and window blinds unwind without visible aid, mysteriously—so the credulous womenfolk assert and firmly believe.

VINE COTTAGE, CHURCH FENTON.

Onward, through fen and dyke-land, down wide green lanes, shut in by deep ditches on either hand, and past swampy patches of unreclaimed ground, where aged trunks of gnarled willows stand forth in the twilight, gaunt and spectre-like, here, by the wayside, is Fenton Grange, built in 1766, on the site of a more ancient structure. Beyond is Fenton Lodge, a very old foundation. Half a mile east we reach Biggin Grange: here we obtain many glimpses and touches of a past age. The house is of two periods, the new portion dates back a little over a century, the other to the Tudor period. This Grange is also famed for its ghost, in form of a mysterious lady, attired in the costume of the seventeenth century —rich brocaded silk—which, an occupant informed us, could ofttimes be distinctly heard rustling, as the spirit wandered to and fro in the silent hours of night. We were shown into the room where this eerie visitant was usually heard, who, if not disturbed whilst wandering, caused very little commotion; on the contrary, if interfered with, the ghost 'takes on' and raves about (for a benighted spirit) most strangely. Many years ago, the farmer then dwelling at the Grange returned home late from Cawood, in a rather jocular mood, having taken a 'wee drappie too much speerit,' and, being thus full of courage, began to mock and imitate the unearthly visitant, but he was so furiously assailed that he never again ventured to disturb the wanderings of the uncanny one.

The township of Biggan is nearly midway between Sherburn and Cawood, and on the north-west side of the Bishopdyke. Biggan—to build (a shelter)—one of the outposts of Teutonic cultivation—in the parlance of the Canons of Helaugh, the 'newbiggyng,' and possibly its beginning does not reach far beyond the Conquest era, as there is no mention of the place in Domesday.

Hereabouts the land is very slightly elevated above the general level of the fens, and here were several homesteads as early as the thirteenth century, as the mention of some of the persons located at Biggan testify: "William-Fitz-Gamel," whose name bespeaks Norse descent, "Alan-de-Newebiggyng," "Peter-de-Brugge," and "Roger-the-Dyker;" also one Robert-del-le-Dyke, of Stokbrigg, gave lands to Healaugh Priory. So we find the settlement at Biggan in the thirteenth and succeeding centuries, and in those early days the hardy pioneers were busy dyking, banking, draining, planting, and gradually reclaiming and raising, and bringing all the low watery swamp wastes and desolate fen, between Barkston and Cawood, under cultivation, whilst Bishopdyke has relieved the land of its surplus of waters, and extinguished the eerie flame of the once frequent will-o'-the-wisp. In the dark months of winter when the winds are abroad and the storm howls, the fens are still eerie and desolate, but to-day a garden compared with the sterile region those patient yeomen of old had to wrestle with. In pre-railway times, a road ran past Biggan to the ferry at Nunnappleton, and from thence to York. It is now disused.

A little distance from Biggan, and adjoining the Bishop's Dyke, stands Mattram Hall, a moated site. Wheater supposes this to have been a hospital, built in honour of St. Mary Magdalene, and endowed by the

Vavasours, celebrated for the foundation of other cells in remote places, where the roads were dangerous, and the district bleak and wild. The place has evidently been of some pretension, but its characteristic features are lost.*

TOWER AND GATEWAY, CAWOOD, FROM THE NORTH.

Away south two hills, notable for their isolation, being conspicuous objects for miles around, loom on the horizon, namely, Brayton Barp and Hambleton Haugh. These conical eminences form a guiding point both for landsmen and sailors ascending the Humber.

Here we cross **Bishopdyke** and enter the road which runs by the side of the dyke to Cawood. The land immediately to the south of Bishop's Dyke is known by the name of 'Rust,' or 'Rest' Park. It was enclosed for a hunting seat by Archbishop Walter de Grey, in the early years of the thirteenth century. The eastern fringe of the park forms the boundary of the 'liberty' of Cawood, Wistow, and Otley. Within the limits of the park are two entrenched positions, but of which scarcely a shred of history remains.

Half a mile south of **Mattram** Hall is a strongly-moated site, called Manor Garth. The house is supposed to have been built and fortified by Archbishop Alexander Nevill, who received a licence from the king to fortify and make a fortress of his 'manor of rest.' The park is now apportioned into farms.

Bishop Wood is immediately to the right of the road leading from Sherburn to Cawood. By the old people it is known as 'Cow-ud Forest,' and they still tell us of bears, wild boar, and wolves, which formerly infested it, as if the thing had only happened in the days of their grandsires. At the present time the extent is not half of that originally planted by the Archbishops. Many a grand hunting scene has been witnessed here; a few of the smaller wild animals still survive, such as the weasel, polecat, and pine martin: the latter, though very scarce, has been seen in this district by the writer, lately. Here, also, frequented a plover, known as the ruffle or ruff, and sixty years ago the forest was quite a hotbed of hag worms or snakes.

CHAPTER X.

CAWOOD.

THIS town is situated on the south bank of the Ouse, a few hundred yards below the mouth of the Wharfe, yet much of the parish lies in the basin of the latter river. The local pronunciation of the place-name—'Cow-ud'—still preserves its meaning: the original settlement of Celtic founding in their 'coed'—a wood, as in Bettws-y-coed. Here, we imagine, some of the old British race, on being ousted from the eastern side of Elmet by the invading Angle, have taken up their abode in this inhospitable marsh and forest of fenland; and here, no doubt, they were left unmolested until the advent of the Dane, who, in the ninth and succeeding centuries, formed settlements all along the river vales.

In imagination we see a vast forest, full of fens, stagnant water, and marshy wastes. The rude dwellings of our remote ancestors stood on the highest ground adjoining the tawny waters of the Ouse, around which was a strong enclosure to protect them, as well from the swords and spears of men, as from the wild beasts of the forest, at that time numerous. As time rolls by, we see passing, the galleys of Imperial Rome, that richly decorated vessel, probably containing Constantine, Emperor of the world, gliding along the bosom of the Ouse to York, the beautiful city of old, and the home of Emperors one thousand eight hundred years ago. Merchants from the East sailed hither, bringing bales of Oriental goods. Great military roads opened communication throughout Britain, and land that had only been waste and dreary brought forth fruit in abundance. When the Romans left Britain, a great change came o'er the scene: ruin, havoc, and desolation in the place of former peace and prosperity. Vessels, filled with Pagans in quest of empire and plunder, arrived from old Saxony, and their descendants are still pressing southward, westward, and eastward in quest of wealth and empire.

THE COMING OF THE SAXON.

An ancient writer says—"The whelps of the 'Barbarian Lioness' arrived in three ships of largest size at the bidding of an ill-omened tyrant. They were soon afterwards joined by a much larger brood, who professed themselves ready to meet any perils for the sake of their worthy hosts, for which they required that certain supplies should be furnished them; these being provided for a time, stopped the 'dog's mouth,' but the strangers, anxious for a quarrel, demanded larger supplies than could be given, which, not forthcoming, the war of centuries between Saxon and Celt commenced."

Over these miseries we pass to the frightful invasion of piratical hordes from Skania, who sailed up the Ouse in their war-galleys, leaving ruin and devastation on all sides. Then along the riversides might be seen the plunder of churches and the glare of burning town and city.

Cawood, standing by the ever-flowing riverway, received its full share of disaster, but from the time of the first Wulstan the castle and town gradually rose to great importance. The last invasion of the Sea Kings was in 1066. Entering the Humber and thence passing up the Ouse, they landed at Riccall, near Cawood, from which place they swept the country around, leaving such havoc and ruin that a century was needed to repair, and to this day the old people of the district tell many a legend about their ancestors fighting the savage Dene, evidently being entirely unconscious of the fact that they are the Denes' descendants.[*]

Two events render Cawood renowned in history: one for sheltering, in his adversity, that great ambitious churchman, Wolsey; also the place where the most celebrated banquet was given by Archbishop George Neville, the brother of Warwick, the king-maker. The first mention of the place is about 935, after Athelstan's celebrated victory over the invaders at the battle of Brunanburgh. Cawood, like Sherburn, was given by the victorious king to the see of York, as a home for the northern prelates. A very fine specimen of ancient gateway and tower of the castle still remain, and early English windows are still prominent features in the adjoining farm buildings.

[*] Trade has apparently given Cawood a fair by prescription. For the towns of his other manor-houses Archbishop Walter de Grey obtained a little concession. On the 23rd August, 1239, King Henry III. grants the Archbishop a yearly fair at his Manor of Ottele for two days, on the vigil and day of St. Mary Magdalene, 22nd of July, and a weekly market on the Monday. At Sherburn a two days' fair also, on the vigil and day of the Exaltation of the Holy Cross, 14th September, and a weekly market on the Friday.

The meadow in front is yet called the 'Bishop's Close.' Around the meadow are distinct traces of the moat. What a series of historic scenes arise as we ponder over the history of this castle !

"Visions of days departed, shadowy phantoms, fill my brain,
They who live in history seen to walk the earth again."

From the twelfth to the sixteenth century this castle was the home or shelter of many of the noblest in church and camp. Henry III. and his Queen rested here awhile when journeying to Scotland to visit their daughter Margaret, wife of Alexander III. Here dwelt Marguerite of France, second wife of Edward I. During the time this old warrior was fighting the Scotch, and when the storm and noise of war was hushed, we can fancy the

A BIT OF CAWOOD FROM THE BRIDGE.

monarch hastening to Cawood, to the society of his beautiful young bride. From this time the castle rose to its greatest height of feudal grandeur. Here gathered around the gallant king were the crusading knights of many an ancient house, who had withstood the shock of arms when fighting the Saracens on the plains of Palestine, and shared in all the dangers of the last great Crusade, and afterwards followed the banner of Edward into the wilds of Scotland.

The old tower now looks desolate and mournfully isolated, debased by the company of farm buildings, but let the screen of five centuries roll away, and the Windsor of the North stands forth in all its majesty. The walls are thick, and, in time of war, strongly guarded : he who comes in peace or war passes over a strong drawbridge,* and thence, through the watch tower,

* Foundations of both can still be detected.

to the castle. Men-at-arms guard the massive gate day and night, the deep moat, full of stagnant water (its traces still to be seen), embraced two sides of the castle or palace, on the other side Bishopdyke and the brown waters of the Ouse formed a natural protection.

Within this area is ample space for the accommodation of king, archbishop, baron, knight and squire, men-at-arms, retainers, cooks, scullions, and every attendant necessary to uphold the dignity of a castle in the days of feudalism. Here would be held many a brilliant tournament, when earl and baron, knight and squire assembled from all parts to join in the honours of the tilting ring. The sound of baying of hounds, and the trampling of horses, proclaim the king is chasing deer in Bishopwood, at that time a forest of great extent, in which roamed herds of roebuck, and smaller animals. 'Tis the evening of the chase, the banquet room is made brilliant with large torches, and the favourite guests of the king are assembled; the jesters, clad in fantastic garments, and minstrels make the hall resound with song and story. Thus, in varied rounds of pleasure or clash of arms, the ever-changing scenes roll by.

GOTHIC WINDOW IN FAR) YARD.

Edward II. and his Queen made Cawood their home on several occasions. After the disaster to the English at Bannockburn, the victors burst over Yorkshire with the fury of a whirlwind, carrying war and retribution to the very gates of York.

In 1319, Queen Isabella, being the guest of the Archbishop at Cawood, two renowned Scottish knights, Douglas and Randolph, with a chosen body of troops, lightly armed, and mounted on small but active horses, by a swift march burst through Yorkshire, with the hopes of making the Queen their prisoner, but by a fortunate accident a Scot fell into the hands of the English, and from him they received warning of the projected attack on Cawood. Hurriedly collecting the force York could muster for protection, the Queen was apprised of her danger and brought to York, and sent thence to Nottingham for greater security, to the disappointment of the Black Douglas and Randolph.

> "Hush ye, hush ye, little pet ye,
> Hush ye, hush ye, do not fret ye,
> The Black Douglas shall not get ye."

In 1464, George Neville, brother of the great Earl of Warwick, last of the barons and king-maker, was elevated to the See of York, and it being customary for every incoming prelate to give a feast, Neville gave at Cawood the most varied and sumptuous banquet ever recorded in history. In the preparation of it nearly 2,000 people were employed. The contents of the bill of fare were as follows:—

"104 oxen, 1,000 sheep, over 500 stags, bucks, and does, 400 swans, 2,000 geese, 1,000 capons, 200 pheasants, 500 partridges, 400 woodcocks, 100 curlews, 400 plovers, 2,000 chickens, 4,000 mallards and teals, 4,000 pigeons, 1,500 hot pasties of venison, 4,000 cold ditto, 2,000 hot custards, 3,000 cold ditto, besides some hundreds of tuns of ale and wine, with spices and delicacies, etc., etc."

Some time afterwards, Neville was stripped of all his estates, arrested, and cast into prison; thus the great banquet would in after years be food for his serious reflection.

Here Wolsey, most famous of churchmen and prince of cardinals, found a home in his adversity. The story of his rise to the highest honours and dignities in the state, and his downfall, is a most instructive lesson in English history. Having incurred the displeasure of the king, he was constrained to deliver up the great seal of office, and ordered to his archiepiscopal residence at Cawood, where he arrived in the autumn of 1530, being received by the people most enthusiastically. By his courtesy and kindness he soon became a great favourite in the neighbourhood. After the work of putting the palace into repair he began to make arrangements for his enthronement in the cathedral at York, a ceremony the performance of which had been delayed by his previous living and ambitious projects about the court. From the summit of his palace he could see the shrine where he hoped to be enthroned, rising in stately splendour above the old city. What visions of future labour and memories of the past would leap before his gaze. Only three days previous to his intended installation he was suddenly arrested on a charge of high treason by the Earl of Northumberland, and forced to set out for London. So great a favourite had he become that the servants and country people would willingly have defended him, but resistance was useless. He was taken from Cawood, which he had learned to love, and, falling sick by the way, he died at Leicester Abbey. A few hours before his death he addressed those ever memorable words to Sir William Kingston, "If I had served God as diligently as I have done the King, He would not have given me over in my grey hairs; however, this is the just reward that I must receive for my worldly diligence and pains; that I may have to do him service only to satisfy his vain pleasure, not regarding my godly duty."

In 1628, George Montaigu, son of a farmer at Cawood, had the greatest honours of the Church conferred upon him, being made Archbishop of York, and dwelling in the castle of his native town. There is a memorial to him on the south wall of the church. Fuller says he was chaplain to the Earl of Essex, whom he attended on his voyage to Calais. He was a man of such personal valour, that out of his gown he would turn his back to no man, and was afterwards made Dean of Westminster, then successively Bishop of Lincoln and London. Whilst residing in the latter place he

CAWOOD CASTLE.
SOUTH GATEWAY.

would often pleasantly say that of himself the proverb would be verified, "Lincoln was, and London is, and York shall be," which came to pass accordingly. He appears to have been an inveterate punster. The see of York being vacant, the King was at a loss for a fit person to succeed to that exalted position, and asked Bishop Mountayne's opinion, whose wit, his best friend through life, did not desert him at that critical moment. Upon hearing the King's question, the doctor replied, "Hadst thou faith as a grain of mustard seed, thou would'st say to this mountain" (at the same time laying his hand upon his breast) "be removed into that see." His Majesty is said to have laughed immoderately, and forthwith conferred the preferment upon the facetious prelate.

During the Civil War, the town, castle, and surrounding parts were the scene of some skirmishing. In 1644, the castle was captured by Lord Fairfax. In 1646, the House of Commons decreed that the Castle of Cawood should be made untenable, and no garrison in future maintained there. After gradually falling into decay, some of its timber and stones were used in the building of the Palace of Bishopthorpe, now the residence of the Archbishop of York.

With the exception of the gateway and tower, and remnants of Norman Gothic windows in the farm buildings, little now remains of the stately palace, the abode of the Primates in the days of feudalism; yet the exact area of the walled and moated enclosure can still be distinctly traced out. The large, lofty barn on the south of the gateway (with its beautiful Edwardian windows in the old brick walls) still remains; it formerly contained an upper floor, and was the banqueting hall of the Archbishop. In this place, where kings and queens have dwelt, lowly cattle are now stabled, and where in former times were held sumptuous feasts, amid rich scenes of magnificence, corn is now garnered and threshed. Such are a few of the incidents of the town and castle, and the shadowy figures of great men. It is well to linger here and consider the changes time has wrought. Yet, though the old baronial days may be rich in story and tradition, let us hope Cawood's future will be brighter than its past.[*]

---

[*] Archbishop Bowett (1407-26) was a generous guardian of the fabric; it was he who built the wall and the great hall. He not only kept the fabric of the castle in good repair, but was especially commended for his unbounded hospitality: "And, truly," as Drake quaintly remarks, "if the consumption of fourscore tuns of claret, which is said to have been yearly spent in his several palaces, can make us guess at the lesser matters, it must argue beef and ale in abundance." To this purpose he built the great hall in the castle of

> "Where have ye gone, ye statesmen great,
> That have left your home so desolate?
> Where have ye vanished, king and peer,
> And left what ye liv'd for lying here?
> Sin can follow where gold may not,
> Pictures and books the damp may rot;
> And creepers hang frail lines of flowers,
> Down the crevices of ancient towers;
> But what hath passed from the soul of mortal,
> Be it thought or word of pride,
> Hath gone with him through the dim, low portal,
> And waiteth by his side."

In 1872 a fine iron bridge was built across the Ouse—a great boon to the inhabitants of this district. Previous to its erection the following incident occurred:—One night the carrier's waggon from York to Cawood was crossing the river by the ferry at the latter place, the usual mode up to that time. The night being wild and stormy, the wind blowing with great force on the cover of the waggon caused the ferryboat to become unmanageable, forcing it down the river, where, coming in contact with a barge, the waggon full of people was upset into the river; fortunately only one life was lost, viz., the carrier, who by giving up his last chance of life saved his wife's. A boatman came to the rescue of two people, the driver and his wife, Bessie, struggling in the river. Leaning over the side of his boat he got hold of both of them, but being unable to save the two, finding his strength unequal to the task, he said, "Ah can only save yan, which 'es it te be?" "Save Bessie," was the noble answer from the drowning carrier, as he fell from the grasp of the boatman into the dark waters of the river; which, if I mistake not, never gave back his body. Nearly thirty years have passed since this sad accident happened, and Bessie Pilmer is still alive and resides in the James Hospital, erected for four poor people according to the will of William James, in the early years of the eighteenth century.

Although to a great extent the charm of Cawood lies in the memories which linger around its castle, yet the town, with its deep-toned brick dwellings and red-tiled roofs, uneven of contour, is full of quaint little pictures; and by way of contrast the buildings are intermixed with portions of finely-chiselled stones from the Huddleston quarries, brought hither in the

---

Cawood, and his manor-house at Otley. His grave was opened in the seventeenth century and a ring found in the coffin bearing the inscription: "*Honneur et Joye*".—"A most appropriate motto," says Wheater, "for one who was probably like Jovinian." The chapel attached to the castle, often mentioned in deeds, stood about midway between the old gateway and river; fragments of this chapel existed in memory of men now living.

first instance for the uprearing of the castle. Time has only given additional hardness and durability to this stone, and also tinted it with a soft silvery grey. So, fragments of the castle can be detected all about the village outskirts and in many an out-of-the-way corner; even the latest new glaring red-bricked structure by the church shows one block of famous Huddleston stone in its walls. Cawood was the port from which the stone from the Huddleston quarries was shipped to York. Various means were adopted in transporting the stone to Cawood—by wains, sledding or floating on punts down Bishopdyke to the Ouse.

[F. Dean.

CAWOOD CASTLE AND VILLAGE, FROM THE RIVER.

Like Boroughbridge and other old places, Cawood possesses quite a number of ancient hostelries, whose quaint interiors, oak-panelled rooms, and ingle nooks are the joy of the tired traveller.

The mediæval splendour depicted on the gateway of the castle, its rich oriel windows, and the beautiful specimens of transition (early English and Tudor) work, displayed in the farm buildings, are too well known for further description.

Wistowgate possesses several pleasing types of domestic architecture, of the Elizabethan period, with picturesque gables. The excellent quality of the brickwork testifies to the care of the builder. Here are evidences of the fairly prosperous condition of the yeoman. There are four interesting granges, of the late Tudor period, in the town, although now shorn to some extent of their old-time features. The Grange, Wistowgate, the residence of the Nicholsons, whose ancestors have dwelt here in direct succession for three centuries, formerly had a fine Tudor roof. There is still a very pretty porch with heavy oaken door well studded with nails, two panelled rooms, and rare bits of furniture. In the garden are several cannon balls, Cromwellian period, found on the land about here, and under the colonnade are life-sized figures of the four evangelists, partly mutilated. These were found at a restoration of the church, buried face downwards by the walls of Cawood chapel. What a dignity and splendour these richly sculptured figures, with other images of saints, would give to Cawood Church of olden times. There are other old features noticeable — the wall surrounding the garden, and the row of aged pollard willows. In the meadows opposite the Grange stands a fragment of Keysbury Hall, belonging to the Lady of the Manor. Here a Court Leet is held every three years to collect

[*E. Bogg.*

A PEEP INTO BISHOPDYKE, NEAR THE SITE OF THE 'OLD SOKE MILL.'

fines for copyhold property.* The land on the south bank of the Wharfe hereabouts is a rich, loamy soil, suited for almost all kinds of vegetable produce, the seed-time and harvest of which finds employment for numerous women workers.

The bridge is the rendezvous for all able-bodied men out of employment, who, with hands deep in trousers pockets, perambulate that quarter; ever and again scanning the river as if expecting some Danish war-prame or the stately barge of the prelates of old, to sweep round the curve of the stream; or, perhaps, hoping for some rich prize to fall to their lot without toiling for it.

In conversation with one of these bridge strollers (an old native) he, with a sigh drawn from far down the aisles of the past, said, " Ay, they had monny rum doin's doon at yon castle. They allus mede their feeasts last 'em for monny a day, and I've heerd it tell't that ya dinner yance lasted oll t' year. Ay, bud them wor rare taimes, ya could eat and drink as mich as ivver ya liked for nowt. They mun hae been rich folks, for when I wur a lad 'ave heerd oad men say, that 'eaps o' gold and silver wor buried on this river side, and a can tak' ye ta a spot where a hide chuck full o' gold lies hid, if onnybody 'ull tak t' trouble ta dig for 't"!

Cawood has not been without interesting characters in the humbler walks of life. There was one John Fowler, or commonly 'Jacky' (*alias* Lord Milton, or Milton Fowler), of whom are told many wonderful stories. Then there was the good-natured and easy-going old miller, who is still

---

* COURT LEET.—The view of frank-pledge, which is a court of record, held once in a year, and not oftener, within a particular hundred, township, or manor, before the steward of the leet; being the King's court, granted by charter to the lords of certain hundreds and manors. Its original intent was to view the frank-pledges, that is, the freemen within the liberty; besides this the preservation of the peace and the chastisement of divers minute offences against the public good are the objects both of the court leet and the Sheriff's town, which have exactly the same jurisdiction, one being only a larger species of the other; extending over more territory, but not over more causes. All freeholders within the precinct are obliged to attend them, and all persons cormorant, *i.e.*, lying therein. But persons under twelve and above sixty years old, peers, clergymen, women, and the Crown's tenant in ancient demesne, are excused from attendance, all others being bound to attend upon the jury if required, and make their due presentments.

It was also anciently the custom to summon all the King's subjects, as they respectively grew to the age of discretion and strength, to come to the court-leet, and there take the oath of allegiance. The other general business of the leet and town was to present by jury all crimes whatsoever that happened within their jurisdiction. Both the town and leet have been for a long time in a declining way, and latterly have fallen into almost total desuetude, and their business has gradually devolved upon the quarter sessions.

kindly remembered, though the original 'Soke Mill,' of Cawood, has long since fallen into disuse. But if the miller was easy-going and careless, his wife was greedy of gain and grain. Scene—Miller's wife to the miller: "Has' ta mootur'd (multured) that corn?" "Ay, lass." "Wha, thoo hesen't auf mootur'd it, a'll mooture it agean." Such is the pith of the story told us by the site of the old Soke Mill. Then there is our worthy friend 'Pepper,' whose eighty-seven years still sit lightly on him, and whose definition of place-names is somewhat original and startling. To him the connection between Acaster Selby, and the mother church of Selby, evidently has no existence, for he told us, with some show of pride, how the name originated from vessels sailing past up the Ouse to York, hence Sail-by (Selby). Many and varied are the stories he told whilst driving us about with his favourite steed 'Violet'— whose colour was white. Of noblemen, the late Lord Wenlock is the one he loves to dilate upon most; from his description, a gentleman by birth and nature alike. For many years 'Pepper' was engaged in salmon fishing, and astounding captures in the past are recounted. He also took part in the celebrated Election between Lord Milton and Wilberforce, which happened over seventy years ago.*

STREET VIEW, CAWOOD.

* A few years ago, an incident occurred just inside this village that goes far to prove the devotion and attachment of dumb animals to one another. The doctor of the place owned a favourite pony, used for visiting district patients. His two dogs, a retriever and a

Let us now wander along the curve of the Ouse, to where the grey tower of the church stands as a sentinel over the tawny water, as it has stood nigh seven hundred years. Near it was a paved ford over the river, and here also stood the tithe barn, now demolished.* The position of the church is admirable, situated on the bank of a tidal river winding about in graceful curves, and everything around contributes to one's sense of peace, pastoral enjoyment and settled content. Our description of the fabric, although a fascinating theme, must be brief. The only portion of the original twelfth-century church remaining is the western doorway and part of the wall adjoining it. The clustered shafts of the south arcade are remarkable for

[E. Bogg.

FONT USED AS A PUMP TROUGH, IN COTTAGE HOSPITAL GARDEN.

* Doubtless the old chapel (originally a small structure) was erected, in the first instance, near an ancient paved ford, which can still be located at low water. This church was either rebuilt or thoroughly restored about the middle of the twelfth century. The west doorway of the north aisle and bowl of the font are all that remain of this Norman church.

---

greyhound, were the especial friends of the pony; the three being inseparable companions either abroad or in the stable. One afternoon, as the doctor was returning from his visits, the pony dropped dead not far from the village. It was dragged into an adjoining field, but nothing could induce the dogs to quit the dead pony through the long, cold, late autumn night. The following day the body was buried deep in the earth. Still, strange to say, the faithful animals refused to leave the spot, scratching a bed in the soil, and for two days and nights kept watch and ward over the grave. Mr. Warrington, who saw them early on the second morning, told the writer the devoted animals were shaking from intense cold.

their slender proportions, and this airy lightness is very pleasing and effective. The two lancet windows and doorway in the south wall of the chancel are very interesting examples of architecture. Part of the dismembered effigy, a memorial of Archbishop George Montaigne, seen in a chest on a former visit, has been restored; the other part is no doubt in existence, and the whole figure ought to have been restored. Allen, in his history of the county of York, written in 1826, says: "Archbishop Mountain is interred in this church and has a handsome tomb." We have a feeling, almost amounting to adoration, for these old effigies, as we stand before them and ponder on the time when they who now sleep trod these very aisles, or knelt in prayer at the altar! Broken tombs, monuments, and effigies are the links that indissolubly bind the past to the present. Another very interesting relic, namely, the bowl of an early English font, now degraded to the use of a pump trough *(see picture)*, is in the garden of the cottage hospital adjoining; this relic of the original church should be removed back into the church from whence it was thrown out some sixty years ago. Outside the east end of the churchyard wall is a panel bearing the impaled arms of the Cawoods of Cawood, and Accloms of Morbey. This site, now unbuilt on, south side of the choir wall and east end of the south aisle, was formerly known as the Cawood Chapel, and it was

CAWOOD CHURCH.

here in the ground, buried face downwards, that the life-sized figures in stone of the four evangelists were found, some years ago; they are now to be seen under the colonnade of the Grange, Wistowgate. The question which naturally arises is: Have the figures been hidden at the Reformation, or during the Civil War, to protect them from destruction at the hands of the Ironsides. The Smiths, Morritts, Nicholsons, Wormalds, Warringtons, and Mountains still reside at Cawood.

Before passing into the Ainsty district, it would be well for us to take a glance at Wistow, the Wykestow of the old nomenclature. In our path through sandy, alluvial, garden-like land, we notice just off the wayside a huge and lightning-blasted oak, standing with gaunt arms extending like some bleached skeleton. This is the haunted oak, or 'Goblin Tree,' and stout of heart were they who at nightfall passed it formerly without fear and trembling. It has weathered the storms of many centuries, and is the sole survivor of its former brethren hereabouts. To fully realise the scenery around Wistow, the place should be visited at two seasons—when the July sun has ripened the fruits of the earth—the potato harvest in full swing on the broad arable—and given splendid frondage to the trees and dressed the wayside hedgerows in plenitude of loveliness; and by way of startling contrast, to fully understand the inhospitable aspect of winter, make a visit in the dark, dreary month of December, when the wide dun fields lie bare beneath a dark grey dome of sky.*

When Wistow was the Wykestow (the name denotes a watery situation) it stood at a very sharp angle of the River Ouse, which has since cut its way through the neck of the loop. The village is now a mile from the river, but the former way of the stream is still visible. Over this old course the

* Some eighty years ago, Cawood and the villages around were infested with hordes of gipsies, whose king was one Largee Young, a man of immense strength. A terror to the neighbourhood, his profession was poaching and thieving. So afraid were the inhabitants of offending him, that for several years he defied the laws with impunity. Being a practised horse thief, he was one night seen by a farmer leading a horse from his stable. Following and overtaking the gipsy in the fields near Hebden farm, the farmer demanded his horse. The gipsy with fearful oaths swore he would murder him. A terrible fight took place, which would probably have ended in the death of the farmer, but fortunately the noise of the strife brought Hebden to the rescue, armed with a large hatchet. The two men proved more than a match for the gipsy king. Young was tried at the Castle; tribes of gipsies from far and near attended the trial; every means possible were adopted by the wanderers to induce the farmers to withdraw from the prosecution, but in vain. Amongst other things offered, as a native quaintly told the writer, was "a quairt pot chuck up wi' gold." The gipsy king was exported beyond seas. The farmer who captured him was for his courage presented with a silver tankard, which, lately kept at an inn in these parts, enabled thirsty ones to drink, while the innkeeper related the story of the capture.

Vikings have steered their high-prowed flat-bottomed 'prames,' for such were the vessels on which the adventurous Northmen—holding life lightly—invaded England. Here just beyond Wistow is the Garman-carr—the Ga-maen: Maen, a boundary—that the Celt and Dane and all others had to respect, the limiting line made for Athelston's Liberty of Cawood, Wistow and Otley. To the rear is the black fen and Boggart Brigg, where Peg Fife skinned a man alive, so the natives still say. The Black Fen is the fountain and origin of the bad fiend—Will-o'-the-wisp—and all that is evil, and the Elf Holes, from whence the elves come tripping lightly in the moonlight, the fount of light and gladness. Thoroughly Celtic in its garmaen, its goblins, boggarts, elf holes, and spark haggs, and the curious, old-world incidents of man-skinning done at the boundary of the Liberty.

The maypole is said to have been a bequest of the fairies, and here the little buxom lasses, sighing anxiously for their loves, were wont to dance a ringhey or reel. Fiends and fairies were deeply interwoven in the minds of the people hereabouts. The scenery among which a child has been reared has a great effect in moulding his after character. Here, cradled and brought-up amongst the fens, it became identified with his everyday life. Seated by the peat fire on a winter's night, when the wind moaned and shrieked mysteriously, he heard the oral tradition repeated from sire to son. And so the belief in fiends, ghosts, and fairies became deeply identified with the penal tradition of the people. Wistow is still a place of old world stories, fancies, habits, and appearances.*

* It was at Scalm Park, in the parish of Wistow, where William Storr, farmer, dwelt in the early years of the eighteenth century. He was a man of quick intelligence for his station in life, and from the journal he kept we find a great fund of information respecting Wistow and the surrounding district, two hundred years ago. The following are two items—of 'Highwayes' he says: "When my father came to Scalme the roadway to Cawood and Wistow was thorow the woods and out at a gate at the garth side of the new hagg for Cawood, and to Wistow out at a gate near the farr end of Mosker Hagg, and so was for twenty years after, but the woods growing so great we was forst to take down Mosker Hagg, being the way to Selby." He also tells us of 'Floods'—"There hath been severall great floods, but one is remarkable because it hapened in summer. It began to rain the 13th of July and continued till Wednesday at noon, and the flood was at its height at Wistow on Setterday at noon. It swam load pikes of hay in the hallings, and I lost there and in the Common Ings fifty load of hay, and the weather was so hott after it that dust flew in the roads very sore, and it did rott the gras upon the ground with the heat of the sun, soe that it was a very loathsome smell to feell all over the lordship, and there was abundance of hay and corn lost in the lordship, and the ground would not keep above half the stock the next year, I mean on low grounds, and because the gras was so rotted away it caused abundance of the Ings to be plowed which never was before. I lost with that flood near upon £100. It was in the year 1706 that the summer flood hapned at Wistow." Descendants of the Storrs still dwell in the district.—*Yorkshire Archæological Society's Journal.*

There is no mention of a church at Wistow in the 'Domesday' survey. The structure is early thirteenth century foundation; the tower, a conspicuous object seen above the roofs and orchard trees. It has been thoroughly restored with great skill and care. Within the chancel lies the effigy of a lady and two smaller figures, supposed to represent her children; the epitaph referring to the above is in Norman French; translated it reads, "You who

WISTOW CHURCH.

pass this way, pray for the soul of Dame Margery; Margery who lies here, for you may Jesus cry mercy." There is a curious memorial—'the End of All'—in the north wall, a skull supporting an hour-glass, and underneath is a coat-of-arms; there are a few incised slabs, bearing every sign of antiquity, and several other features of interest. Wheater says that in 1474 there stood in the churchyard of Wistow, but not attached to the church, a chapel called St. Hilda's Chapel, and the Bishop's report states that it was in a dilapidated condition, although the Prebendary of Wistow ought to have kept it in a proper state of repair. The principal image, they state, had been withdrawn from the church, and that they have neglected the very ancient custom of strewing the church with straw. This little chapel of St. Hilda may have been a very old foundation, and its dedication to the great Scandinavian Saint speaks strongly as to the origin of the inhabitants of Wistow.*

Away to the west is Olive House and Olive Bush. These points of the once dark and drear fenland seem to tell of the Norseman Olaf, the St. Olaf, and the long train of dark days and drear nights of ague-racked agony to be endured for generations before the swamp-covered land became the paradise of cultivation it now is, and the terrors of olden times became mere sounding names.

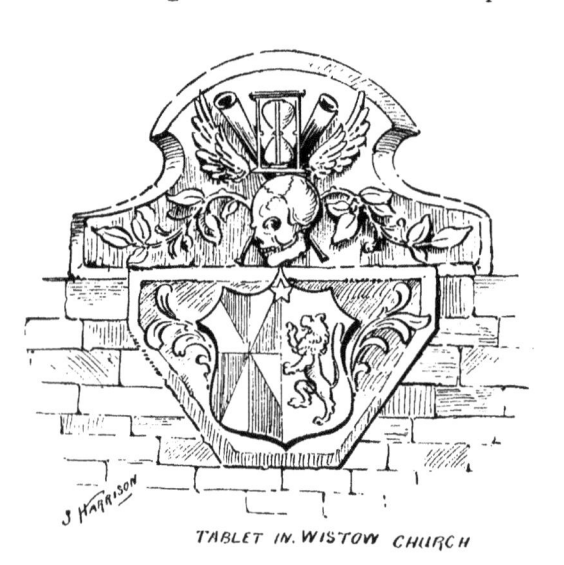

Just beyond the sleepy village is Boggart Bridge, and some two miles away over the low-lying meadow and root-land, the chief feature in the landscape etched forth is the tower of Selby Abbey, architecturally a church producing a wondrous charm, and inevitably impressing the mind of the traveller, who gazes on it, with its superb west front and massive early Gothic work. Around this monastery the little market town of Selby has gradually arisen. A few words must suffice for description. The spirit of the beautiful is instinct in everything here. The massiveness and dignified grandeur of the Norman, Gothic, and Transitional nave, the enriched character of the decorated choir, contrasting with the heavy Norman work; the pleasing variety of the triforium and clerestory, and the exquisite, pointed

TABLET IN WISTOW CHURCH

* The four parcels of land within the manor of Wistow are:—Hornington Hagg, Pile Hagg, Westall Hagg, Paulden Hagg. Statute measure, 976 acres : 1 : 9.

and graceful early English—blend architectural styles into pleasing harmony. Even the chequered gleam and shadow on the pavement is sublimely beautiful within this " solemn temple." We glance at the Jesse window, with its wondrous story, gem-like in colour and luminous conception ; let us tread softly the pavement worn by the " noiseless foot " of sandalled monks, lest we awaken their long sleep, as we silently contemplate the ornate beauty and massive grandeur, the graven stones and monuments, stored with undying thought, appealing to all who really love and venerate their country's shrines—and Selby Abbey is indeed truly one of the most magnificent and beautiful.

The Missionary Benedict, whose coming to England in the 'Conquest' era led to the foundation of this Abbey of Selby, has left a fine word-picture of this sylvan scene. Perambulating the district which included the first possessions of Selby and speaking with the freshness of the actual landscape before his view, he describes it as "a most pleasant place, covered as well with frequent groves as crowned with an ample tidal river, like an earthly paradise. Situated on the bank of the Ouse at the southern quarter of the city of York and (as to Selby) only some ten miles distant from it, the intervening windings of the river are covered on every side with woods and groves, which provide much beauty in a pleasant place; among these many big groves,

WEST DOORWAY, SELBY ABBEY.

(G. F. Jones.

excellent in quality, properly lie near and belong to this domain. In the profits of the water, this vicinity furnishes much; the lakes and dams abounding in fishes." How delightful to have the lines of such a picture fixed by a poet's eye! Its charm in the vista, he adds, including his own home. "In the meantime, a monastery as fair as notable, sits in its revered mass. .. The tower of the church, far off from those walking, can be seen on the public roads from every part, and with it the roofs of the offices arising beside it as in steps, appear and are pointed out; and also whatever is brought to York by ships from parts beyond the seas, or carried away from it to other parts of England, is wont to pass before the gates of the monastery of Selby," just as they must pass before the tower of the Archbishop's palace at Cawood. More than eight hundred years have passed since that description was penned, yet it can still be applied, word for word, to the district then referred to. Somnolence is one of the grand features of the Ouse and lower Wharfe; its aspect, its serenity, its landscape, are the enduring marks of self-sufficient existence. What is, was, and, let us hope, will henceforth continue to be.

We are wandering over historic ground, and by a river rendered famous in the Sagas of old. Here is Wistow Lordship: the large number of shapely-dressed stones from the Huddleston quarries prove the place to be of ancient foundation; Monks Lane, an old-time way, passing through the Haggs to Wistow, tells of a time when the spiritual brethren were predominant in this district. Yonder to the east, just beyond the banks of the Ouse, the substantial tower of Riccall Church rises high and square above the roofs of the lowly village, blending finely with the rich green frondage of elm and ash, in which it is embowered. This wide stretch of lowland is remarkable for its noble temples, whose grand towers, romantic and beautiful, rise out of the landscape like island-peaks in the ocean; but it is not of the church we would speak, nor the ornate beauty and noble grandeur of its Norman-Gothic entrance portal, with its four ranges of moulding springing from shafts with capitals ornamented with grotesque figures; and with its wondrous symbolism of Christianity triumphing over Paganism.*

Riccall—the Richehal, Ric-hael—the hall of government, is a place of unmistakable antiquity. It was here in the Ouse that Hardrada, the

* In Riccall churchyard still flourishes a mulberry tree, nigh three hundred years old, its planting marking an order made by King James I.—faddist in many things, unpractical and before his time in others—his idea being to encourage the propagation of silkworms and the manufacture of silk by such means.

renowned king of Norway, moored his five hundred ships which had borne his vast army of Norsemen from the wilds of Scandinavia and the Orkneys to the conquest of England. A beck enters the Ouse between Wheel Hall —(wheel is often used in connection with Yorkshire rivers, meaning an expansion or backwater)—and Riccall, and, from its wide river vale aspect, has formerly been an arm of the Ouse, deep and wide enough at the flow of tide for vessels of small draught to enter, and in this indent, the natives

[Valentine & Son.

THE CHOIR, SELBY ABBEY.

(the very descendants of the Danes) tell us—the 'Deanes'—Norsemen, moored their war keels. From thence they marched overland through the great forest of Ouse and Derwent to York. The Saxon army of defenders met the invaders at Fulford and thus barred their entry into the city, and there, says one writer, where the smooth green turf now covers the ings with its delicious sward, Saxons and Danes faced each other in mortal strife; but at nightfall the famous banner, the land ravager of the Norsemen, floated triumphant over the field of battle. Marching on to York the victors took possession of it, but hearing that Harold was advancing to the rescue, they retreated, choosing their position on the Derwent at Stamford Bridge, where on the 25th of September, 1066, Harold, on whose prowess rested Saxon England, came in sight of the invading hosts of Scandinavia. The contest was fierce and terrible, both sides doing deeds of undoubted valour: around the bridge long raged the keenest fury of the battle. A giant Swede[*] for some time defended it with the power of his single arm, but was at length slain by a spear thrust from beneath the bridge. The old wooden bridge stood a little higher up the river than the present structure, its former position can still be determined. After performing prodigies of valour, the Norwegian king and Tosti were slain, with thousands of their army.

Many memorials of this famous battle have been found: swords, battle-axes, pikes and other armour. The remains of a half-circular trench joining on to the river at both extremities shows the entrenched position the Norsemen occupied west of the river at the onset of the battle. Danes Garth and Danes Well, battle flats and evident signs of earthworks on the east side of the river, are all suggestive of this great struggle. And again on the west bank, by Chapel or Chantry Field, is a raised earthwork, sixty yards long by eight or nine feet high, and said by the villagers to be a burying place of the slain from the battlefield.[†] Stamford Bridge is a spot

[*] This giant Norwegian—the northern Horatius—who defended the bridge, was one of the warriors who had accompanied Harold Sigurd to the Greek capital on the Mediterranean coast, and had shared in all his great Eastern victories by sea and land, and his mighty sword had helped to carve a path through the infidel host to the walls of Jerusalem, where he had worshipped before the Holy Sepulchre, and afterwards washed in the waters of Jordan. The old wooden bridge which he so long defended was standing until near the middle of the eighteenth century.

[†] Previous to the battle, King Harold sent an envoy and twenty horsemen, both men and horses completely mailed, to try and win over his brother, and so split up the invaders. Coming into the presence of Tosti, the spokesman said: "Harold, thy brother, sends thee greeting, and the promise of peace, also that thou shalt have the whole of Northumbria; and rather than thou shouldst become his enemy, he will share the third part of the kingdom with thee." "And what," answered Tosti, "if I accept this offer, will be given to Harold Hardrada?" The trooper replied: "He has, indeed, said what he would grant him of England's soil, seven feet space, but as men say he is a giant he shall have eight." Then replied Tosti, "Go and tell your king to prepare to fight, for no man shall ever say that Tosti, son of Godwin, broke faith with Harold, son of Sigurd, and joined the ranks of his foes." Both sides prepared for combat, the invaders being composed of adventurers from many nations and climes; but the troops mainly to be relied on were the warriors the giant king had often led to victory, he being the greatest warrior of his age. Mounted on a magnificent black charger, his gigantic figure enveloped in armour of burnished steel,

where the antiquary will love to linger. The village, with its clustered roofs, is not uninteresting: the Derwent flowing in the foreground, and away in the background are the white chalk roads winding across the brow of the Wold Hills. But we are diverging from our subject, let us return over the many miles which intervene between Stamford and Riccall. The fighting and chase continued, numbers were drowned in the Derwent and Ouse. The Saxon chronicle says that " The English from behind hotly smote them until they came to their ships, some were drowned and others also burned, and thus in divers ways they perished, so that few were left to carry back to Norway the dismal story."* In this hour of victory Harold graciously allowed the remnant of the army to return on condition they would for ever observe peace and friendship to this land. Thus of a fleet of five hundred prames bearing a mighty host of warriors who proudly entered the Humber a few days previous 'burning with high hope,' only twenty-four ships were needed to take back the survivors. Deep was the sorrow and loud the wailing amongst the Norsemen for the loss of their brave king and the destruction of his army. Even the flapping sails and creaking of masts sounded like a funeral dirge, as the few vessels crept slowly and mournfully down the Ouse and out of the Humber, and thence homeward across the wild North Sea, to spread the dismal story of evil omen and death. For generations after, the sad story was told by fathers to sons, of that fearful fight and carnage at Stamford, where the blood of a kindred race, Angle and Norse, changed the clear waters of the old Ouse and Derwent to crimson.

Here on the banks of the Ouse and lower Wharfe we are in Danes land. The Danes never rested until the North-Humber country was

* While the immense fleet was in preparation, many vague previsions of gloom pervaded the Viking host. "One man dreamed that the fleet had sailed, that he saw flocks of crows and vultures perched on the masts and sails, and that a witch-wife, seated on an island, holding a drawn sword in her hand, cried out to the birds: 'Go, and go without fear; ye shall have plenty to eat, for I go with you.' Another man dreamt that he saw his comrades landed in England, that they were in presence of an English army, and that a woman of gigantic stature rode on a wolf, to which she gave human bodies, which it held in its jaws and devoured one after another. Hardrada dreamed that he saw his brother, St. Olaf, and that the warrior-saint warned him, in vague words, that the expedition would terminate in disaster."

picture him! with his grizzly warriors, the sea kings, around him, and the famous standard, " The Land Ravager," floating o'er them. Towering above his army he sang his famous war song, telling of great victories won by the Norsemen; and as he sang of the mighty deeds of Rolla and chiefs of old, the blood mantled his cheeks, and ere he had ended his battle-song the wild enthusiasm of the Norsemen was beyond control.

R

conquered. The ship was the Norseman's pride; up the riverways they sailed, fought, plundered and settled along the banks, as the range of place-names yet testify, and to-day the Norse element in this district is predominant. To these wild sea rovers we, to a great extent, owe our love of liberty. The admixture of Norse blood still flows strong in our veins, their language in our speech.

In our journey to Ryther let us follow the bank of the sinuous Ouse, with its rich undergrowth and umbrageous foliage, past slumberous Kellfield and all that remains of its former castellated and moated manor-house. It would be as well to mention in passing along the bank of the Ouse that curious phenomena, the eagre or sea tempest: the tidal inrush of water up the estuaries. The highest, and consequently the most dangerous, is that nearest to the new moon, to autumnal or vernal equinox. At neap, low tide, the inflow of water can only be slightly marked. On the level stretch of river, between Cawood and Kellfield, the whole body of springtide water sweeps in one large wave, followed by a succession of smaller ones, and meeting the descending river rises like a wall of water to the height of six or seven feet, and travels upwards at the rate of seven to eight miles an hour. Boats and keels are, at times, washed from their moorings, and persons fishing peaceably by the river are often caught unawares and immersed

[E. Bogg.
A BEND OF THE OUSE AT CAWOOD.

up to the middle by the rapid influx of water—hence the shout of warning when the wave is seen swiftly approaching. At Cawood the men call out: 'War aigre—war (ware) oot, it's coming, look out!' whilst the lads playing by the river shout on its approach, 'War oot for t' worly aigre' (whirling, from the succession of waves). The word is pronounced variously, as 'eygre,' 'eagre,' and 'eager,' Anglo-Saxon 'eagor,' 'egor'—the sea water. We can easily understand the feeling of awe the sight of this body of moving water, surging up the estuaries of certain rivers would have on the minds of the half-wild men from the land of Scania; and we can also understand how this spirit of the water and sea-giant of old became the Ægir or Sea God of the Norsemen, and that strange, unaccountable feeling of awe and mystery (we might say worship), which it produced lingered in the minds of the people dwelling by the banks of the Ouse and Trent far into the years of the last century. At Cawood we cross by the bridge to the south side of the river and turn in to the old 'Commercial' for refreshments, an excellent inn, typical of old days. We rest in the ingle nook, have a pleasant chat with the landlord on bygone times and things; then leaving Cawood, with thoughts of its past history still in mind, we take the road to Ryther, through the flat lands, to some perhaps monotonous, yet affording fine views of a lowland river winding deep under overhanging willows. In the middle distance a red brick or whitewashed farm stands out to relieve the miles of flatness. In the far distance a tower or spire and tapering poplars, with the roofs of Fenton and other villages, complete the scene.

Hereabouts in the loose sandy subsoil the mole, which is often of a creamy colour, proves very troublesome to the farmers. Under the molehill are three chambers, the bottom-most being the home or nest, the upper chambers are generally stocked with headless worms, a provision of the sagacious mole against a rainy day. This maiming of the worm does not destroy life, but deprives it of the power to creep away, hence the mole generally retains in its larder a fresh supply of live food. We are told by an authority that the mole lives almost wholly upon the red earthworm of the fields. It has been seen to refuse to touch hard-skinned creatures like the beetle or armoured wood louse, although the softer-skinned grub or maggot of flies is devoured when chance allows. As we have observed, the mole's 'fortress' consists of an upper gallery and a chamber, or 'keep,' in which it ordinarily lives when at rest. There is a third and larger chamber, which is placed where two runs meet at some little distance from the 'fortress.' Here the mother mole rears her young. The upper excavation, or top chamber, from its domed, tunnel-like character, if not intended for the purpose, is nevertheless a sort of trap for worms, which wriggling their way as is their habit through the soil, and bringing up fine earth to the surface by night, or after rain, tend to break through and congregate in the gallery, balling themselves, as is also their habit, as one by one they happen to strike. Once in the smooth-walled receptacle, they cannot escape except by the 'run' of the mole. Such as do follow the line of the least resistance are almost sure to make a meal for the blind burrower. The old mole-catcher here is quite a character and familiar figure in his well-worn velvet coat. The damp and fogs of the fenland have, however, marked him for a victim, for he rather jocularly told how "Yance ah went weel eneaf ah twa sticks (legs), but noo ah ev̇ te hev foure."

VIEW ON THE OUSE BETWEEN CAWOOD AND RICCALL.

CHAPTER XI.

WANDERING along, we soon obtain a glimpse, nestling amongst trees in the meadows, of Ryther's ancient church, in whose peaceful aisles rest mailed knight, crusader, and nun, their embellished tombs telling of warfare in the battlefield, or the more saintly fight of the just. Ryther, now a secluded and very uneventful village, was a place of some importance in "the days when the earth was young," and Tubal Cain was a man of might. We do not suppose Tubal dwelt at Ryther, nor does he belong to this story. The place-name is perhaps a disguise of the Celtic word "Rhayader," a cataract or waterfall, and suggestive of this are the two streams which fall into the Wharfe from either bank opposite the village. But the more probable derivation is from the Norse "Riodr," a settlement in a forest-clearance; and a few remains of the old oak forest of the Percys may be seen over the river. The earliest associations of the place are with long settlement and its consequent stability. Its church of pre-Conquest foundation and dedicated to "All Hallows" was the only one between the Wharfe and Brayton. The antiquity of its territorial family cannot be estimated from the effects of the Norman conquest. Their heraldic badge, three crescents, is said to be a mark of distinguished conduct, won during the Crusades. The place is doubtless of Norse origin, and here the Viking fleet, in armour glittering with barbaric embellishments, the Raven Standard fluttering in the breeze, have often passed up and down by the riverway. The place-names from the mouth of the Wharfe to Hubberholm in its upper reaches, bear out the story of the supremacy of the Dane in this river vale.

The church stands on slightly rising ground some two hundred paces from the river; opposite, on the northern bank, stands Nunappleton. Just to the west of the church are fragments of a well-defined moat, enclosing the site of the former castle of the Rythers, and parallel with the moat on the west is a fen dyke—"the Fleet," which on reaching the precincts of the village expands into a wide-flowing estuary. The road to Cawood skirts this expansion of water for some little distance. The water-mark on the line of posts, erected to guide people at flood-time and on the dark nights of winter, gives the village quite a Dutch aspect and adds a distinctive charm and character to the place. The homes of the cotters are all to the west of the beck hollow, which cuts the connection between the church, Hallgarth and the village. A high raised causeway, the stones laid so as to shed water readily, gave sole access to the church, and is another quaint feature of interest telling its own story, and a strange eventful one too,

TOMBS. RYTHER CHURCH

AFTER THE RESTORATION.

reaching over the centuries; of the happy bride led to the altar, or grief-stricken mourners bearing all that is mortal of friend or kin to the tomb, in days and at times when such passage was not without its moving incidents by flood and field.

RYTHER CHURCH.

Architecturally a treasured shrine of historic remains, the delightful simplicity observed within the interior harmonizing quaintly with the charm of its surroundings. Here the most unimpressionable cannot fail to be arrested by the venerable form and the prevailing antiquity, as it were, blending tradition and romantic story, and themes sufficient to rouse the least fertile imagination into active interest. It consists of entrance porch, nave, south aisle, and chancel; the solid simplicity of the chancel arch, devoid of ornament, shows the rude character of the semi-barbarous early Gothic work. The first Danish or Saxon church, possibly erected not later than the ninth century, has been a very lowly edifice, including chancel and about half the length of the present nave. The chancel arch and two rude round-headed windows built in the north wall are relics of the early structure. The growth of the church is very apparent: the lengthening of the early English nave, and the after addition of the early-decorative south aisle, which required the introduction of the hagioscope in the old arch, so arranged that the Ryther family, seated in this aisle, could witness the Elevation of the Host; also the difference in character of the two piscinas: the one in the north or original wall—Norman; the other in the south wall—early decorated. Built into the outside walls are fragments of an earlier church, specimens of diaper work, and other antique features illustrative of the growth of this church and the reason of its varied styles of architecture.

It is very rarely one finds such a display of tombs and effigies of warriors and ladies as are to be seen here, reaching the entire length of the south aisle; and although much of their history is forgotten, maybe they still rest on from century to century. How hushed and solemn is the hallowed spot as we linger by these monuments of the dead, shafts of glimmering sunlight gilding the effigies with an almost ethereal radiance! The first is a fine tomb of fine alabaster, on which reposes the sculptured figure of a knight in plate mail; a helmet, minus the crest, is on his head, and a hound lies at his feet. The collar round the neck represents the 'sun in splendour'—a

INTERIOR OF RYTHER CHURCH BEFORE THE RESTORATION.

badge for distinguished conduct given by Edward IV. At each end of the tomb are arcaded canopies, in which are the figures of three knights in armour and three ladies; on the side are four spaces with canopied enrichments containing four knights and four ladies. There are various suggestions as to whom this tomb may commemorate : I think it is the Dean of York, the Rev. A. P. Purey-Cust, who weaves quite a romance around it. It most probably represents a knight of the Ryther family, slain at Towton fight; it is, indeed, a chaste and stately monument, and

[*E. Bogg.*

SAXON CHANCEL ARCH AND HAGIOSCOPE, RYTHER CHURCH.

goes far to prove the importance of the Ryther family in " the brave days of old." The next tomb of Portland marble, decorated with tracery and bunches of grapes, is fine in detail and finish ; around the edge of the cover have been inserted ribbons of metals and also shields, enamelled in heraldic colours, but which have been ruthlessly removed by the hands of the despoiler : this is supposed to be the tomb of Sir Ralph de Ryther. Resting on the floor, near an ogee arch in the church wall, is the figure of a lady in the costume worn during the latter part of the thirteenth century ; her hands, resting on her breast, clasp a heart, which she seems to be in the act of presenting to the church. At the extreme end of the aisle is the time-worn effigy of a Crusader in chain armour; by the side of the warrior rests his lady, wearing a wimple, her hands clasped in the attitude of prayer—

> "Full seenly her winple y'pinched was."

A William de Ridre, whom the effigy is supposed to represent, was a celebrated warrior in the time of Edward I.; he manfully assisted that monarch in the Crusades and Scotch Wars. The hardship and cost of these long campaigns seem to have brought the family into rather straitened circumstances, for, in 1308, Sir William de Ridre, Knight, acknowledges that he owes one William, a clerk, forty shillings, which, in default of payment, may be levied on his goods and chattels. The poem on the siege of Caerlaverock says

> "William de Ridre was there,
> Who a blue banner did bear,
> The crescents of gold so radiant."

John de Ridre, his son, was also a great favourite with Edward II. He was the king's constable of Skipton Castle during the great raid of the Scots under Randolph and the "Doughty Douglas," and he seems to have continued his active military career; in 1321 he was constable of Corfe Castle, a royal appointment of value, and a year or two later we still find him constable of the castle and honour of Skipton, and also keeper of Purbeck Chase.*

John de Rithre's services were equally accepted by Edward III. on the 16th July, 1327, in an order to Thomas Deyvill to deliver to John de Rithre the issues received by him from the manor of Scarthecroft during the time when he had the custody thereof, as the manor was taken into the king's hands by reason of the quarrel of Thomas, late Earl of Lancaster; and not to meddle further with the said manor, which was held of John by Robert de Rithre, deceased. On 5th July, 1327, is an order to the exchequer to cause Matilda, late wife of Robert de Rithre, to whom the king committed the custody of two parts of Robert's lands, in his hands by reason of the heir's minority, of the extent of the manor of Scarthecroft, charging her with the extent of the manor of Rithre, the escheator being ordered not to intermeddle further with the manor of Scarthecroft, and to restore the issues thereof, retaining in the king's hands the manor of Rithre, because it was

* The change of d to th, and the converse, is a common one in vulgar folk-speech; so in this case, if the place-name has a Norse derivation, the present-day spelling is the least correct.

found by inquisition taken by the escheator that Robert held at his death the manor of Rithre of the king as of the honour of Pontefract, and that he held the manor of Scarthecroft of John de Rithre by the service of a quarter of a knight's fee, and that William, son of the said Robert, is his next heir, aged twelve years.*

There are other features worthy of notice. The window in the east end of the south aisle, interspersed with fragments of old glass, containing the arms of the Rythers; noticeably the three crescents or, on a field azure with three cushions, argent and ermine, has an historic importance. On the floor of this aisle are inscribed stones and brasses to the memory of John Robinson, of Ryther, and his descendants. The five stone altar slabs and the Norman font are features to muse over. An inscribed stone within the chancel reads: "Here lies the body of Idonea de Gainsbro', prioress of Nun Appleton; she died in 1334." In the fields near Bolton Percy a large tombstone of another prioress was some years ago found, at the time of its discovery serving as a cover for the head of a drain. It is now to be seen on the floor at the west end of Bolton Percy Church. Great credit is due to the architect and Rector for the skill and care exercised in the judicious restoration of this ancient fabric of Ryther.

The family castle has long ago been dispersed; fragments of the deep moat are still seen and the impress of the hall in the cultivated fields and gardens fully attest that the castle of the old knightly family who took their name from the village stood here. The field west of the church is to this day called "Hall Garth," or Castle Field. An aged man, near fourscore years, who pathetically said, "Ahm t' last o' me breed," still recalls how in his time the foundations of the castle were used as a quarry for the surrounding district until barely a stone remained to tell the story of former greatness. The meadow east of Hall Garth and north of the church is called Coney Garth, and in it great quantities of bones have been unearthed. Regarding the above name, Coney, there is a letter extant, in which a Sir William Ryther writes to a friend requesting him to send some coneys as he is making a coney garth to his hall at Rither. As an evidence of the antiquity and importance of this family, a Ryther of Ryther witnessed the foundation charter of Appleton Nunnery over the river in 1154.

* April 3rd, 1361, Archbishop Thoresby paid Robert Ryther, Lord of Ryther, twenty pounds sterling, being the price of twenty four oaks bought of him for the use of restoring the cathedral.

Sir William de Aldburgh, of Harewood, dying without issue, the castle and lands came into possession of his two sisters. Elizabeth married Sir Richard Redman, knight, of Westmorland; Sybill, Sir William Ryther of Ryther; and it is rather singular that these two families and their descendants inhabited Harewood Castle jointly for several generations; the last to reside there was a Sir Robert Ryther, towards the close of the fifteenth century, and he was interred in Ryther Church. A Sir William Ryther, born 1405, married Isabella, daughter of Sir William Gascoyne, of Gawthorpe, son of the renowned judge.

The family of Ryther appear to have died out early in the eighteenth century. The present Earl of Harrowby is supposed to be the nearest representative. In the matter of economy the Rythers do not appear to have been a prudent family, thus, gradually, they became dispossessed of their lands. Of this fact one Robert Ryther, of Belton, bears witness, for in his will proved May, 1696, he devised and settled his estates upon his sixth cousin —John Ryther of Scarcroft —upon failure of his own issue, and gives his reason for so doing—"To preserve the lands in our ancient family, which is now very inconsiderable in comparison of the great estates heretofore enjoyed in the counties of York, Lincoln, and elsewhere, by our extravagant ancestors."

THE FERRY, RYTHER.   [E. Bogg.

Space forbids further description of this interesting village. Passing the ferry and the fine curve in the river we reach Ozendyke, an old foundation, its name expressive of the situation : it is a small hamlet between Ryther and Ulleskelf. The wild hop clambering luxuriantly in the hedgerows is worthy of notice. Let us follow the bank of the river. The charm of such a walk is the perfect peace and solitude : we wander through a profusion of tall grass, wild flowers, and giant hemlock, the high banks winding in great curves like incoming waves, the river rolling slowly onward in its deep bed so solitary and silent, as if weary with its long journey : musing thus we reach Ulleskelf. The vulgar pronunciation—Uskell—appears more meaningful than the later refined name.

When the early English work in York Minster was being executed, Uskell was the point where the stone was shipped. At that time the village was held by a family bearing the territorial name, who appear to have done no more to immortalize themselves than to give freely of their lands to the Hospital of St. Peter at York, a deed for which the generous donors have a right to receive full credit. There is an antiquity about the place reaching backward to Celtic days. Bronze and flint implements of warfare and fragments of ancient pottery have been unearthed hereabouts from time to time. The settlement, however, is chiefly due to Norsemen.

The village does not present any particular attraction. The Hall, formerly the home of the Shillito family, who were lords of the manor, has, of late years, been often tenantless ; consequently, an air of fallen dignity clings around it. For the first word-photograph of this somnolently luxuriant place we have to trust to the invaluable John Leland, his report being very acceptable :—" From Towton to Uskelf village, about a mile, where is a goodly house longing to a Prebend in York, and a goodly orchard, with ornamental walks. The ground about Uskelf is somewhat low and meadowish, as toward the fall of waters about Nunappleton. The parish of Ryder is but a mile from Uskelf. From Uskelf to Tadcaster three miles by good corn and pasture ground and some wood." Those who are not used to walking will consider John Leland's miles very long ones. This village possesses two inns, where the fishermen who resort here from Leeds and other towns find suitable refreshment.

Instead of taking the very inviting road to Grimston, with its leafy avenue and the undulating lands in front, well wooded with fine trees, from which peep mansion, church, and tower, the other path might be taken leading across the fields, by the side of the river. From these meadows, in the eventide, Ulleskelf makes a charming picture. The village is seen through the intervening orchards, with the smoke rising, as it were, from amongst the trees; all jarring contrasts of colour being softened into rest and harmony. After a mile's walk by the side of the river Grimston church will be noticed; as seen from the bank it is indeed a most pleasant picture for the eye to rest upon.

A BEND OF THE WHARFE AT ULLESKELF.

Standing on this spot when the sun had drooped below the western sky, and just before night spread her mantle over the light, the beauty of the scene was beyond description; some two miles away in the distance the ancient town of Tadcaster appeared like a fairy city in the after-glow. The waters of the Wharfe seem dreary as they near the end of their journey, flowing on sluggishly and melancholy; but on this night even the river shone resplendent from luminous light in the evening sky. Turning from the river, we look across the meadows, where no sound is to be heard save that of sleek cattle cropping the dewy grass. We see the old church tower, with the small but pretty village of Kirkby in front; behind, on the gently undulating lands, is the noble park of Grimston, where gigantic trees fling their shade over many a grassy dell. Above the park on this night spread a rift of purple cloud, along whose edge, and westward, trailed a rippling fleece of vapour, the beautiful harmony of whose colour required the brush of a Turner to delineate. Against this background, church tower, graceful poplar, and the more spreading tree, stood out clear and distinct, every leaf, twig, and branch showing out their wondrous grace and beauty of form.

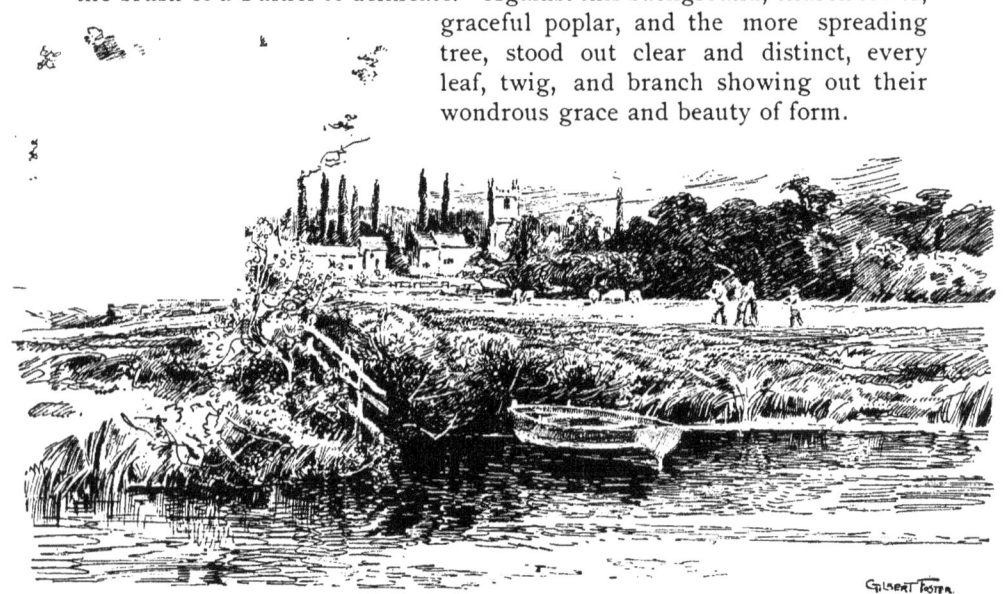

GRIMSTON AND KIRKBY WHARFE.

The distinction belonging to Grimston and Kirkby Wharfe, including Ulleskelf and Ryther, is that they are about the only settlements south of the Wharfe made by Norsemen. Grim, the founder, whose name means "the man with the helmet," was, no doubt, a warrior of the usual proclivities—taking all he could get hold of. The old hall, where the Viking brood of this ancient rover found shelter, was the predecessor of the one burnt down in the lifetime of William Grimston, who was born in 1640; the latter being succeeded by another on a more eligible site. The original mansion was moated and of timber, no doubt. Although Grimston House is a worthy mansion, and has been the seat of nobility and the resting-place of kings, it is by no means a representative of mansional dignity. The charm of the place is sylvan, its dignity is derived from the early English church. The mediæval features of Kirkby Wharfe have been somewhat neglected, although they are of high interest. The manor belonged to the family of Ryther of Ryther and Scarcroft, from whom it descended to the Ashes, and, during the reign of Elizabeth, was purchased by the Plumptons of Plumpton.

The church is a rectory belonging to the Prebend of Wetwang, who pays an annual pension of five marks of silver to the Vicar. The vicarage being of the patronage of the Prebendary is endowed only with the whole altarage of the place and of the tithes of the curtilages therein, in the name of the vicarage. In 1561-2 an augmentation of £20 yearly was made to the vicarage out of the fruits of the prebend of Wetwang. The first fruits of the vicarage in the King's Books, 1525, are £4 16s. 8d., tenths, 9s. 8d.

CHURCH TOWER, KIRKBY WHARFE.

The surroundings of the church standing just within the boundary of the park are extremely beautiful. A picturesque village green, magnificent groves of trees, antique farm buildings, lovely gardens, lawn, and sweet lush meadows all around. The interior has undergone judicious restoration and it possesses many evidences of undoubted antiquity. There are a few specimens of old glass, Dutch school, sixteenth century, and very curious. The Londesborough Chapel contains a sculptured panel (subject, "Adoration of the Magi"), fifteenth century marble. The carved work of the screen is modern and is a good example of the florid Flemish renaissance style. Some of the modern glass, especially the east, windows are very poor indeed. There are two fonts—the Norman and one of recent date. Apart from the old font, the most interesting remains are fragments of two very curious crosses found under the floor of the church, on which are carved rude representations of our first parents. Art was only in its infancy, or just awakening from long slumber, when these stones were fashioned; they also point to the fact that a church has stood on this spot since British times. The country around was at that date one vast forest. In the meadows near, enormous trees have been laid bare several feet below the surface when draining, pointing to a former lower level of the land. The name, Old Street, which led hither from Tadcaster, suggests a Roman occupation of this place.

The churchyard contains small stone coffins and a tomb cover emblazoned with crest and arms.

Grimston House, on the rising ground to the west, was formerly one of the seats of Lord Loudesborough, previous to which it was a residence of Lord Howden: now the home of J. Fielden, Esq. Half a mile from the mansion brings us into the London highway, the great coaching road of the first half of the eighteenth century. A few hundred yards away, in the vale below, the little river Cock winds its way through willow garths and joins the Wharfe near Grimston Grange.*

[F. Bogg.
ANGLO-DANISH CROSS, KIRKBY WHARFE.

* The Testamentary Burials are especially instructive, especially that recording the devotion to the ancient faith of this family of Leedes, of North Milford (a small hamlet adjoining Kirkby Wharfe). In it we have a picture of the great change too rare and striking to be passed over with unheeding lightness:—

27th April, 1540, Christopher Cattall, vicar of Kirkby-super-Wharf, made his will, whereby he commended his soul to God Almighty, the Virgin Mary, and all saints in heaven, and gave his body to be buried in the quire of the p.c. of K.

23rd September, 1459, Nicholas Leedes, parson in the Cathedral Church of York, made his will, proved 21st December, 1459, and bequeathed his soul, *ut supra*, and his body to be buried in the quire of the p.c. of K.

3rd May, 1546, Thomas Leedes, of N. Milford, gent., made his will, proved 5th March, 1546, giving his soul, *ut supra*, and his body to be buried in the high quire of the p.c.

18th April, 1602, Thomas Leedes, of N. Milford, Esq., made his will, proved 6th July, 1602, whereby he commended his soul to God Almighty, his Creator and Redeemer, to V. Mary and all Saints, and gave his body to be buried in the queare where his brother Leedes lyeth buried. Reserving out of his lands in Pocklethorp and Nafferton the yearly rent of £3 6s. 8d. unto the Catholic prisoners which shall remain from time to time in the Castle of York, for the Catholic faith and for their conscience; and if it shall please God to restore the Catholic service to His church as it was in King Henry 8th's days, and in the last four years of Queen Mary, then his will is that the said rent shall be divided between two honest Catholic priests for ever, the one to celebrate divine service in the p.c. of Kirkby-upon-Wharf, and the other in the p.c. of Kepaxe, and that they may for ever pray for the souls of Anne, his late wife, of his father and of his mother, John Brandesky and Robert Henneage.

7th March, 1678, George Stanhope, of K.W., gent., made his will, proved —— whereby he bequeathed his soul to God Almighty, his Creator, hoping in Jesus Xt. his Redeemer for salvation, and his body to be buried in the p.c. of K.W., near his deceased ancestors.

2nd March, 1477, Thomas Grenehill, vicar of Kirkby-super-Wharfe, dying intestate, administration of his goods granted to Robert Hawley, gent., of Ruston parish.

THE WILD FLOWERS OF ELMETE.

BY F. ARNOLD LEES, M.R.C.S.

THE "FLORA," as the various kinds in the aggregate are called, of Elmete is neither meagre nor without instruction and interest, even for the non-botanist. Because all plants depend somewhat for their variety upon the sort of soil they grow in, those of Elmete are mainly of one type—limestone-likers, technically calcicoles; owing, of course, to the fact that the area of the district, in the main the shallow river basin of the Cock beck, is one with underlying magnesian limestone strata, obscured only here and there by what is known as glacial drift—the mingled stone, gravel, and clayey detritus which the ice-age left as a legacy to the arid stony slopes its glaciers overpassed in their slow, grinding course, south-by-east, down the vale of York to the Humber sea. This geologic fact it is which makes the wild flowers of 'the little kingdom' of one kind or type. Limestone flowers are not the less but the more interesting on that account to the wanderer in search of them. For example take the glossy gamboge-coloured goldilocks —an early buttercup of the copses and hedge-bottoms, not of the meads; it is very common, and as pretty as variable in hue of bloom and cutting of leaf, all over Elmete; yet in walking north-east from Leeds, say, or north from Castleford, or south-west from York, this goldilocks would not be seen shaking out its yellow tresses until the lime tract of Elmete had been set foot upon near Roundhay limehills, or Ledstone, or Towton-field. So even a common wayside flower has an added charm from restriction and environment.

Keeping our 'marches' in mind, the bounds within which we may best set the floral gems of Elmete are those eternal and unvarying ones of season. In Spring, Summer, Autumn, and ay! even Winter, there is something characteristic, vegetally, in Elmete; that is, something not found in the same salience elsewhere in the serpentine stripe of Wharfeland, which, be it known, is nearly five hundred square miles in extent.

To begin with Winter, the season of rest and recuperation, but in which much hidden growth is being made, and next year's leaves are in process of formation within the scales of the buds of many and many a twig. Often, ere February impends, its 'fair maid' the snowdrop will flake (or fleck) with pure but living snow the glades of beechwood and elm holt from Grimston and Hazelwood to Aberford and Ledsham; divergent rainbows of green leaf-blade—promise of brighter glories in the same places later on—to right and left of its slender flower stem. With Lent will come the wild daffodil in many a coppice and spinney. But long ere then the orange and rose-pink fruit of the spindletree, "that in our winter woodland looks a flower," as Tennyson, with the poet's eye, put it, will have gone the same way as the crimson yew berries of Oglethorpe, and the black bunches of privet grapes, and the glassy red mezereon and Wayfaring-Gueldre bush fruit; that is to say, down bird's throats, and so into the leaf mould below the bare twig perch, in good time to germinate, and, unnoticed, but surely for all that, as moons wax and wane, as seasons come and go, renew the verdure, reproduce the leafing, flowering, fruiting item that makes the bosky woodland and the hedgerow what each veritably is—'a thing of beauty, and a joy for ever.' Does anybody object that berries are not wild flowers, it were good to remind them that the 'flower,' although oftentimes much the least showy, always precedes the fruit, and that what excites our admiration, for its shape or colour, is also often the least essential part of the blossom. Holly trees and, one season in three, holly berries are not wanting in the hedges of Elmete to give force of character to that marly bank or that hanging wood, in shade from May to October, but neither the Holly, nor the Whin dedicated to the kiss because one or other of its species is in fashion for bloom nigh all the year round; nor the opulent Broom—none of these, though occurring here and there in coverts, are either so fine or so comparatively plentiful as in other sandier or more grit-stony parts of Wharfeland beyond the boundaries of what may be, in the Irish sense, loosely termed 'the barony' of Elmete.

In spring, when it merges into summer almost, is Elmete's natural "Floralia," its revel of form and tint of faery. Then is it that lily o' the valley carpets the beech groves of Becca by Aberford. Then, when sky and earth have ceased to meet at the feast of bluebells where some spinney slopes steeply to the stream of Cock, the chequered snake's-head fritillary will modestly, with hanging head, obtrude itself among the parkland at Hazelwood. Grimstone's demesne will reveal the purple martagon lily in its sylvan shades; and, most beautiful of all, in many a wood from Micklefield at one extreme to Bramham at the other, the stately 'dovetower,' or columbine in variety of colour from pale lavender to deepest purple-shot blue, will be found displaying at the summit of its softly green and downy shafts a coronal of perching culvers. Later on yet a little, and "high-taper," the flannel-leaved mullein, will, in the same or stonier spots, such as are afforded by the numerous long-since-worked quarries; now overgrown with treillage of travellers' joy and bryony vine the "mandrake" of the herborists; uprear its wands of chrome flowers. In shady groves, in fifty spots, careful search among the dog's mercury covering the ground with its grey-green palmy plumes, will reveal the herb Paris or true lover's knot, most singular of wild flowers, and in its colours, a clear grass green almost unique. Picture four green leaves topping a bare stem, over this a green cross, superimposed and alternating with the arms of which is another green cross; the last two sets being narrow, for they are the flower envelopes, not leaves although green; within these crosses, at the hub of the spoked wheel as it were, eight stamens (male organs) cruciately alternate with the spokes, and are yellow-green likewise; the centre of all is what looks like a pointed green button, the ovary, which in early autumn, when the green rosette has almost faded, becomes a blue-bloomed berry. Not unpretty, this Herb of equal parts (*par*, *paris* is the Latin for it) is a most singular one, and, more singular still, the cross of true leaves, normally four, is occasionally made up of three, triangularly set; sometimes, again, there are *five* leaves; not very rarely six; quite rarely seven: so does it set botanic Adams at defiance, and try to belie its name! Possibly true-lover's Knots can be tied in a variety of ways also.

The other two *green* flowers of Elmete are the tiny moschatel of leafmouldy hedge-bottoms, an inconspicuous spring wilding; and the green hellebore with fan-fingered glossy leaves and a pallid green-buttercup blossom, which flourishes in the garth-fence by Kidhall, and has been known there since Blackstone peregrinated about 1746. It, too, grows at 'Beck-ha' banks, Aberford, again above the famous and fatal rivulet of Cock. Not broad but swiftly running, at times between steep banks, at Towton ford it accounted for the lives and deaths of many brave men.

As summer comes up the flowers of Elmete keep pace with it, and in bewildering variety of beauty prank alike its highways and byways. First there are the roses, white of York, excessively spiny, forming impassable thickets in places, a low branching bush with profuse creamy blossoms, never a tinge of Lancasterian red on their velvety petals—a rose whose motto might well have been that of its County-men: "Touch me not" *(Nemo me impune lacessit)*. It is abundant at Towton, although also found in many other parts: it is no calcifuge as is the foxglove (quite a rare flower in Elmete), for it will grow and spread on seashore sand, but it clearly has a preference for the dry soil that mostly prevails above limestone rock. Still, in Elmete, the downy red rose of Lancaster (scientifically *Rosa tomentosa*) is not unfrequent, with the paler open-blowing and pink-flushed dog-rose, and all three sorts grow on Towton Field; but the folk-lore conception that the mingled blood of the combatants is typified in the mingled hues of the rose-bloom is, of course, botanically a fable. The rustic clock of midsummer day is the Elder or burtree blossom. In Elmete, as elsewhere, a little before the woodbine and after the roses most years, its heavy-scented blossom, small individually but large in mass, begins to set ghostly pale-faces in their frames of hedgerow verdure towards dusk of the days between the 21st and 24th of June. Then summer has well come, and it is not long before the green black-briony berries begin to turn red, and their halberd or heart-shaped leaves a coppery bronzy purple. The great Bindweed, likewise, now ramps over the sloe hedges, and sets its silver trumpets of blossom at intervals, spirally, up its leaf-wreathed arms. A week later and the great Throatwort has rung its watchet to white bells in a mute carillon in the damper woods and hedgebanks from Parlington to Bramham. The waysides are gay now with the bedstraws, the 'great white' and the 'ladies' yellow,' massed and contrasting finely with the rose-purple basil, the madder marjoram, and last but not least that handsome ditch-bank flower the Fleabane, whose cottony crinkled leaves, and gold-disked, yellow-hair fringed flowers are said, on the 'principle of signatures,' exploded herborist fancy, to be the sovereign preventive against one insect torment at least. This flower of Elmete is not everywhere, but is particularly common about Barwick, and on the ancient 'way' from Wendel Hill to Kidhall. One rare flowering plant of Kippax Park must here have mention because it grows nowhere else in Elmete. This is the baneberry *(Actæa spicata)*, a neat fresh green cut-leaf bush, with pyramids of pretty white bloom, not unlike the *Spiræa* of home-pot fame and the late spring flower-market. It is plentiful in places by the shady foot-road from Kippax to Allerton.

Then, again, the singular Bee orchis grows near the beacon in Ledstone Park, and at Bramham and Huddlestone, and is properly a guest of full summer, with the great white butterfly orchis: the botanic eye, however, is needed to detect the vegetable mimic among the bent. The Twayblade, too, so often miscalled the green-man orchis from the shape and stem-stringing of its amber marionettes, is both curious and not rare.

Comes Autumn, and what flowers are there? They are none so numerous, yet some are of striking mien. First in point of time there are two orchises: the bastard Helleborine, with broad ribbed leaves and dull purple and amber spikes of flowers, that grows in clumps or singly in the semi-wooded quarries that long ago yielded the building stone for York Minster, and many another storied edifice; and the lowly Chesterfield-spired ladies'-tresses Orchis, which, with its spirally-twisted plait of blossoms, each set on the stem at a different angle, lives to reward sharp eyes in the open quarries and stonier pastures of Barwick's Tower Hill itself. There is also the orange-flowered gentian or Yellow-wort, affecting similar bare broken ground, and even more commonly the bitter Felwort or autumnal gentian with lavender to purple tubes of blossom. Though not conspicuous this item in the flower sum of the year, coming to hand when all colours but yellows are on the wane, is neat and acceptable enough. And there is yet another flower-face of distinct physiognomy: almost without warning in the close-cropped pastures about Aberford, Barwick, and Parlington, and perhaps in other fields of the 'barony' as well, we seem (to the initiate) to be back or to have leapt forward to spring and crocus time! There, jutting from the damp turf, is the naked-flowering Colchicum, its oval crocus-like bloom of clear pale puce on a soft silvery stem without a leaf-blade to guard it from the shivery equinoctial winds! Its leaves are produced in spring, its flowers now; and it comes from the mould a surprise, first and last, like the armed men that grew from Jason's teeth, as mythology tells, a real yearly reminder of Towton fight, for it grows on the classic field; and, to keep up the similitude, though it shows bravely at an inclement time above ground, yet keeps its reproductive receptacle subterraneously, and perfects its seeds safe and snug away from the killing influence of cold!

In very late autumn, last of the year's proper blooms, more or less over all Elmete there is the 'mantling ivy,' Dickens' favourite flower, and another green one, so valued from the decorative aspect; the heavy tods of which, crowning some ruin of dead wood or stone, are begemmed with globular honeyed thyrsi, dear indeed to starved hybernating mothdom, that, fire-eyed, crowd to the feast on shiny opaline nights of October, when, as disembodied spirits are supposed to do, for a brief space, they 'revisit the glimpses of the moon.'